Telling the Fuller Truth

Telling the Fuller Truth: The Race & Reconciliation Initative at TCU, 2020–2025

EDITED BY

Amiso George, Karen Steele, and Jenay Willis

TCU
Press

Fort Worth, Texas

Library of Congress Cataloging-in-Publication Data

Names: George, Amiso M., editor. | Steele, Karen, 1965- editor. | Willis, Jenay F. E., editor.
Title: Telling the fuller truth : Race and Reconciliation Initiative at TCU, 2020-2025 / edited by Amiso M. George, Karen Steele, Jenay F.E. Willis.
Description: Fort Worth : TCU Press, [2025] | Includes bibliographical references and index. | Summary: "Dialogue about race, racism, and the Confederacy is uncomfortable, but meaningful it can foster true understanding and healing. This book addresses the race and reconciliation efforts of Texas Christian University through the Race and Reconciliation Initiative (RRI): a five-year academically based historically focused initiative designed to investigate and document TCU's relationship with slavery, racism, and the Confederacy. This academic endeavor draws upon the talents and experiences of faculty, staff, students, and alumni to research and raise awareness of racism and inequality at TCU, helping us work toward a campus culture where everyone is respected and valued. Part one provides a new narrative of TCU's first 150 years with special attention to race and racism. Part two includes essays from faculty, students and community members who explore a variety of topics related to the race and reconciliation work at TCU. The book not only serves as a catalyst for future scholarly investigations of these important issues in the understudied areas of TCU's history but also equips campus leaders faculty and staff with strategies to expand students experiences and understanding of TCU's history. The collection in sum offers one institution's road map to thinking about racial diversity in the history and current practices of higher education. This book is an invitation to explore these difficult landscapes together to learn from our past and to imagine a future unburdened by the ashes and fears of old"-- Provided by publisher.
Identifiers: LCCN 2025033735 (print) | LCCN 2025033736 (ebook) | ISBN 9780875659329 (paperback) | ISBN 9780875659411 (ebook)
Subjects: LCSH: TCU Race and Reconciliation Initiative. | Texas Christian University--History. | Discrimination in higher education--Texas. | Educational equalization--Texas. | School integration--Texas. | Reconciliation--Political aspects--Texas. | Racial justice--Texas. | Minority college students--Texas. | Fort Worth (Tex.)--Race relations.
Classification: LCC LD5311.T382 T45 2025 (print) | LCC LD5311.T382 (ebook)
LC record available at https://lccn.loc.gov/2025033735
LC ebook record available at https://lccn.loc.gov/2025033736

TCU
Press

Fort Worth, Texas

TCU Box 298300
Fort Worth, Texas 76129
www.tcupress.com

Design by Bill Brammer

We dedicate this book to the individuals and communities who made the RRI possible. In particular, we pay homage to the individuals and communities whose experiences were deeply impacted by TCU's race and reconciliation efforts and who came in conversation and community with the RRI as a place of individual and communal healing.

CONTENTS

List of Illustrations **viii**

List of Contributors **xi**

Editors' Note **xiv**

Introduction **xv**

Part One

TCU's Founding Years (1873–1923) **1**

TCU's Transition to Integration (1941–1971) **26**

TCU's Recent History (1998–2020) **47**

Part Two

Frederick Gooding, Jr., Ubuntu as a Tool for Reconciliation **86**

Marcellis R. Perkins, Take it Easy While We Reconcile This! **96**

Sylviane Ngandu-Kalenga Greensword, Finding Charley **106**

Jenay Willis, Speaking the Truth: Telling Y[Our] TCU Story **119**

Theresa Gaul, Jessica Mundy, Lori Salazar, Shafiq M. Said, Victoria M. Washington, Taking a New Route: Creating TCU's Indigenous Campus Tour **127**

C. Annette Anderson, Judge Softly: TCU Students Walking Alongside Native Communities as Allies **142**

Carrie Liu Currier, Asian Pacific Americans in Higher Education and the Politics of Identity at TCU **150**

Kelly Palida Phommachanh, Creating Community for Asians, Asian Americans, and Pacific Islanders at TCU **162**

Cecilia N. Sánchez Hill, TCU and Fort Worth Mexicanos During the Progressive Era (1900–1924) **172**

Sean Atkinson, Embracing the Culture of Our Community: The Story of Mariachi Sangre Royal de TCU **180**

Images

Part One

Photograph from the Sallie Clark Collection **2**

Slave rental note made to J. A. Clark **6**

Program from 1905 Texas division of the United Daughters of the Confederacy **12**

Photo from the scrapbook of Mattie Cooper Harlin **14**

Detail of TCU servant house **16**

Article in *Skiff* recalling electing "Black presidents" at TCU **17**

Program from Mammoth Pageant at Fort Worth Coliseum **23**

Ridglea wall topped with barbed wire separating Black Como from white Ridglea **28**

Portrait of Abdullah Ben Kori, possibly TCU's first student and faculty member of color **31**

Portrait of Elba Altamirano, possibly TCU's first Mexican student **33**

Alumni letter to President Sadler **34**

Provost Moudy's statement on desegregation **36**

James Cash, TCU's first Black basketball player **42**

James Cash at unveiling of his statue next to Schollmaier Arena **44**

Chancellor Michael (Mick) Ferrari **48**

Chancellor Victor J. Boschini, Jr. **50**

Letter to department heads, sent in fall of 2017 **55**

TCU's Native American monument **64**

Divine Nine Pillars **65**

Intercultural Center **65**

Portrait of Allene Parks Jones **66**

Design model for Sesquicentennial Plaza **67**

Additional Images

Hand holding a sticker with the Race & Reconciliation logo **81**

Heritage trail walking tour, Spring 2022 **81**

TCU's second annual Reconciliation Day, April 2022 **82**

Detail from RRI panel discussion with James Cash, November 2022 **82**

TCU's fourth annual Reconciliation Day and recognition of founders of ethnic and area studies programs at TCU, April 2024 **83**

TCU's third annual Reconciliation Day, featuring Indigenous drummers and recognition of the founders of the Native American and Indigenous Peoples Initiative **83**

TCU's third annual Reconciliation Day, April 2023 **83**

RRI honoring TCU alumnus Ronald Hurdle with the Plume Award, February 2024 **84**

TCU's fourth annual Reconciliation Day, featuring student artist Claudia Tiffany Rodriguez **84**

Part Two

Race & Reconciliation sign, installed August 2020 **87**

TCU's first Reconciliation Day, April 21, 2021 **92**

RRI "plumes" as homage to TCU's Frog Fountain **94**

Reconcile This! logo **97**

Rhondda Thomas of Clemson University interviewed by Marcellis Perkins and Frederick Gooding, Jr. **100**

Rhonda V. Magee interviewed by Perkins and Gooding for their first live recording of *Reconcile This!* **100**

Frederick Gooding, Jr., and Marcellis Perkins, cohosts of *Reconcile This!* **103**

Granbury Depot, which houses official administrative
county records **110**

TCU's third annual Reconciliation Day included recognition
of the founders of the Native American and Indigenous
Peoples Initiative **112**

Thorp family reunion during TCU's second annual
Reconciliation Day, April 2022 **113**

Family tree of Charley Thorp and his descendants **116**

Map of TCU's Indigenous campus tour **129**

TCU sundial, the first stop on TCU's Indigenous campus tour **131**

TCU pollinator garden **133**

Indigenous lodge and Frog Fountain on the campus commons **136**

Based on Quanah Parker by Comache/Kiowa artist
J. NiCole Hatfield (Nahmi-a-Piah) **138**

Based on Mrs. Jack Treetop-Standing Rock 1908 by
Comache/Kiowa artist J. NiCole Hatfield (Nahmi-a-Piah) **136**

World premiere of Sangre Royal by TCU wind band and
mariachi, September 2023 **182**

Members of the Mariachi Sangre Royal de TCU during
the fourth annual Reconciliation Day, April 2024 **185**

CONTRIBUTORS

C. Annette Anderson (Chickasaw and Cherokee) is a licensed clinical social worker, a council member for the Indigenous Institute of the Americas, and a member of TCU's inaugural Native American Advisory Circle. She has presented programs and mentored pedagogical projects at TCU and was a keynote speaker at TCU's Native and Indigenous Peoples Day Symposium in 2023.

Sean Atkinson is dean of Fine Arts at the University of Montevallo; previously, he was associate professor of music and music theory at TCU and served as director of the School of Music from 2021 to 2024. He was a member of the RRI Taskforce during the 2021–2022 academic year.

Carrie Liu Currier is an associate professor of political science. She was director of TCU's Asian Studies program, chair of the political science department, and is the current director of the Texas National Consortium for Teaching about Asia (NCTA), an initiative funded by the Freeman Foundation to facilitate teaching and learning about East Asia in K-12 schools nationwide.

Theresa Strouth Gaul is director of the TCU Core Curriculum and a professor of English at TCU. She was a co-recipient of the RRI Plume Award in 2023 for her collaborations in co-founding the TCU Native American and Indigenous Peoples Initiative.

Amiso George is a professor and former chair of the department of strategic communication at TCU. A Fulbright scholar and fellow of the Public Relations Society of America (PRSA), she is chair of the Race & Reconciliation Initiative at TCU.

Frederick Gooding, Jr., is the Dr. Ronald E. Moore Professor of Humanities and associate professor of African American Studies at TCU. He served as the inaugural chair of the Race & Reconciliation Initiative from 2020 to 2022.

Sylviane Ngandu-Kalenga Greensword, who was the inaugural postdoctoral fellow for the Race & Reconciliation Initiative, is an assistant professor of professional practice in TCU's Honors College, where she teaches cultural studies. Her work centers on ethnic identity and cultural performance in the African diaspora.

Cecilia N. Sánchez Hill earned her Ph.D. in history at TCU. Her dissertation combines history, ethnic studies, and curriculum studies to demonstrate how politicians and educators have used schooling as a tool of white supremacy to maintain social hierarchies. She served as a graduate assistant in comparative race and ethnic studies during its first three years as a department.

Jessica Mundy is a Ph.D. student in the TCU English department studying Early Modern British literature, especially adaptations and appropriations of Shakespeare's plays.

Marcellis R. Perkins served as the inaugural graduate research assistant for TCU's Race & Reconciliation Initiative from 2020 to 2022. Perkins completed his Ph.D. in higher education leadership in 2024.

Kelly Palida Phommachanh is a first-generation, Lao American doctoral candidate in the higher education leadership program at TCU. She served as the RRI graduate research assistant from 2022 to 2024.

Shafiq M. Said is a Ph.D. student in the TCU English department studying post-9/11 Arab American literature.

Lori Salazar earned her B.A. at TCU in 2022 and is pursuing her master's degree specializing in literature and film studies in the TCU English department.

Karen Steele is professor of English; formerly, she served as director of Women and Gender Studies, chair of the English department, and inaugural dean of the School of Interdisciplinary Studies. Since 2020, she has been a member of Team RRI.

Victoria M. Washington is a Ph.D. student in the TCU English department studying contemporary American Black literature and hip-hop.

Jenay Willis is an assistant professor of higher education at the University of Mississippi. She served as the postdoctoral fellow for the Race & Reconciliation Initiative from 2023 to 2024, where she directed the Oral History Project (OHP) and worked in partnership with Team RRI and the research team to study TCU's history with slavery, racism, and the Confederacy.

EDITORS' NOTE

We opted to capitalize the "B" in the word "black" as a designation for people of African descent but not the "w" in "white" as a description for people of Euro-American descent, following the practice of most media outlets and established custom in contemporary scholarly writing. We also opt, in Part One, for the word "Indigenous" over the word "native," given the latter's colonial complicity with racialization and racism.

Introduction

IN SEPTEMBER 2023, during the 60th anniversary of the bombing of the 16th Street Baptist Church in Birmingham, Alabama, where four young Black girls were killed by Ku Klux Klan members in a shocking terrorist attack, Supreme Court Justice Ketanji Brown Jackson reminded her fellow Americans about the importance of remembrance culture: "We cannot forget because the uncomfortable lessons are often the ones that teach us the most about ourselves. We cannot forget because we cannot learn from past mistakes we do not know exist."[1] TCU's Race & Reconciliation Initiative—established following the summer of racial reckoning in response to the murder of George Floyd on May 25, 2020—is driven by a similar commitment. We seek a fuller truth of our past so that we can learn from our mistakes, but also so we can cultivate new ways of belonging for all members of our campus community.

As an academically based, historically focused initiative designed to investigate and document TCU's relationship with slavery, racism, and the Confederacy, the Race & Reconciliation Initiative (RRI) researches TCU's history and raises awareness of racism and racial inequality, helping us to work toward a campus culture where everyone is respected and valued. Examining TCU's nearly 150-year history, the RRI has focused on the histories and experiences of those whose racial identity is underrepresented on our campus, notably faculty, staff, and students who are Black, Indigenous, Latinx, and Asian Pacific American. According to Frederick Gooding, Jr., RRI's inaugural chair, "Our study of TCU's history will provide critical perspective, deepen understanding, and result in recommendations for action and healing." In the pages that follow, readers will discover how TCU, a private, predominantly white university (PWI) that has grown to over 13,000 students and possesses a national reputation, has changed a great deal over its first 150 years. Yet our history reveals the many large and small ways that TCU is still working to learn from and repair its past mistakes with regard to race.

This collection documents RRI's journey over its five-year mandate. The goal is to share, through archival research, oral history, reflective essays, and case studies, what we have learned through this mandate and how this research can be utilized by faculty, staff, students, and alumni to inform and strengthen their understanding of TCU's history.

Part One, which consolidates our survey reports over our first four years, provides a fuller history of TCU through its close attention to race. While we could not cover every event or story in TCU's history of slavery, racism, and the Confederacy, we provide a deeper dive into three "slices in time" to TCU's past: its founding years, its transition to integration, and its recent history.

The founding years begin in the late-nineteenth century, with the establishment of TCU in 1873 by brothers Addison and Randolph Clark. The Clark brothers, affiliated with the Disciples of Christ Church, established TCU to fill a gap in education that the state of Texas was unable or unwilling to provide for all its citizens. Visionaries within the context of their time, the Clark brothers established TCU during a time of great social and political upheaval and rampant violence. While the Clark brothers were not beneficiaries of slave labor, they both fought for the Confederacy, even if their service was reluctant and short lived. Even so, the cultural climate of TCU during its founding years applauded and supported slavery and the Confederacy, as well as the subordination of Black, Indigenous, and other people of color in the United States.

TCU's transition to integration, which focuses on the years 1941–1971, examines the many challenges posed by legally mandated and culturally entrenched racial segregation in U.S. society and on TCU's campus, as well as the prolonged and arduous efforts to desegregate TCU's campus in the decades following World War Two. From gradual and unofficial desegregation in the 1940s and 1950s—off campus and in select graduate programs only— to TCU's official desegregation in 1964, TCU's transition to a desegregated campus elicited powerful opposition and pushback. Moreover, desegregation did not mean integration; indeed, the first years of TCU's desegregation were difficult for the pioneering students, staff, and faculty members of color at TCU. In the fall of 1964, five Black high school graduates were admitted but did not return the following year. A year later, in 1965, when fourteen Black students were admitted, these students decided to remain united, to support one another, and to commit to graduating on time. They would graduate with the class of 1969, the first fully integrated class.

TCU's recent history, which focuses on the years 1998–2020, documents the marked shift at TCU when students' collective voices played a pivotal role in catalyzing necessary changes with regard to race and racism. Under the visionary leadership of Chancellors Michael Ferrari and Victor Boschini, Jr., student and faculty activism—together with curricular and programmatic revisions by faculty and staff—produced dynamic changes to student and faculty demographics, athletics, and infrastructure that worked to build a more inclusive campus. Demands by students also inspired the establishment of the Race & Reconciliation Initiative in 2020, when the University began the important work of acknowledging and addressing the role of slavery, racism, and the Confederacy in its own history.

Part Two showcases the insights of TCU faculty, students, and community members whose research and teaching about Black, Indigenous, Latinx, and Asian Pacific American history and culture synergistically contributes to the mission of RRI. Frederick Gooding, Jr., the Dr. Ronald E. Moore Professor of Humanities, discusses the leadership challenges, opportunities, and lessons he learned as the inaugural chair of RRI and proposes concrete strategies for applying *ubuntu*, a South African concept of "humanity to others," to the work of RRI. Marcellis R. Perkins, a recent graduate in TCU's higher education leadership doctoral program and the inaugural graduate research assistant for RRI, highlights a dynamic method for humanizing research about race: *Reconcile This!*, a popular podcast that he and Gooding created to share the work of RRI that has attracted an international audience. Sylviane Ngandu-Kalenga Greensword, who launched and directed the RRI Oral History Project when she served as the inaugural postdoctoral fellow for RRI, explores another human dimension of archival research in discovering the story of Charley and Kate Thorp, a formerly enslaved couple who contributed immensely to TCU in its first decade in Thorp Spring. Greensword also powerfully reflects on the experience of locating and later meeting Charley and Kate Thorp's descendants, who came to TCU on our second Reconciliation Day in April 2022. Jenay Willis, who directed the RRI Oral History Project as the postdoctoral fellow for RRI from 2023 to 2024, elaborates on the process of researching, planning, executing, and documenting oral histories of our campus community; she also reflects on how all of us might make immediate and prospective uses of this open-access resource.

Carrie Liu Currier, who for many years directed TCU's thriving Asian Studies program, deconstructs the "model minority" myth and educates readers on the diversity of the Asian Pacific American (APA) population, their place at TCU, and how they have been deminoritized in higher education. Her essay captures one of the key elements of the mandate of the RRI: raising awareness of racism and inequality. Currier's chapter is in productive conversation with Kelly Palida Phommachanh, a Ph.D. student in higher education leadership and formerly a graduate research assistant for RRI, who provides a case study for creating community for Asian Pacific Americans at TCU.

Proposing strategies to work toward a campus culture where everyone is respected and valued, the collaboratively authored essay by Theresa Strouth Gaul, a professor of English and Indigenous Studies, and English Ph.D. students Jessica Mundy, Lori Salazar, Shafiq M. Said, and Victoria M. Washington, explore the deliberate and unexpected "new route" to creating an Indigenous campus tour at TCU, providing the campus community and others an opportunity to recognize and reconcile with locations on campus that are meaningful to Indigenous communities. The chapter was designed to be read in fruitful dialogue with C. Annette Anderson's reflection on allyship. Anderson, a Chickasaw and Cherokee and member of TCU's Indigenous Advisory Circle, reminds readers of the importance of moving with "genuine respect, communication, and understanding with the original stewards of TCU land," by listening to and learning from Indigenous peoples.

The final two essays explore TCU's uneven, century-old relationship with Fort Worth's Latinx community. Cecilia N. Sánchez Hill, who recently completed her Ph.D. in history at TCU with a dissertation on Mexican American education in Fort Worth, examines the relationship between Mexicanos, Fort Worth, and TCU during the first two decades of the twentieth century. Highlighting the missionary activism of Mateo Molina, a TCU professor of Spanish and French and later a student at Brite College (the former name of Brite Divinity School, a separate institution to TCU with a shared heritage, affiliation, and tradition), Hill suggests Molina's holistic care for Fort Worth Mexicanos still stands as a model for TCU today. The final chapter by Sean Atkinson narrates the recent history of establishing TCU's first mariachi band, Sangre Royal de TCU, bringing to the fore how community, culture, and music are linked. Along the way, Atkinson, dean of fine arts at the University of Montevallo and formerly an associate professor of music and member of the Race & Reconciliation Initiative Taskforce, reminds readers of how this music, which has long been a part of the cultural fabric of Mexicanos, can foster stronger connections between TCU and its Fort Worth Latinx community.

In what follows, we encourage readers to confront uncomfortable truths about race, racism, and the Confederacy at TCU and engage in meaningful dialogue that can foster true understanding and healing. While the chapters might serve as a catalyst for future scholarly investigation of these important but understudied areas of TCU's history, they also serve to support campus leaders, faculty, and staff in strategies for integrating race into the student experience. The collection, in sum, offers one institution's roadmap to thinking about racial diversity in the history and current practices of higher education. As we continue to grapple with issues of race, racism, equality, and belonging, we can do so more effectively by understanding a fuller history of our university. This book is an invitation to explore these difficult landscapes together, to learn from our past, and to imagine a future unburdened by the ashes and fears of old.

The work of the Race & Reconciliation Initiative reflects the efforts of many individuals —faculty, staff, students, alumni, and community members—who have come together to research and share what we have learned in our first five years. Part One is indebted to the intellectual and creative efforts of those who served on Team RRI or the Race & Reconciliation Initiative Taskforce over our first five years (2020–2025): Sean Atkinson, Tosin Alao, Sue Anderson, Florencio Aranda, Jean Marie Brown, Gregg Cantrell, Amy Ceniceros, Kenneth Chapman, Haylee Chiariello, Leslie Ekpe, Holly Ellman, Ashley English, Allan Gallay, Amiso George, Frederick Gooding, Jr., Sylviane Ngandu-Kalenga Greensword, Timeka Gordon, Lynn Hampton, Lauren Laphen, Clifford Harrell, Alex Hidalgo, Jacque Lambiase, Adam McKinney, Marcela Molina, Trung Nguyen, Marcellis Perkins, Kelly Phommachanh, Brandy Quinn, Sarah Robbins, Nancy Ruiz, Mary Saffell, Briana Salas, Lucius Seger, Rebecca Sharpless, Karen Steele, Callie Strelow, David Swillum, Tracy Syler-Jones, Uma Tiwari, Aisha Torrey-Sawyer, Taliah Williams, Tracy Renee Williams, and Jenay Willis.

Part One

TCU's Founding Years
(1873–1923)

THE FORCES THAT LED TCU founders Addison and Randolph Clark to establish Texas Christian University in 1873 illuminate some of their views of enslavement, the Civil War, and the Confederacy. The long Texas history of enslavement and violence, which led the state to join the Confederacy in the Civil War, left a powerful legacy in the war's aftermath. The violence of the war years remained intact, and in some ways grew worse, as the state proved unable to curb rampant lawlessness. Such lawlessness stemmed from hostility towards the emancipation of the enslaved and also from an inability to influence government to provide basic safety for all. Criminal activity went largely unchecked, and the government failed at building schools and providing education for the state's children—a failure of proportions unknown in all the other states.

The Clark family's drive to create a university was an attempt to fill this educational void. The action of founding an institution of higher learning indicates that the founders of TCU opposed the dominant ethos of many white elites who despised or ignored the societal benefits that education can bring to individuals and to society. During a time period in which the state of Texas provided limited investment in education and suppressed the participation in civic life by Black and Indigenous people, as well as people of color, the Clark brothers began their work as teachers and institution-builders. Randolph Clark explained that he and his brother intended to devote their lives to running a school that was influenced by neither church nor state; instead, they embraced the purpose of character building, studying the Bible, and training students for a "complete human life, physically, intellectually, and spiritually," enabling students to find themselves and choose their life's work.[2]

TCU's founding was a direct reaction to the decimation wrought by the Civil War, which continued in the wake of the war. Its founding had little

Photograph from the Sallie Clark Collection, c. early 1900s

to no direct connection to either enslavement or the Confederacy. Enslaved Black labor, for instance, did not contribute substantially to the creation of wealth for the university. Although the Clark brothers' father, Joseph Addison Clark, benefited from slave labor, the two brothers possessed limited financial resources. Nonetheless, throughout the South there arose organizations, and a general white culture, that celebrated and memorialized slavery and the Confederacy. This culture whitewashed the horrors of enslavement and embraced racism and white power. Early in its history, TCU students, faculty, and trustees joined in the celebration of these fantasies about the past to maintain white dominance and exclusivity, while institutionalizing the social, political, and economic inferiority of Black and Indigenous people and people of color in American society. This dynamic created a "norm" that persists to the present day in which the needs, desires, experiences, and assertions of people of color are assessed by whites as "different," "unnecessary," and "unwanted"—that is unless they converge with the white culture's definitions of what is necessary and proper at TCU and for the society at large.

Long-Term History of
Enslavement in Texas

Historians have increasingly identified the centrality of enslavement to Texas. From the sixteenth century to the end of the American Civil War, the enslavement of people was ubiquitous. The earliest Spanish conquistadors entering Texas from Mexico captured Indigenous peoples whom they shipped south to become enslaved laborers.[3] For centuries afterwards, Texas was a source as well as a way station for the continuous shipment of Indigenous peoples from not only Texas, but also from the Great Plains and other parts of the Southwest to Mexico.[4] Eighteenth-century Spanish settlements in Texas conducted slave raids to obtain Indigenous captives and purchased slaves from Indigenous captors. Apaches, in particular, sold Indigenous captives to the Spanish until Comanches opened a trade in Apache slaves that dominated the Texas landscape, culminating in thousands of Apaches being shipped as slaves to Cuba. As late as the mid-nineteenth century, the busiest trading post in the north-central region of Texas, Torrey's Trading Post No. 2 (just outside of Waco), was a key spot for Comanches and other Indigenous peoples to bring enslaved Indigenous and Black people—the latter mostly stolen from plantations to the east and southeast—who were sold to local whites.[5] All of this slaving violence precipitated and perpetuated a culture of intergroup violence that lasted for centuries.[6]

In the early nineteenth century, white immigrants from the United States arrived in Texas with their enslaved Africans and heightened the slaving violence with and against Hispanic and Indigenous communities. The white slaveholders migrated to Texas for inexpensive lands to produce cotton on slave plantations.[7] With the rising tide of anti-enslavement in the northern United States, many of these immigrants, particularly after the Anglo rebellion against Mexico that culminated in Texas independence, saw themselves creating and advertising their new country as the last slaveholders' republic.[8]

Divisiveness of the
Civil War in Texas

With the 1860 election of Abraham Lincoln to the United States' presidency, most of the slaveholding states seceded from the United States. Texans voted overwhelmingly to secede and join the Confederate States of America, though the German immigrants in the Hill Country and the counties to the north of Dallas and Tarrant counties voted firmly against secession. In Texas's northern counties, while there were few plantations, enslaved Black communities comprised 10–15 percent of the total population.[9]

Enslaved Black people, both apparently and in fact, did practice resistance in the northern and central Texas counties at a higher rate than in the plantation areas. This dynamic emerged from the enslaved themselves, who sometimes forged alliances with local Mexicans and Indigenous Americans.[10] Fear of dark-skinned populations influenced Southern whites to exert great hostility against Black communities as well as against whites who might work in concert with Black people or with the United States government. Most of the white population strongly supported the maintenance of the social and legal inferiority of Black Americans, even if they did not support secession.

In October 1862, Confederate sympathizers rounded up alleged Northern sympathizers in the North Texas counties and subjected them to trials by an illegal court on charges of treason. The subsequent civilian violence extended into Fort Worth and other areas south of the city. This violence played a leading role in intimidating and silencing those in Texas who dissented from the Confederacy, those who favored the United States government, and those who challenged the racial hierarchy that placed whites at the top and people of color at the bottom of the social order.[11]

Once the Confederacy's authority was established in the state, many felt that it was the duty of citizens to defend the area.[12] The Clark family fit that pattern. Writing years later, Joseph Lynn Clark explained, "When Texas became one of the seceding states…, and Lincoln called for volunteers, an act that was interpreted as a prelude to the invasion of the South, factionalism ceased and Texans throughout the state rushed to the defense of the Southern Cause."[13] Addison Clark joined the Confederacy in 1862, leaving his father engaged in commercial enterprises, shipping most commodities to the war area but also supplying local retailers. While there are few records, it appears that the founders' father Joseph Addison Clark made considerable profits during the war years. Missing from retrospective family reporting are indications that the labor of enslaved persons might have facilitated the family's financial advancement.

Randolph later depicted his older brother Addison as anti-war, not for political as much as for religious reasons: "Addison had been taught from childhood that Christians should not go to war." So, why did Addison Clark enlist in the Confederacy? Randolph concluded, "It was easier to preach non-resistance than to practice it in the face of an invading army."[14] Addison Clark formally enrolled with the Confederate armed forces in Grayson County and was mustered in Collin County as a 2nd Lieutenant, Co. D. 16th Texas Cavalry. Randolph joined him at the end of the war, though not as an enrolled soldier. In an undated early draft of his *Reminiscences* manuscript, Randolph Clark speculated that his father was "maneuvering to keep [Randolph] out of war." He bemoaned, however, "the time was coming that I would have to go without the privilege of volunteering."[15] Later, he wrote, "I consider that year of my life misspent. And believe as mother did … that Christians cannot make war."[16] In 1868, with the impeachment of President Andrew Johnson, Joseph Addison Clark wrote the following: "I think there has been a fight in Washington. I have been expecting it. If I knew that this country would be ruled by Mongrels and negroes I would want to go somewhere [else]."[17] In his memoirs, Randolph claimed that their motivation to serve in the Confederacy was not pro-enslavement but pro-region: "They [Texas soldiers who enlisted] settled no doctrine of state's rights, and were opposed to enslavement. The South was their home, it was invaded, they answered the call to defense."[18]

During the Civil War, the Clark family abandoned North Texas, in part because of the dangerous situation of deserters and partisan raiders. The sponsoring father of TCU founders Addison and Randolph Clark, Joseph Addison Clark, owned a "negro" in 1860 valued at $1,000. Other records indicate that, previously, the elder Clark had owned an enslaved thirteen-year-old boy in 1850 and rented out a slave, George, for the year 1856 at a cost of $150. Joseph Addison Clark had earned enough during the war to purchase a farm, a ranch, and 100 horses. In 1864, there is a record of a

Joseph A. Clark in Hill County who possessed five slaves—this might have been him. Joseph apparently bought property in the northeastern corner of Hill County and gained an interest in a flour and lumber mill in Alvarado, near the property, which he later moved to Cleburne.

During the Civil War there were no battles in the counties of North Texas, as local conscripted and volunteer soldiers for the Confederacy were sent to the east. The Civil War, however, indelibly shaped the region, and the Clarks' cultural memory of the Confederacy remained a part of their identities. In fact, the brothers' intention to establish a school may have been influenced by their reverence of General Robert E. Lee. Randolph's son Joseph Lynn Clark later wrote that "the admiration of the brothers for the beloved leader of the armies of the South was ... greatly enhanced by his acceptance of [Lee's] presidency of Washington College, at Lexington, Virginia.... [T]he brothers continued to follow the fortunes of their hero in his noble efforts of rehabilitation of the South through the slow process of education."[19]

Note made to J. A. Clark in which John Harris agrees to pay $150 for the use of Clark's enslaved boy, George, for one year and also to provide the boy with two suits of clothes and two bed blankets. Dated February 1, 1856.
Photo courtesy of TCU Special Collections.

The Clarks' affiliation with the Disciples of Christ was also essential to their vision of establishing TCU. Joseph Addison Clark, following his wife's lead, had joined the Disciples of Christ in 1842 and preached throughout his life.[20] Both Addison and Randolph Clark followed in their father's footsteps teaching and preaching. To date, there is no evidence that Joseph Addison or his sons preached on the topic of enslavement. Sermons were rarely written down, and little documentation exists regarding the Church's stance on enslavement other than what was published in religious journals. Disciples preachers were typically traveling evangelists who concentrated on personal salvation while infrequently commenting on social matters.[21] The Disciples of Christ generally tried to ignore the issue of enslavement to avoid the sectional divisions that had split other denominations in the United States. There was little sign of anti-enslavement sentiment among Southern followers of the Church.[22]

There existed a long tradition in the United States for churches to establish private academies, colleges, and universities. Inspired by their father, who was a teacher, and by the Church's coeducational leanings, the Clark brothers operated a coeducational seminary in Fort Worth. The Clark brothers then transitioned to create a far more comprehensive educational institute—the Add-Ran Male and Female College, later renamed Texas Christian University. They soon moved to Thorp Spring, away from the "sinful" influences of Fort Worth's notorious "Hell's Half Acre," which earned infamy for the gambling, drinking, and prostitution that accompanied portions of cowboy culture.

Thorp Spring, the first location of what would be Add-Ran Male and Female College, had been established by Pleasant Thorp in 1854. According to Barbara Thorp Wilkins, one of Pleasant Thorp's descendants, Thorp Spring was near the hunting grounds and campsites for Caddos and Comanches and an Ioni Indian village. Wilkins notes that after the Federal troops withdrew following secession, the area was vulnerable to "escalated Indian attacks."[23] Hoping a school would be a valuable economic asset to the community, Thorp erected a school building; in 1873, he invited the Clarks to move their school to Thorp Spring.[24] Expanding their enterprise to a college, the Clarks obtained a charter from the state in 1873 and named their institution Add-Ran Male and Female College, after Addison's young son, who died prematurely in 1872. Membership to the first Board of Trustees was restricted to members of the Christian Church, and in 1873, the college was recognized as a school of the Christian Churches in Texas.[25] On the first letterhead of the school, A. Clark is listed as President, R. Clark as Vice President, and J. A. Clark as Proprietor.[26]

The financial crisis of 1873 imperiled the Clark family finances such that they could not complete payment for the building at Thorp Spring, where the College intended as permanent residence, and they were forced to move to other accommodations within Thorp Spring. At this time, the brothers took control of the school as their father relinquished his managerial responsibilities.[27] The Clark brothers tapped into a strong desire in North Texas for higher education, giving them no trouble attracting students: in its new home, the college thrived; by 1893, enrollment grew to 445 students. Several more buildings were added, including one funded "through the generosity and leadership of Major and Mrs. J. J. Jarvis."[28] Jarvis, who served as a Confederate major, became head of the Trustees.

Add-Ran Male and Female College was designed to be a racially segregated institution. It never would have occurred to its founders that it would be anything other than that. In post–Civil War Texas—and well into the twentieth century—any Texas school that had ever contemplated admitting a Black student (or an Indigenous student or a student of color) with white students enrolled would have immediately lost all its white students, faculty, and financial support. Even so, Black, Indigenous, Latinx, and white peoples and communities in the South had always been closely interwoven, as the story of Charley and Kate Thorp reveals.

Charley and Kate Thorp, a formerly enslaved couple who worked at the college for its entire time in Thorp Spring, reveal a great deal about TCU and race in its founding years. Born a slave in Caldwell, Texas, in 1852, Charley Thorp (whose rarely used legal name was Henry W.) and his mother Jude had been purchased by Pleasant Thorp and brought to Thorp Spring in about 1855.[29] Emancipated when the war ended, Charley Thorp stayed in Thorp Spring, likely helping to build the stone structure that first housed AddRan College. When the Clark brothers opened their school, Charley went to work for the Clarks and soon proved indispensable to the new institution. Joseph Lynn Clark, Randolph's son, left the best account of Charley's duties:

When the Clarks opened the school in the Thorp building, Charley was em-
ployed for janitorial service; as the school developed, he gradually accepted
wider responsibility for practically every detail, aside from academic activities,
not specifically belonging to someone else. He saw that the buildings were kept
in repair. He advised on improvement. He repaired frozen water pipes. He
made winter fires in the classroom stoves, and filled the oil lamps, and when
the duty was not assigned to a reliable student, he rang the big bell that
regulated the school's daily schedule. He prepared the auditorium for the
Sunday services and sounded the bell that called the community to worship.[30]

But Charley's contributions to TCU and to the Clarks went far beyond
these mundane, if vital, duties. Charley helped the brothers enforce their
strict prohibition of alcohol on the campus. The nearest saloon was three
miles away in Granbury, but as Joseph Lynn Clark explains, if there were
ever any suspected "infringement" of the rules, "Charley was the FBI." Charley was the unofficial "fire chief" of the hamlet, and "his skill and patience
in the sickroom was notable."[31] In his memoir, Joseph Lynn Clark goes on
to relate the story of an Add-Ran student, W. H. Forrester, who in 1894 fell
seriously ill with typhoid fever. For thirty days, Charley nursed Forrester,
and when he was well enough to travel, loaded him into a wagon and drove
him to his parents' house, a journey of eighty miles. Charley's extraordinary
service in this case was such that the local newspaper in Granbury called on
the community to take up a collection to pay Charley "for his faithful and
careful nursing" of Forrester, emphasizing "our citizens should not let his
earnest labor go unrewarded."[32]

Randolph Clark relates another story about Charley that indicates something of Charley's character. Clark's wife Ella had fallen "dangerously ill"
while Randolph was away preaching at a revival. Anticipating that Ella's
illness might be so serious that Randolph would need to be sent for, Charley harnessed a buggy that he would need to ride the twenty miles to the
nearest telegraph office to summon Randolph. But when he saw the doctors
"anxiously counseling," Charley made the decision to go ahead. He rode the
twenty miles, sent the message to Randolph "in words that could not be mistaken," and then waited all the next day and into the night until Randolph
arrived. Recalling this story, Randolph noted that "this is only a small part
of a life spent in like service."[33]

In about 1882, Charley married Kate Lee. Listed on the census as a "mulatto," Kate was probably the daughter of an enslaved woman owned by Moody Lee, who was the mother of Randolph Clark's wife, Ella Lee Clark. After her mother's death, Kate remained as a member of the Lee household. It is also possible that Kate and Ella shared the same biological father, making them half sisters. But in any case, they grew up together and had a close, lifelong relationship. Kate came to Thorp Spring with Ella and Randolph, where she met and eventually married Charley Thorp. They had several children. Kate worked as a domestic servant for the Randolph Clark family and, according to Joseph Lynn Clark, served the Thorp Spring community as a midwife and nurse.[34] Charley and Kate Thorp both made substantial contributions to TCU's early years in Thorp Spring. Sylviane Ngandu-Kalenga Greensword provides a more extensive history of Charley and Kate Thorp in Part Two of this collection. Other Black people likely worked at Add-Ran during the school's years in Thorp Spring, even if only the barest of clues hint at their presence. In his family memoir written in the 1960s, Randolph Clark's son Joseph noted that since the nearest school for Black children was three miles away in Granbury, education for the children of Kate and Charley Thorp and any other Black children connected with Add-Ran "was neglected, a lamentable situation."[35]

TCU's Waco Years, 1895–1910

In 1889, the Clark brothers transferred ownership of the college to the Christian Church of Texas and changed the college name to Add-Ran Christian University. In 1893, it reached its peak enrollment for the Thorp Spring years, with 445 students. But for the Clarks, the added stability wrought by the transfer of ownership also meant that they no longer controlled the school's destiny, and in 1895 the new board of trustees reached a monumental decision: The university would move to Waco.[36]

Disciples of Christ members in Waco played an integral part in bringing the college to their city. The elders of the Central Christian Church bought the property for $30,000. In moving to Waco, the university placed itself in the heart of a region whose dedication to the old Confederacy was never in doubt. Waco was one of the northern ends of the Texas plantation belt. But northwest Waco, where TCU settled, was on the open prairie, a grassland that once stretched into Canada. The physical remoteness of the campus ensured that the Black community had little direct contact with the College. Few Black people lived nearby, and those who worked on campus would have had to walk several miles, ride an animal, or take the segregated street-car, which took precious cash. TCU was almost two miles from the nearest Black neighborhood, which had built up around the site of the Freedmen's Bureau school on North Seventh Street near Colcord. We have the name of only one of those early employees, Benjamin Jones. Jones, a Black man born in July 1863, was listed in the 1900 Waco city directory as "working" at Add-Ran College.[37]

TCU students and faculty on the Waco campus openly participated in the "Lost Cause" rhetoric that was endemic during this period. One of the most aggressive proponents of the "Lost Cause" was an organization named the United Daughters of the Confederacy (UDC), which spread to Texas in 1895. In November 1903, the UDC organized "a strong chapter" with twenty-two members at TCU. The *Skiff* approved of this development, explaining, "Most of the girls in the hall have fathers, uncles, or grandfathers who championed the cause of the South from '61 to '65," concluding, "It is T.C.U.'s mission to aid in all commendable work and doubtless this move which has for its purpose the remembrance of the valorous deeds of our Southern heroes will be strongly supported, as it should be."[38] When the Texas chapter of the UDC met in Waco in 1905, the G. B. Gerald chapter held an opening reception that TCU faculty members attended; several TCU faculty took to the stage. In addition to three days of reports, addresses, and prayers, attendees heard poems and musical numbers, including the poem "My Old Black Mammy" and the song "My Old Black Mammie." We have no record of TCU students attending, although one might surmise that members of the student UDC would have made the trek across town for the events.[39] The Old South appeared in various other guises on campus as well. A 1905 reprint from the *Houston Post*, published in the TCU student newspaper the *Daily Skiff*, extolled the return of captured Confederate battle flags from the U.S. War Department.[40]

The *Skiff* reveals that student journalists also routinely made racialized references in their reportage. These pieces are only occasionally signed, so

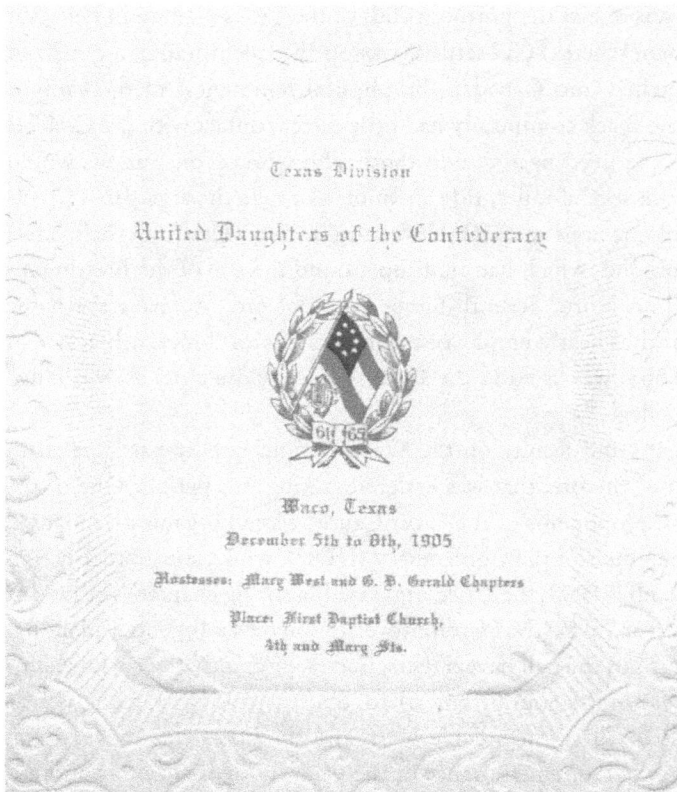

Texas Division

United Daughters of the Confederacy

Waco, Texas

December 5th to 8th, 1905

Hostesses: Mary West and G. B. Gerald Chapters

Place: First Baptist Church,
4th and Mary Sts.

Program from the meeting of the 1905 Texas Division of the
United Daughters of the Confederacy, held in Waco, Texas.
Image courtesy of TCU Special Collections.

the authors remain anonymous. A description of "Waco today" in 1903 described Latinx people as "the sombreroed montezuma" [sic] and a Black man as "the ebon son of Ham." One writer praised the reign of King Cotton.[41] A month later, the newspaper detailed the arrest of "a Negro" for horse theft, following a call to the sheriff by TCU business manager Aaron C. Easley and also referred to the suspect as "the darkey."[42] A writer in April 1903 praised Robert E. Lee as "that sterling old hero."[43] In 1906, a writer for the *Skiff* observed that they were "not advocating lynching at all," but that with enough words they would show that "[lynching] is not antithetical to the great primal laws and principles of Democracy. Mob-law is not named rightly as anarchy and this is the thing we object to."

New Home, Old Attitudes:
TCU's Return to Fort Worth,
1910–1923

On the evening of March 22, 1910, the TCU main building in Waco caught fire and was gutted in a matter of hours. Although the other buildings on the campus still stood, the university had insufficient insurance to rebuild its main structure. The trustees received invitations from several cities, and in the end, they decided to move the campus to Fort Worth. The Waco period ended quickly and shockingly. In 1912, the university sold the remaining property to developers, and TCU in Waco was no more.

Fort Worth famously embraces its identity as the place "Where the West Begins," a motto that *Fort Worth Star-Telegram* publisher Amon G. Carter institutionalized on his newspaper's masthead in 1923. A quick look at the history of Fort Worth and Tarrant County, however, lays to rest any doubts about its Southern heritage. In 1860, Tarrant County, which was still very much on the frontier, was home to 740 enslaved Black Americans, owned by 158 whites. By 1864, with an influx of southerners fleeing the ravages of the Civil War, those numbers had swollen to 1,744 people enslaved by 346 white owners. Those laborers were valued by Tarrant County at $1.5 million, by far the largest category of capital assets in the county. Tarrant County's climate was not conducive to the production of cotton on large plantations, but enslaved labor was utilized on small farms and in livestock raising, milling, construction, and a variety of other industries.

TCU moved to land that was the ancestral homelands of the Wichita and Affiliated Tribes, who lived here for generations. By the time TCU re-established itself in Fort Worth in 1910, the Black population of Tarrant County was sizably larger, having increased to 15,572 out of a total population of 108,572—a substantial Black minority for a city that thought of itself as western.[44] The growing city participated fully in the South's rigid system of segregation, with separate schools, residential neighborhoods, businesses, and public accommodations for Black, Indigenous, and Latinx communities—and whites. The idea of TCU admitting Black, Indigenous, or other students of color—at least American students of color—as students still lay nearly a half-century into the future. Since the enactment of the statewide poll tax in 1902 and other legal and extralegal means of discouraging po-

This photo appears in the scrapbook of Mattie Cooper Harlin, which notes a list of teachers, including "Mr. Addison Clark, President" and "Mr. Randolph Clark, Vice President," as well as a list of "girls of the boarding house" with forty-two names. Note the lone Black woman off to the side and around the corner of the building. Who is she? Why is she not identified? What other questions should we ask about her placement in what seems to have been a posed photograph? *Photo courtesy of TCU Special Collections.*

litical participation, people of color had been largely excluded from voting. Black, Indigenous, and other people of color held no public offices and could not sit on juries. Apart from a small middle class of teachers, ministers, and business-owners in the Jim and Juan Crow economy, most people of color (including Fort Worth's small Mexicano community) worked as domestic servants or in other manual labor occupations that protected most white workers from performing the daily drudgery of keeping the school running. Instead, TCU filled positions such as housekeepers, cooks, and groundskeepers exclusively with Black workers.

Life for TCU's Black workers was not easy. When students moved into the first two state-of-the-art brick dormitories—Jarvis Hall for women and Clark Hall (on the site of the present-day Sadler Hall) for men—the university faced the quandary of how to keep the students fed and the buildings and grounds cleaned and maintained. In segregated Fort Worth, the nearest Black neighborhood was Terrell Heights, four miles east of campus, and the duties done by cooks and other workers required very early mornings and late evenings. Consequently, the university built a "servant house," a low-slung, white frame barracks on the west edge of campus behind the main building (now Reed Hall), one structure in a small complex of service buildings that included a stable, tool shed, various workshops, and the university power plant.[45] It was a classic expression of the southern tradition of housing domestic workers in servants' quarters behind the "big house," where they would be close at hand for duty but otherwise hidden away. Even the architecture of TCU's original buildings—in the neoclassical style with stately Ionic columns—hearkened back to the great plantation houses of the antebellum South. The quarters in the servant house were no doubt cramped and lacking in privacy. For most of those workers who did live off campus, getting to work involved a lengthy walk or a ride in the back seat of the city's segregated streetcars, which would have been expensive and time-consuming to do on a daily basis.

While white students knew, and often even spoke fondly (if condescendingly), of the school's Black laborers, the very familiarity between the two groups meant that the students felt little hesitation in involving the Black "help" in what the students viewed as harmless campus hijinks. The most notorious of these pranks, in which students used Black workers essentially as "props" for a racist practical joke, involved the annual election of a freshman class president. In all but two years between 1912 and 1923, the students followed this script: The first week of the fall semester, a meeting of the freshman class would be called for the purposes of electing a class president. Since the freshmen were virtually all strangers to one another, a helpful upperclassman would stand up and make an impassioned speech in favor of a certain named candidate, upon which the gullible freshmen would elect the recommended candidate by acclamation. The upperclassman would then escort the new class "president"—a Black janitor, cook, or gardener—into the room, with the predictable "hilarious" response from the gathered crowd. It goes without saying that such episodes were demeaning to the Black workers who were being used in this manner. But it is also notable that they apparently never refused to participate: Abe Green, S. H. Thompson, Joe Allen, Roland Briscoe, Hattie Cole, Haywood White, Arthur Hunter, Jeremiah Lindsay, and Roosevelt Bailey all understood that if they valued their jobs and hoped to avoid whatever repercussions might come with being branded

TCU's "servant house," located behind what is today Reed Hall, c. 1930.
Photo courtesy of TCU Special Collections.

"uppity" or "insolent," they had better play along with the white students' jokes.[46]

Racist jokes and the use of racial epithets were so pervasive on campus that they never elicited any commentary that we know of. So common was such fare in the pages of the *Skiff* that a brief list of representative items will suffice to illustrate the point: a 1911 report on a program of the Shirley Literary Society that referred to a sophomore "who had more announcements than a n*****'s dog had fleas"; a 1913 letter from a former TCU student living in New York City, complaining about "'thick-lip' Africans sitting 'jam-up' side by side with whites, in every street car"; a 1915 story complaining of professors who fail to keep their classrooms properly ventilated, causing the rooms to smell "like a negro hut where about five negroes had slept with everything closed tight all night"; a 1918 story about students obtaining chickens for a picnic "'n*****r' fashion" (that is, by stealing them); a 1919 story about a Halloween party in a women's dorm told in Black dialect and using the n-word four times; a 1921 poem about a woodpecker which included the lines, "He works like a n**** / To make the hole bigger"; an account in the 1923 *Horned Frog* telling of a devastating flood in April of

Article in the *Skiff* recalling tradition of freshman class "electing" Black presidents at TCU, Nov. 6, 1936. *Photo courtesy of TCU Library.*

that year near the university, among whose refugees were "frightened little n****"; a 1923 poem titled "African Golf" about Black men shooting dice, which begins with the lines, "Five coal black n**** with heavy scowls / All sat together, cheek and jowl."[47]

Nor was campus racism confined to the written word. Minstrel shows were at their peak of popularity in the America of the 1910s, and both performances and graphic depictions of blackface were common. In 1914, prior to a big football game against Austin College, students held a "pep carnival" in which one of the main features was a booth with "Negro Minstrels," whom the *Skiff* described as "heavy-weights, spade-footed, kinky headed, pug-nosed, and as black as the ace of spades." The *Horned Frog* depicted the TCU men's quartet, led by student John Spurgeon, as stereotypical blackface children in a racist 1916 cartoon.[48]

TCU's Black workers, however, *would* have had the opportunity to witness one particularly egregious piece of campus racism. In the 1914 "pep carnival" mentioned above, another featured attraction, apart from the minstrel show, was a game called "Hit the Negro Baby." A common feature of fairs and carnivals in the Jim Crow South *and* nationwide, "Hit the Negro Baby" (usually with the other n-word in the title, and sometimes also called "Hit the Coon" or "African Dodger") involved paying a Black man or boy to stand behind a canvas sheet with a head-sized hole cut in it. Fairgoers then would pay to get three tries at hitting the "dodger" in the head with baseballs or eggs. The game was so dangerous that, in 1917, New York became the first state to ban it, but it remained popular in Texas into the 1940s. (Modern dunking booths were invented as a tamer alternative.) We do not know whether the booth at the TCU student fair actually used a live person as a target—sometimes the "Negro baby" was just a graphic representation of a Black person. One can hope that one of the university's Black workers was spared the danger and humiliation of being called on to serve as the live target in this instance, but even the less-dramatic version of the attraction was demeaning enough.[49]

The end of World War One and the Bolshevik Revolution in Russia ignited not only a Red Scare and a wave of anti-immigrant hysteria in America but also the worst crisis in Black-white race relations since Reconstruction. The race riots and repression that broke out in Texas and throughout the nation in 1919 spurred the growth of the resurrected Ku Klux Klan. By

1920, the "new" Klan had spread throughout Texas. Klansmen constituted a majority in the state legislature by 1923, and Texas sent a known Klansman, Earle Mayfield, to the U.S. Senate. Fort Worth became one of the Klan's strongholds; over the next few years more than six thousand white Fort Worthians joined Klavern No. 101, the city's local chapter. Pro-Klan candidates captured all local offices. Businessmen found that they couldn't get city contracts unless they joined the order. The 1920s Klan tried to maintain a veneer of respectability; it claimed to be a citadel of Protestant religious values and public morality, punishing bootleggers, adulterers, and anyone else who ran afoul of its fundamentalist Christian moral code. But like the Klan of the Reconstruction era, it also engaged in much covert violence, the victims of which were often immigrants, Catholics, Jews, and Black people.[50]

The widespread influence of the KKK affected TCU, of course. Even before the arrival of the new Klan in Texas, white Fort Worthians were inclined to view the Klan positively. In 1916, the city held its "first annual Halloween Mardi Gras," which was attended by the "entire student body" and featured a "parade led by the T.C.U. Band." Following in the procession immediately after the float from the TCU art department was "a troup of Klu Klux Klansmen" [sic]—whose presence suggested that when the new Klan was actually organized in the city, it would find a warm reception.[51] Three years later, in 1919, readers of the *Skiff* were greeted by the bold-faced headline on page 1: "Ku Klux Klan Revived." It turned out that the story was not about the KKK at all; rather, it was about a late-night raid by pajama-wearing male students on the women's dorm, which led to buckets of water being flung between the warring groups of students—a sort of combination panty-raid and wet-t-shirt contest. What was revealing about the story was that it made no mention, oblique or overt, of the Klan. In the South, white readers all would have gotten the joke: the Klan was known for midnight assaults on unsuspecting victims.[52]

By 1922, the Klan was so omnipresent that it had become a sort of cultural touchstone. Another reference that year to the Klan in the *Skiff* reinforced how familiar with—and how nonjudgmental—TCU students were about the hooded order. TCU had recently adopted an academic honor code, in which students were required to report any incidents of cheating. The *Skiff*'s story carried the headline: "The Invisible Empire of T.C.U.," a reference to a name that the Klan gave itself. The story explained the analogy: "It has often been said in speaking of the invisible empire of the Ku Klux Klan that you never can tell when you are talking to a member of that invisible empire. Just so, when you are cheating, some one may have his eye on you."[53]

Yet there is no record of an actual chapter of the Ku Klux Klan ever being established on campus or of TCU students joining the Fort Worth "klavern." Doctrinally, the Disciples of Christ denomination generally steered clear of the Protestant fundamentalism with which the Klan was so closely associated. Still, individual students were attracted to the order. In 1922, TCU history major William J. "Jack" Hammond, who had been vice president of the campus's Christian Endeavor chapter and president of the TCU Ministerial Association, "preached a sermon in the interest of the Ku Klux Klan" at the Ross Avenue Christian Church in Dallas. The *Skiff* gave no details on the sermon, only speculating, tongue-in-cheek, that Hammond might have been "looking for a free membership into this great organization."[54]

Klansmen were equal-opportunity bigots; they disliked any group that they deemed less than "100 percent American," including people of color, immigrants, and non-Protestants. TCU likewise was no stranger to ethnocentrism. Fort Worth had relatively few non-white minorities in the early twentieth century. There were only about 121 Mexicano households in Tarrant County when TCU moved there in 1910. Seven times that many had arrived by 1920, due to the dislocations wrought by the Mexican Revolution and the lure of jobs in the meat-packing industry, but as a percentage of the population, the overall numbers remained very low.[55]

Not surprisingly, "Mexicans" (distinctions were rarely drawn between Mexican nationals, Mexican immigrants, and Mexican Americans) came in experiencing their share of stereotyping at the hands of TCU students. A common trope of the era was referring to athletes and athletics as "of the Mexican variety." This was a reference to an athlete who was lazy or unmotivated, tapping into a longstanding stereotype of Mexicans. (The *Oxford English Dictionary* identifies use of the adjective "Mexican" in the early-twentieth-century U.S. to designate "anything of inferior, fraudulent, or makeshift quality," and the first example it gives is a 1912 *New York Evening Journal* referring to "a Mexican athlete.") So, the 1916 TCU yearbook could refer to an intramural football game between the university's medical and law students, complimenting the law students for not confining "their athletic activities to the Mexican variety," or note that "varsity athletes show[ed] their versatility by engaging in Mexican athletics" at a sports banquet.[56]

TCU's fiftieth anniversary in 1923 coincided with the high point of the second Ku Klux Klan in Texas. In Fort Worth and statewide, the Klan went into a steep decline after the press exposed some of its more extreme acts of violence, and by the second half of the 1920s, its heyday was over. But whether the Klan's brief reign was a cause or a symptom of the extreme racism of that era—and it was probably a bit of both—TCU had clearly participated in the bigotry of the period. Yet there were always occasions when the better angels of the university's nature emerged, even if briefly.

Better Angels

In May 1903, an unnamed writer in the *Skiff* made a somewhat surprising declaration: They proclaimed Black leader Booker T. Washington "one of the greatest living men, because his work is unique, the modern Moses, who leads his race and lifts it through education, to even better and higher things than a land overflowing with milk and honey."[57] The TCU writer, of course, extolled the more conservative Booker T. Washington rather than the more progressive W. E. B. DuBois. Yet the TCU writer did acknowledge the race problem of the South and advocated for education rather than other alternatives as a solution.

Black education received a boost closer to home in 1913. That year, readers of the *Skiff* learned about the recent opening of the Jarvis Christian Institute (later Jarvis Christian College), a segregated Black Disciples-affiliated college in Wood County named for Maj. James Jones Jarvis and his wife Ida Van Zandt Jarvis, who donated land for the college. The Jarvises were also major benefactors of TCU, and the *Skiff* noted approvingly that "Texas is making a step toward educating the negro."[58] Eight years later, Randolph Clark wrote a glowing account of his visit to Jarvis Institute. The elderly co-founder of TCU had gone to Jarvis with Charley Thorp, whom he described as "our old college janitor, watchman, and general caretaker of the old Add-Ran," to help Thorp enroll his youngest daughter in the school. Clark, ever the disciplinarian, was particularly impressed with the strict moral code that the institution enforced, and he praised the Black school for its "marked results."[59] Jarvis Christian Institute was part of the structure of Jim Crow in Texas, but in an era of such virulent racism, its very existence and the cordial ties between it and TCU were nonetheless noteworthy.[60]

In the first decades of the twentieth century, progressive lecturers frequently spoke on campus, sometimes on racial topics, and they seem to have received respectful hearings. For example, in December 1911, TCU hosted a visit from Dr. Willis Duke Weatherford, who spoke on "the Negro Problem in the South," and the *Skiff* reported that "not only were many new thoughts presented to the audience, but a new feeling was created toward the negro. Those who heard this lecture now realize how little we have done for the Black man and what a meagre change we are giving him."[61] TCU student Louise Dura Cockrell saved in her college scrapbook a flyer for a "Mammoth Pageant" titled "Up From Slavery," which featured a performance by Florence Cole Talbert, a renowned Black coloratura soprano, and "a cast and chorus of two hundred," which benefited the local "Colored Branch" of the YMCA. Notably, Cockrell's father, former TCU professor and current Fort Worth mayor E. R. Cockrell, delivered "Bits o' Thought" prior to the performance.[62] TCU students often did seem eager to learn about cultures beyond the U.S. borders. In 1921, the Nobel Prize–winning Bengali writer and educator Rabindranath Tagore spoke in Fort Worth, as part of a tour of Texas universities, with the *Skiff* remarking on the "large crowd" that had gone to hear the "noted" polymath, despite very disagreeable weather.[63] The following year, TCU welcomed Dr. Yu Yui Tsu, a Chinese scholar and diplomat, whom the *Skiff* described as "one of the foremost statesmen of China." Tsu's visit to TCU was, according to the *Skiff*, intended to produce "a more sympathetic feeling between the countries which are so far apart in both manners and miles," and the newspaper declared that students who attended one of his several speeches at TCU "were treated to an unusual privilege."[64] The following year, U.S. Commissioner of Indian Affairs Cato Sells spoke on campus "on the subject of the American Indian." Sells sought to enlighten his student audience on the current state of Indian affairs, noting, among other things, that "a larger percentage of the Indians attend school without compulsion than white students with compulsion."[65] So, although the TCU campus remained a bastion of whiteness, that bastion was never hermetically sealed off from the broader, more diverse world. Students who wanted to expand their minds were given modest opportunities to do so.

One of TCU's most significant efforts at minority outreach came at the hands of Modern Languages professor Mateo Alvarez de Molina, a native of

"Up From Slavery"

Mammoth Pageant

At the Coliseum

Monday
Nov. 21, 1921

at 7:30 p. m.

Benefit Y. M. C. A. (Col. Branch)

FLORENCE COLE TALBERT (Detroit, Michigan), winner of diamond medal at Chicago Musical College in 1916 and greatest coloratura soprano of the Negro race, is taking the leading part as the Goddess of Music, supported by a cast and chorus of two hundred. Special Scenery—Birth of negro folk songs portrayed.

One-half auditorium reserved for whites.

Tickets on sale for whites:

Collins Art Store and George's Drug Store, North Fort Worth.

For Colored: Y. M. C. A., Col. Branch, 912 Jones St., and Prospect Drug Co., North Fort Worth.

Prices: $1.00, $2.00, $3.00. All school children 50 cents. These tickets will be delivered through the principals of the schools.

First appearance in this city.

This pageant is endorsed by the Mothers Council (White) and many of the reputable music clubs of the city.

Actual conditions giving rise to the birth of the negro folk songs, exhibited by a chorus of 200 of the best voices of the city.

"Bits o' Thought," by Hon. E. R. Cockrell, mayor of the city; Mr. M. H. Moore, Supt. City Schools; Mr. R. C. Balaam, Gen. Sec. Y. M. C. A.

Program from the Mammoth Pageant at the Fort Worth Coliseum, featuring the celebrated coloratura soprano Florence Cole Talbert, November 21, 1921.
Image courtesy of TCU Special Collections.

Valencia, Spain (or possibly a native of Mexico), who joined the TCU faculty in 1909. Molina, an ordained minister, had studied in France, Argentina, and California, before coming to Texas and was fluent in Spanish, French, and English. Although he had a degree from a Spanish university and was on the TCU faculty, he also enrolled in Brite College (later, Brite Divinity School). In the meantime, he founded a mission to Fort Worth's small Mexican community in 1915, which he ran for many years. Cecilia N. Sánchez Hill explores this history in greater depth in Part Two.

The mission operated a night school and a church, and it furnished clothing and meals to the impoverished residents of the city's north side. TCU faculty and students often helped with the enterprise, both with their labor and financial contributions.[66] In the 1910s, TCU had a college-preparatory academy in addition to its collegiate departments, and it admitted at least one Mexican student, Jesus Rivera of Laredo, who had been baptized by Molina. Rivera, however, soon dropped out of TCU, for reasons that were never reported.[67] Still, despite the ethnic slurs or stereotypes directed at those of Mexican heritage, in 1914 the *Skiff* published a written version of a talk given in the campus chapel with the headline, "Mexicans Are Much Like Americans." Noting that that Americans "do not have a monopoly on industry, honesty, and integrity," the essay argued that "people of all nations are very much the same in true character."[68] Similarly, a writer in the *Skiff* two years later declared that "the calamity howler who speaks all-wisely and in vulgar epithetic terms of the Mexicans, is, as a general rule, an ignoramus who knows as little about the Mexican people as a hog does the side-saddle."[69] When a former TCU student, Riley Ailen, wrote back to the *Skiff* to tell of his experiences teaching in a Mexican American school in Marfa, he informed his former classmates that the Mexican children "were good students in spite of so many disadvantages, and the idea that these Mexican children are stubborn and hard to teach is a great mistake."[70]

TCU's efforts to be open-minded about Mexicans carried over into its attitudes toward Jews, a group which, in that era of rampant nativism and xenophobia, was often considered a separate "race." A 1912 entry in a campus oratorical contest by TCU student J. Lindley Wood was titled "The Jew and Civilization," and it argued that Jews had been unjustly persecuted.[71] Several Jewish students attended the university, and the *Skiff* periodically commented favorably on their activities. In 1920, as the Ku Klux Klan was being revived in Texas, Rabbi Dr. George Fox spoke on campus, where he was introduced by TCU President Edward M. Waits. Fox's talk was overtly political, noting the "disconcerting amount of insincerity and dishonesty eating at the heart of the nation today" and calling for the election of "capable officials." According to the *Skiff*, "the student audience showed its appreciation of the splendid talk of Dr. Fox by vigorous applause."[72]

As TCU concluded its fiftieth year, the campus seemed prepared to face something of a racial reckoning. Several TCU students had attended a national Student Volunteer Conference, part of a group dedicated to international Christian missions, in Indianapolis, and when they returned to campus, one of the attendees, Kenneth Bonham, submitted a "student comment" to the *Skiff* in which he argued that "race prejudice is based upon a fallacy—a mistaken theory of race superiority. The difference in accomplishments of the races was due to the difference in opportunities and not in capacities!" Another TCU student, Vida Elliott, returned from the conference and reported her belief that "the call of the world is to unite nations, races, and classes in Christ."[73]

For half a century, TCU's founders, administrators, faculty, and students had been part of a society that systematically denied people of color the fundamental rights guaranteed by the Constitution and the treatment ostensibly required by their Christian faith. Randolph Clark bore his share of the responsibility for that injustice. Real change would eventually come to TCU, but it still lay in the distant future.

TCU's Transition to
Integration (1941–1971)

THE ROAD TO INTEGRATION at TCU was long, difficult, and painful for many people. Since its founding in 1873, TCU existed in a world of white supremacy, and in many ways, it reflected that reality rather than combatted it. As the history of TCU's founding years details, the university was a creation of its place, in the South, and of the specific time in the life of the United States and Texas. Over its early years, Jim Crow laws governed segregation by race. Such practices ruled the South, Texas, Fort Worth—and TCU.

As "desegregation" directly refers to reversing the written rule of racial separation, it may be useful to define the more nuanced term "integration." In this context, integration is to be understood as not only desegregation, but also the physical, cultural, administrative, and academic inclusion of people of color within the TCU community. This section details the university's efforts (and barriers to such efforts) to integrate its student body, faculty, administrative staff, curriculum and coursework, athletics, and student life. It highlights the distinction between how the administrators and campus community at that time viewed this transition and how we, today, view the issue. Indeed, the debate of the mid-century was centered on whether and how to end segregation, whereas the contemporary TCU community's focus has shifted to the pursuit of integration.

In our research, the Race & Reconciliation Initiative incorporated the experiences of many racial and ethnic identities beyond Black Americans, yet it is important to note that segregation and integration refer predominantly to the treatment of Black people, as the latter were the targeted population of such practices. For instance, in 1963, J.M. Moudy, provost and vice chancellor for academic affairs, discussed how the ongoing, explicitly intentional "policy of excluding Negro students from Texas Christian University" contrasted with TCU's admission of dark-skinned international students.[74] Likewise, although our research addresses the long-held exclusion of Tejano / Mexicano students until the 1960s, students of Indigenous, Asian and Asian Pacific American, Middle Eastern, and Latin American descent appear on several occasions in TCU yearbooks that precede our 1941–1971 time frame.

TCU and Race in the Fort Worth Community

As in many U.S. cities, Fort Worth urban planning functioned as geographic racism, the segregation of communities of color and low-income residents, where they often lacked adequate city services. The residential pattern of inequality lingered throughout the twentieth century, as exemplified in the 1947 Ordinance that prevented roads from connecting the white Ridglea neighborhood to Black Como, leading to the building of a high brick and barbed-wire fence known as the "Ridglea Wall."[75] Although the two communities were only a block apart, the 1960 census reveals that Ridglea was 100 percent white and Como 98 percent Black.[76] In addition to standing as a stark symbol of Como's racial segregation, the "wall" hindered Como residents' ability to access basic public amenities, such as the library, which was on the Ridglea side.[77] On the Como side of the wall, neighborhood residents have reported, to this day, frequent flooding due to municipal neglect and poor infrastructure.[78]

Despite the highly visible markers of racial divide, the City of Fort Worth was awarded the All-America City Award in 1964. This recognition honors "communities that leverage civic engagement, collaboration, inclusiveness, and innovation to successfully address local issues," illustrating the extent to which folkways of segregation were ingrained in cultural norms.[79]

The neighborhood around Ridglea Country Club was not alone in engaging in explicit practices of segregation. Colonial Country Club, TCU's immediate neighbor, opened in 1936 as a "men only" establishment. The Colonial would not admit its first Black member until more than five decades later, after brokering an agreement with the Fort Worth Chamber of Commerce. The change was economically motivated, made out of concern that the Professional Golfers' Association (PGA) would exclude the Colonial

Ridglea Wall. *Image courtesy of TCU Library.*

from the 1991 Tour,[80] at a time when the South's most prestigious and exclusive golf clubs were recalcitrant holdouts in admitting members of color (and women).[81]

The Fort Worth neighborhood known as Little Mexico also endured patterns of racial hierarchy and segregation through urban planning. In 1935, TCU history professor and City Councilman W. J. Hammond (Progressive Democratic Party) voiced his concern over civic issues such as public housing and the growth of slums in Fort Worth. He commissioned his fellow professor Austin Porterfield, who specialized in the scientific sociology of crime and family relations, to evaluate city neighborhoods.[82] Two years later, after Hammond had been appointed mayor, Porterfield and his team of TCU graduate student researchers determined that Little Mexico had a high index of disorganization, amoral behavior, and intellectual deficiency. Their reports illustrated the common fear of physical proximity and miscegenation with Mexicans, who were considered a racial group despite their official classification as whites.[83] As a result of Porterfield's study, the City of Fort Worth and the local Housing Association displaced Little Mexico residents, and the neighborhood was dismantled as the white-targeted Ripley Arnold Housing Project took shape in the late 1930s.[84] Supporters of this project, who documented the Mexican families' incomes in great detail, denied all racist motivations: "the Mexican problem, relative to housing, is not a matter of racial prejudice or discrimination but purely an economic circumstance which will make difficult their participation."[85] Tarrant County College-Northeast history professor Peter Martinez, a founding member of the Historians of Latino Americans (HOLA) of Tarrant County,[86] identified an exhaustive list of flaws in this study. Yet the Housing Association's readiness to accept and implement its findings exemplifies the prevailing views on racial determinism that classified Mexicans as immoral health hazards. It also illustrates how members of the TCU community used their academic authority to widen the gap in the city's racial proxemics.

The Supreme Court's 1954 decision to desegregate schools did not yield overnight results in Fort Worth public schools. White resistance to desegregation persisted, prompting two Black families to file a lawsuit against the district in 1959.[87] As a result of a federal court order, Fort Worth Independent School District (FWISD) began desegregation in 1963, when the School Board implemented a "stair-step" plan that integrated one grade per year.[88] The district remained under federal government oversight until 1994.[89]

Global Context: World War Two and the Cold War

When the U.S. became fully engaged in World War Two in 1941, it had greater needs for workers and workforce development; thus, significant investment was made in the training and recruitment of Black men in Texas and in Fort Worth. White instructors were recruited to provide training at the Negro War Industries Training School, a Fort Worth campus of the National Defense School. The war also brought groups from Europe and East Asia, who sought refuge in America. Their arrival would be visible in higher education, too. For instance, Texas Wesleyan University welcomed two Japanese students from relocation camps in 1941 with the War Department's approval. In the wake of World War Two, fierce competition and an ideological war for supremacy ensued between the U.S. and its allies and the Soviet Union and its satellites. Racially segregated TCU was not immune to communist criticism regarding the unequal treatment of Black people. In

1963, J. M. Moudy, then TCU's provost and vice chancellor for academic affairs, cautioned the TCU community against racist practices on campus that might give credence to communist arguments.

In the 1940s, decolonization was also in full bloom as former European colonies were advocating for political independence in Asia, Africa, the Caribbean, and Latin America. Even though the U.S. supported several pro-independence leaders to largely rally them against the communist bloc, student activists (at home and abroad) pointed the finger at America, highlighting its ill treatment and oppression of U.S. populations of color. At the national level, civil rights activity also began after World War Two, and TCU moved slowly with the nation. Conflicts such as the Korean and the Vietnam wars opened the eyes of young TCU students to parts of the world and ethnic identities that, for them, were largely underexplored, leading some to question the justice of international and racial privilege.[90]

Integration in North Texas Universities

In 1954, the Supreme Court ruled in *Brown v. Board of Education* that all public schools, and by extension all public facilities, must desegregate. The majority ruling clarified, however, that the desegregation could occur with "all deliberate speed." In some locations, "deliberate speed" took two decades. The reluctance of Texas educators to desegregate public universities meant that private establishments experienced little pressure to integrate at all.[91] Most universities followed a common pattern to desegregation. They first admitted Black graduate students, then Black undergraduates in special programs such as evening courses that did not lead to the full experience of student life. For private universities, desegregation of the main undergraduate campuses would take place on average ten to twelve years after that of the graduate schools. Among public universities in Texas, the University of North Texas (UNT) in Denton was the first to admit Black students at its main campus, between 1950 and 1956. The University of Texas at Austin admitted Black undergraduate students in 1956 as well, and other universities soon followed.[92] Private North Texas universities followed in the early 1960s with Southern Methodist University (SMU) being the first and Rice University the last. In 1958, SMU, TCU, and Baylor had desegregated their graduate schools.[93] Baylor officially voted to fully desegregate in 1963, and TCU officially desegregated its main campus in 1964. The exact dates of each step in desegregation for each college or university is not easily accessible because many did not maintain public records of Black enrollment and instead elected to desegregate quietly and discreetly.

Early, Silent Presence of Racial and Ethnic Minorities

"Quietly" was the golden rule for higher education desegregation in North Texas, and TCU was no exception. Despite a small and quiet presence of people of color since the early 1900s, the early 1950s marked a transition in the university's racial landscape. In 1951, President M. E. Sadler addressed the board of trustees and acknowledged the enrollment and physical presence of Blacks in TCU programs.[94] In Sadler's report, which was summarized in TCU's student newspaper the *Skiff*, he sought to reassure the campus community that TCU retained its segregationist policy in barring Blacks from enrolling. The few exceptions were carefully planned to take place out of sight and outside the main campus classrooms: in the evening, off-campus, and via individual conferences.

Portrait of Abdullah Ben Kori, possibly TCU's first student and faculty member of color.

When TCU formally dropped its racial barriers in 1964, the presence of students of color was nothing new. University publications, such as the *Skiff* and the *Horned Frog* yearbook, featured several illustrations of the enrollment, academic employment, and active participation of racial and ethnic minorities. Nevertheless, their otherness was mollified by their international status. As early as 1902, for example, Abdullah Ben Kori was admitted to TCU as a student. Born in Tripoli in the Syrian province of the Ottoman Empire (present day Lebanon), Ben Kori attended schools in Beirut and Rome before moving to the United States in 1900. He graduated with a Bachelor of Arts in 1904 and then remained at TCU to pursue a master's degree, during which time he also served as a professor of modern languages. Upon completion of his graduate degree, Ben Kori was promoted to department head, likely the first student and first faculty member of color at TCU. He spoke and taught German, French, Spanish, Italian, Modern Greek, and Arabic.[95]

While the yearbooks note that Abdullah Ben Kori hailed from Tripoli, few TCU documents discuss his race or specific ethnicity, possibly because his Middle Eastern origins and Arab ethnicity were interpreted as white. In 1906, he relocated to Forest Grove, Oregon, and changed his name to Alexis Ben Kori, occasionally using "Abdullah" as his middle name. Other photographs, such as that of Vida Cantrell, class of 1915, have prompted speculation about the possible presence of students of color "passing" as white during the university's first decades.[96]

Integrating the Student Body: The 1940s

The first overt examples of Indigenous, Asian American, and Latin American students on TCU's campus can be traced to the early 1940s. While white students, such as J. C. O'Neal and brothers Van "Hoss" Hall and Johnnie Hall, were given the epithets "Chief from the Indian country" and "the Indian," solely due to their outstanding football performances,[97] the *Horned Frog* and the *Skiff* indicate that Jack Jordan, a registered Cherokee, attended TCU in 1941.[98] Likewise, the enrollment of Tommy Moy, an Asian American student from New York, did not appear to trigger much resistance. Moy was an actively engaged student, involved with the TCU fencing team as an athlete,

Portrait of Elba Altamirano, possibly TCU's first
Mexican student. *Photo courtesy of TCU Library.*

then as a coach; he was also on the yearbook staff. He remained at TCU to
pursue a graduate degree. While discrimination against Tejanos abounded
in Fort Worth, the university welcomed students from Latin America. Elba
Altamirano (born of a British mother and Mexican father), for example, was
recruited from Mexico City; she earned a scholarship to pursue graduate
studies at TCU in 1944. The first identified Chicano to graduate from TCU
was Victor Vasquez, class of 1965.

Black students also studied at TCU in the 1940s, albeit off campus, and
only in evening classes. These students were mainly military officers, who,
due to university-obtained government contracts, were taught by TCU faculty members. The classes, which were under the auspices of the Evening
College, did not lead to a TCU degree.

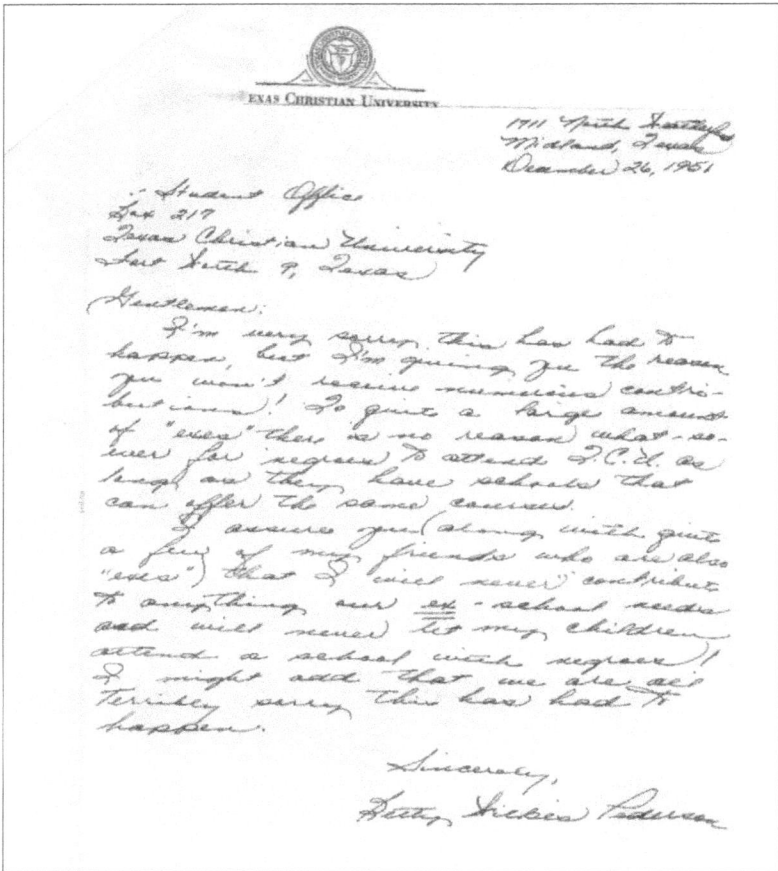

Alumni letter to President Sadler protesting the possibility of desegregating TCU, 1951.
Photo courtesy of TCU Special Collections.

Indigenous students gained increasing visibility following World War
Two. Articles and captions in the *Skiff* and the *Horned Frog* detailed the
tribal affiliations of several students, starting in the 1950s. Otis Albert Penn,
an Osage from Pawhuska, Oklahoma, attended TCU in 1948.[99] Other Indigenous students would follow. In 1952, Claire Taylor, Maxine Linn, and
Donna Gay Knox, three high school graduates from Arizona, joined the
Horned Frogs. In 1953, Joyce Hammett enrolled as a twenty-one-year-old
transfer from Oklahoma A&M. A radio major, she would soon become
KTCU's station manager.

The first cracks in segregation for Black students at TCU emerged in the 1950s, but they were neither subtle nor celebratory. Rumors about possible Black integration began to circulate in the media, to the great dissatisfaction of TCU's leadership. The mere possibility of Black integration generated ire by some members of TCU's campus community, as illustrated by the written complaint of one TCU alum, which in part stated, "I will never contribute to anything our ex-school needs and will never let my children attend a school with negroes!"[100] To reassure such persons, President Sadler wrote that TCU did not have Black students enrolled, but the university was merely complying with government request to educate soldiers.[101]

The Supreme Court decision *Sweatt v. Painter* (1950) required that universities admit all qualified students to their graduate programs, and in 1951, the TCU School of Education began offering evening courses to Black teachers. The courses were segregated, however, and offered off campus at Gay Street Elementary School. This program was designed for Black teachers seeking college credits to fulfill new certification requirements. Two program participants who had enrolled in 1951, Gay Street Elementary Principal Lottie Mae Hamilton and Fort Worth teacher Bertice Bates, had earned enough credits to earn a master's degree. Yet TCU initially refused to grant degrees to these Black students. After years of deliberation, these two educators obtained their diplomas but were not allowed to attend the still-segregated commencement and graduation ceremonies in 1956 (Hamilton) and 1960 (Bates). Such off-campus offerings were discontinued in 1956; when the TCU School of Education desegregated in 1962, numerous Gay Street program participants enrolled to complete their master's degrees. Among the first to graduate on campus were Juanita Cash (mother of James Cash, discussed below) and Reva Bell, who were granted their diplomas in 1965.[102]

The Brite College of the Bible (which had a separate board of trustees but was located on the TCU campus) integrated its graduate programs in 1950, noting that its obligation to prepare youth for a life of service in Christ's Kingdom superseded the right to deny Negroes admission based on the assumption that it is a private school.[103] James Lee Claiborne, the first Black student at Brite, enrolled in 1952 and graduated in 1955. Daniel Godspeed and Vada Phillips Felder would soon join him. These three graduate students, all married and living off campus, were not allowed to eat on campus, and Brite set up separate food service for them in Weatherly Hall, a set up similar

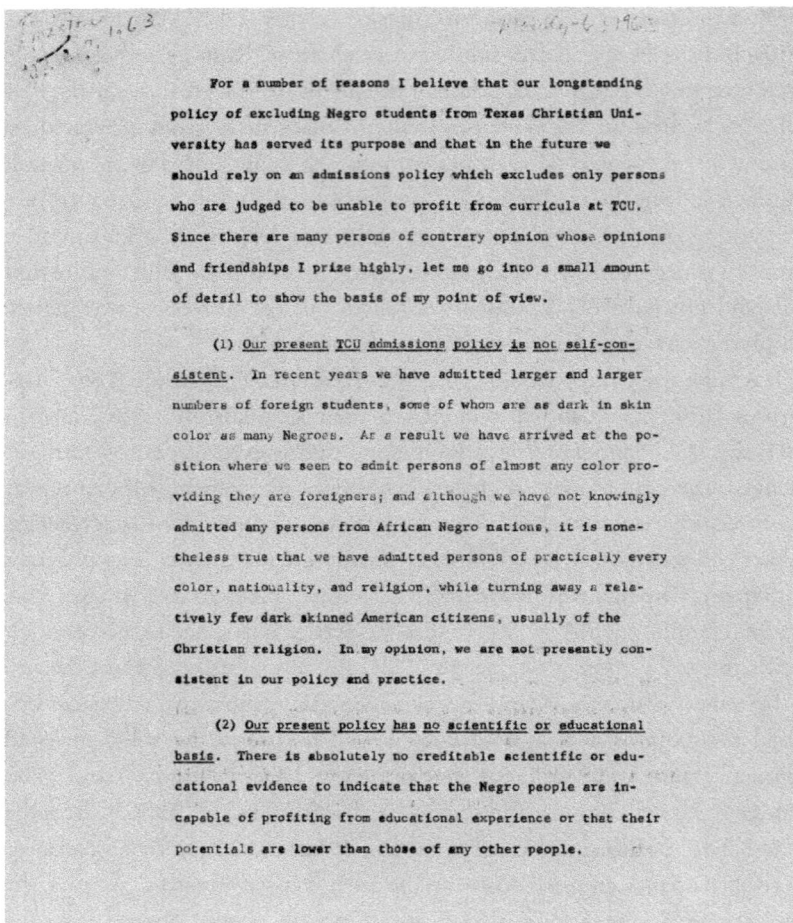

For a number of reasons I believe that our longstanding policy of excluding Negro students from Texas Christian University has served its purpose and that in the future we should rely on an admissions policy which excludes only persons who are judged to be unable to profit from curricula at TCU. Since there are many persons of contrary opinion whose opinions and friendships I prize highly, let me go into a small amount of detail to show the basis of my point of view.

(1) Our present TCU admissions policy is not self-consistent. In recent years we have admitted larger and larger numbers of foreign students, some of whom are as dark in skin color as many Negroes. As a result we have arrived at the position where we seem to admit persons of almost any color providing they are foreigners; and although we have not knowingly admitted any persons from African Negro nations, it is nonetheless true that we have admitted persons of practically every color, nationality, and religion, while turning away a relatively few dark skinned American citizens, usually of the Christian religion. In my opinion, we are not presently consistent in our policy and practice.

(2) Our present policy has no scientific or educational basis. There is absolutely no creditable scientific or educational evidence to indicate that the Negro people are incapable of profiting from educational experience or that their potentials are lower than those of any other people.

Provost Moudy's statement on desegregation, 1963.
Image courtesy of TCU Special Collections.

to the Seminary at Southern Methodist University (SMU). In 1959, Brite alumna Vada Felder invited Martin Luther King, Jr., to Fort Worth to speak at Brite. Despite its independent status, Brite's physical location required TCU approval for such events. The university refused permission for King to speak on campus, and, instead, the event occurred at the newly desegregated Majestic Theater. Harold Lunger, professor of social ethics at Brite, hosted a reception at his home for King and other Brite faculty members.

Despite Brite's modest efforts to admit a handful of Black students in the 1950s, TCU was in no hurry to desegregate its undergraduate programs, even with the need for a qualified and educated Black workforce in Fort Worth. In 1962, a dire shortage of Black nurses in Black hospitals led Harris School of Nursing, which had its own board of visitors, to pass a resolution stating that it would admit students to its nursing program "without regard to race, color, or creed."[104] The first Black students enrolled in 1962. This group included the trailblazing Allene Jones, who, like the Black Brite students, was married and older than typical undergraduate students.

Even as Black students began to enroll at SMU and Arlington State College (now the University of Texas at Arlington) in 1961 and Baylor in 1963, the TCU Board of Trustees dragged its feet. In 1962, faculty members at Brite and the Harris College of Nursing had begun to exert pressure on the board for integration of the whole TCU campus to support the Black students who were in their colleges: Harris needed TCU to offer lower-level classes for Black students before they took their nursing training, and Brite wanted their students to be able to enroll in undergraduate classes along with the general student population.

In June 1963, James Moudy, who was then provost and vice chancellor for academic affairs, issued a statement to the board of trustees that no TCU department should exclude Black students from admission.[105] Although this statement was certainly instrumental in orchestrating desegregation, Moudy's six-point rationale was hardly enthusiastic about such change to come. First, he noted that the presence of international students of color on campus, including some of darker complexions, contradicted the university's systematic denial of admission to American students of African descent. Secondly, he highlighted the mental and intellectual equality among races, dispelling any belief in Black people's inability to learn and benefit from a TCU education. Moudy reminded the board that since the most prestigious universities that TCU sought to emulate had desegregated campuses, desegregation was a key strategy for institutional effectiveness. Additionally, the Christian principle of racial equality should, according to Moudy, serve as a moral compass to consider applicants according to their human worth instead of their race. Moudy paired this tension with the American principle of human equality, especially in a Cold War climate. Indeed, as he reiterated to the board, his concern was that refusing Black enrollment might give proponents of communism room to argue that the American education system was morally corrupted by racism and bigotry.

In keeping with Moudy, TCU's Student Government Association, led by senior undergraduate Mark Wassenich, petitioned the board of trustees in November 1963 to drop racial barriers.[106] After much discussion, on January 29, 1964, the board moved to integrate TCU, the seventh of eight Southwest Conference universities to do so. Only Rice, whose founder expressly forbade desegregation in the university charter,[107] was later than TCU to integrate. While the structural bar came down, the trustees sought to reassure white stakeholders that TCU would largely remain a white campus.[108] In March of that same year, TCU approved a five-year formal affiliation between TCU and its sister institution, the historically Black Jarvis Christian College, which was established in 1912 by TCU founders and board members. TCU became financially and academically responsible for Jarvis, setting the curriculum and hiring the faculty as well. "Separate but equal" was the law of the state. Indeed, the Disciples of Christ, which was affiliated with TCU, had greater governing authority over the Black denominational college in Hawkins, 125 miles from Fort Worth in East Texas, to help keep in place that distinction between Black and white students. Nevertheless, while the Black student population remained relatively small at TCU, the mostly white student population would nevertheless drop by 24 percent after desegregation.[109]

TCU's Challenges with Desegregation

Desegregation did not mean integration; the first years of TCU's desegregation were difficult for the pioneering students, staff, and faculty members of color at TCU. In the fall of 1964, five Black high school graduates were admitted but did not return the following year. According to Marian Brooks Bryant, who was among these five students, the climate was so unwelcoming that they chose to leave TCU and enroll in other universities and colleges.[110] This erasure was strategic, as Chancellor Sadler feared that publicizing the number of Black undergraduates might generate negative publicity, as he detailed in a letter to the registrar. His decision was modeled on other recently integrated universities, to which Sadler referred for counsel. He stated, "If we want to keep a little private record [of the number of Black students who enrolled at TCU] for our own selves, that might be all right."[111] Assistant Chancellor Melton Amos disagreed, as he believed this was a matter of public knowledge, despite a similar desire to keep details under wraps: "I sincerely hope that when registration is over, we can make a short, accurate statement that will make a one-day story—then be forgotten," he wrote back.[112] Subsequently in 1965, a year after TCU's first Black undergraduates enrolled and then transferred to other campuses, fourteen Black students were admitted. Because their predecessors had warned them of the hardship ahead, these fourteen students decided to remain united, to support one another, and to commit to graduating on time. They would graduate with the class of 1969, the first fully integrated class.

Integration was experienced differently among students, depending on a student's race, ethnicity, and other factors. Despite the university's standard practice of treating desegregation "quietly" in its advertising and media coverage, students were aware of the changes that were occurring, and most had strong opinions about what was happening on campus.[113] Although student opinions were the result of personal experiences, they were deeply informed by academic knowledge of national and world events. In other words, the education they received at TCU and through news outlets available on campus guided their perspectives more than their personal feelings did. Just as TCU's administration demonstrated apprehension and disapproval of interracial courtship, so too did TCU's student body. The pioneering Black students who ushered in desegregation, on the other hand, were shaped by several common experiences. For example, while macroaggressions against students of color were few, microaggressions were not. The students of color who persisted did so because they were focused on their end goal—getting a degree—not their student experience.

Curriculum, Faculty, and Staff

As a liberal arts university, TCU provided coursework that reflected some of the diversity of world cultures. This curricular diversity did not, however, cover U.S. racial groups, such as Black, Indigenous, Latinx, or Asian Pacific American identities. In this regard, TCU aligned with most U.S. universities at the time. Sociology, anthropology, modern languages, history, geography, and the art departments offered classes on the Americas and Europe. In 1940, the only classes that discussed Asian and African civilizations or the development of the British Empire did so exclusively in the context of their subaltern relations to the European metropole.[114] Except for the graduate course offerings documented above, TCU's curriculum imparted little about U.S. racial or ethnic minorities until 1945, when the sociology department started offering a course that grouped ethnic subcultures and other marginalized groups. The American Minority Groups class was an ambitious attempt to study all these minorities in one semester. If the focus on minority "problems" was typical of its era, it was also limiting, given that this problem-oriented approach was the only opportunity for students to learn about non-white identities.[115]

TCU course offerings provided greater attention to Indigenous history, geography, and cultures. For example, in the 1930s and 1940s, courses such as Pre-history of the Western Hemisphere, American Indian Civilization and Culture, as well as Colonial Contact between Natives and Europeans were offered. In the next two decades, there were also lectures and curated exhibits on Southwest Indian handicraft.[116] Likewise, the departments of art, history, sociology, and anthropology offered Indigenous-related coursework and sponsored scholarly research.[117] The scope of these classes was largely limited to a white perspective, however, and all their instructors were white. Not until 1974, with the arrival of Gail Pete, a part-Choctaw, part-Cherokee academic who specialized in Indian art, did this curriculum get delivered by a faculty member who understood the subject through an experiential lens.[118] TCU sociologists studied Chicano culture through the lens of social ills. While the history department offered courses on Mexican history, it did not offer coursework on the history of Mexican Americans, despite its broader representation in Fort Worth and in Texas. Nevertheless, some graduate students, such as Arnoldo DeLeón, a Mexican American alum who started graduate school at TCU in 1970, pursued this research.[119] DeLeón reported being the only Mexican American in TCU's doctoral program in history (the few other Hispanics were Cubans).[120] Working under Donald E. Wooster, a Latin Americanist, DeLeón wrote a master's thesis on great migrations in Mexican American Texas (1910-1920)[121] and a dissertation on Anglo attitudes towards Mexicans in Texas.[122]

Asian and Black contributions to the diversity of world cultures were virtually invisible in the university's first hundred years of existence. Academic Affairs considered an Asian Studies program in 1972, motivated by the ambition to increase American students' awareness of China in the context of the Cold War; at the time, universities nationwide were competing to hire the few experts in this field.[123] TCU did not establish a minor in Asian Studies until the 1990s, discussed below.[124] Programming on the subject of Black Studies was initiated in late 1967, almost four years after desegregation began. Given the national context of Black Studies, which was just emerging at this time, TCU was relatively ahead of its counterparts. By way of a series of six public lectures, the Experimental College invited speakers from TCU and Jarvis Christian College to lead a noncredit, tuition-free course for students, faculty, and the community. The *Skiff*'s coverage highlighted the approach of A. L. King, an assistant professor, to teaching Black history, which included many examples of Blacks' contributions to American history and society.[125] This experiment led, in 1969, to the first Black history class, From African Civilizations to Contemporary Era in America, which compressed 3,000 years of history on three continents into a three-credit hour, one-semester course.[126]

Despite small interventions in TCU's course offerings in the 1960s and 1970s, Black, Indigenous, and students of color could rarely see themselves in the TCU curriculum, nor could they recognize themselves in the textbooks assigned. They did not accept the epithets professors often used in speaking to and about them.[127] They certainly did not identify with the faculty, who were, until the late 1960s, almost exclusively white. In 1968, TCU alumna Allene Jones joined TCU's School of Nursing, becoming TCU's first Black faculty member in Harris College; in 1974, alumna Reva Bell became the first Black faculty member in the School of Education.[128] Until 1983, they would remain the only Black faculty members at TCU.[129]

Athletics

As TCU's leadership was preparing for desegregation in 1962, Chancellor Sadler charged his assistant Amos Melton to explore the integration of athletics at fellow Southwest Conference institutions. TCU proceeded with

James Cash, TCU's first Black basketball player, 1969.
Photo courtesy of TCU Marketing and Communications.

caution by observing how Baylor and UT navigated this transition. Despite TCU's formal declaration of integration in 1964, athletics strategically dragged its feet. The football arena constituted a space where community members could and did vocalize their discontent. As SMU's Jerry LeVias, the first Black athlete to receive a scholarship in the Southwest Conference, discovered in 1965, TCU fans were not ready. They heaped physical and mental abuse on LeVias, including death threats, when SMU played the Horned Frogs.[130] According to the *Skiff*, "Trainers wouldn't tape his ankles for fear of touching his black skin. Teammates emptied the showers when he stepped in."[131]

The same year that LeVias was drafted, TCU offered a basketball scholarship to James Cash, a senior at I. M. Terrell High School, and the son of Juanita Cash, who was among the first Black master's students to graduate from TCU's School of Education. James Cash was TCU's first Black athlete at TCU and the first Black basketball player in the Southwest Conference. He would later become the first Black member of the TCU Board of Trustees and the first Black faculty member to receive tenure at the Harvard Business School. In November 2022, TCU unveiled a statue of him and hosted a ceremony where Cash received an honorary doctorate, a proclamation by Tarrant County Commissioner Roy Brooks, and a proclamation by Fort Worth Mayor Mattie Parker, marking November 11, 2022, as Dr. James Cash Day. The statue of Cash is the first (and, to date, only) campus monument that honors a person of color at TCU.

Like many of his peers in the TCU class of 1969, Cash has numerous fond memories of his TCU years.[132] Although he experienced microaggressions, they occurred only occasionally; he benefited from the privilege of being a student athlete for a sport that, in comparison to football, attracted relatively smaller crowds. Linzy Cole joined the Horned Frogs a year after Cash, becoming the first Black football player at TCU. Like Jerry LeVias, Cole received death threats to discourage him from playing on the field. In a similar fashion, TCU's first Black cheerleader Ronald Hurdle was not allowed to perform routines with white female cheerleaders during football games.[133] He too received death threats to bar his inclusion on the field. Although he was elected to the squad in 1969, Hurdle was not a full participant until late 1970, due to the omnipresent fear of interracial romance and unlawful miscegenation. Likewise, in the autumn of 1970, Jennifer Giddings's crowning

James Cash at unveiling of his statue next to Schollmaier Arena, November 11, 2022.
Photo courtesy of TCU Marketing and Communications.

as the first Black Homecoming Queen at TCU, and in the Southwest Conference, was somewhat dulled when Chancellor Moudy's greeting took the shape of a handshake instead of the expected, traditional hug.[134]

The crowning of a Black Homecoming Queen contributed to TCU's reputation as a champion of diversity. Giddings's race was not a hindrance to her popularity. Her afro-styled hair (which was highly politicized in the 1970s) did not diminish her poise or her beauty. These expressive liberties of ethnic and gender identity, however, did not extend to the football team. In 1971, Coach Jim Pittman requested that all players should remain "well-groomed" and clean shaven. While this appeared to be a race-neutral policy, a survey of the team rosters revealed that all but one of the players with facial or voluminous hair were Black. Additionally, Black football players endured discrimination in their classrooms and other parts of student life and were routinely denied food at the training tables; when Pittman policed the hair of his Black athletes, it was the last straw.[135] In February, four football players—Larry Dibbles, Ervin Garnett, Hodges Mitchell, and Ray Rhodes—withdrew from the squad. Their position was that they should not be required to sacrifice their ethnicity (their afros) and their masculinity (their facial hair) to be accepted.[136]

Along with Jennifer Giddings and other Black student organization leaders, the athletes addressed the campus community via a press conference, where they listed ways that campus life needed to improve, particularly regarding race-related policies and practices.[137] The students requested an explanation for the exclusion of Giddings from the recent Cotton Bowl Parade. They also asked for the hiring of Black counselors (a minister and a psychologist), as such professionals would be more understanding and aware of the challenges that Black students encounter in a predominantly white institution.[138] In the area of academics, the group called for a more inclusive curriculum, as well as an increased Black faculty presence. Finally, they demanded more transparency concerning the rejected application of Jimmy Leach, a Black man whose enrollment was denied amidst allegations of racism. While the university met some of the demands, such as hiring a counselor, others were either dismissed, explained away, or given minimal attention. It would take several more decades before student demands—on matters such as the hiring of minority faculty, a diversity and inclusion officer, and the creation of a Black Studies minor and ethnic studies programs—were met.[139]

Student life

Most references to people of color in TCU's documents during these years pertain to entertainment, such as a 1948 yearbook image of students clamoring for Duke Ellington's autograph after a concert or extended attention to sports after integration; however, as TCU moved into the 1960s, there is some evidence that a modest number of students of color participated in some aspects of campus social life. A photograph in the 1963 *Howdy Week* booklet (since 1949, a welcoming orientation tradition where returning students host a series of social and informational events for new students) depicts a Black student riding a bumper car with several white TCU students. The young man's identity and student status were not provided. In February 1963, the student congress welcomed Black comedian Dick Gregory and the minister Thomas Griffin as part of a seminar on race. Later that semester, Ralph Bunche, Under Secretary to the United Nations, visited TCU and spoke to an audience of 1,000 people in the student center on the realities of racial prejudice in America.

In October 1968, a group of TCU undergraduates attempted to experience shared interracial proxemics as they enrolled in an exchange program with Jarvis Christian College (JCC), a historically Black college affiliated, like TCU, with the Disciples of Christ. The program took place as the two universities were four years into the 1964 Jarvis-TCU affiliation, whereby TCU had assumed oversight of Jarvis's finances and academics. JCC students enjoyed an entire week as TCU students, attending classes and residing in TCU dorms. TCU students, who reported to the *Skiff* the poorer conditions of Jarvis's infrastructures, did not remain at our sister institution past the first day.[140] The partial failure of this exchange program highlights the separate and largely unequal state of higher education in Texas.[141]

Several aspects of student life remained segregated beyond the time covered in this section. Greek life, for instance, would not see any interracial fraternity or sorority until 1979, and no Black student would be accepted into a historically white Greek organization (where Blackface performances were frequent) until 1981. On the other hand, 1967 marked the beginning of a new tradition: the practice of mock slave auctions as fundraising events. The *Skiff* would promote these events annually until 1984.

As TCU neared its centennial in 1973, it had made major strides in catching up to American society regarding integration. The student involvement in making such strides was a clear example that the mission of "educating individuals to think and act as ethical leaders and responsible citizens in the global community" was well underway. Nevertheless, much work still lay ahead, even as it does today.

TCU's Recent History
(1998–2020)

AS THE SECTION ABOVE SUGGESTS, student involvement as early as 1971 played a critical role in enacting adjustments at TCU. The student demands of 2016 and 2020, as we will see, prompted even greater changes. Student involvement was and is instrumental in pushing to address and improve institutional change across TCU. Over the last two decades, students have spoken individually and collectively to their needs for greater institutional support, from mentoring to financial aid to a multicultural center of their own. Students repeatedly called for TCU to prioritize hiring faculty and staff who were skilled in using their diversity as a resource in their teaching. They also longed for a curriculum that imparted skills in navigating difference, as well as greater resources and programming to ensure every student felt welcomed and valued. Demanding modifications at each of these levels equipped students to enhance their sense of belonging at the university, especially for those from historically marginalized racial and ethnic backgrounds, such as Black, Indigenous, Asian Pacific American, and Latinx, acknowledging and including those whose voices have often been disregarded by TCU.

This final section of TCU's history reveals how students' individual and collective advocacy has substantially influenced TCU's response to race and racism, especially in regard to leadership, academics, athletics, and infrastructure. Students remain key change agents at TCU. While it took administrators, faculty, and staff to implement important transformations over the last twenty years, students were—and still are today—the most powerful advocates in addressing issues of race and racism and creating and sustaining a sense of belonging for all.

Leadership

The role of the chancellor, who is charged with advancing the mission, vision, and the strategic goals set forth by the board of trustees, is critical to understanding how TCU responded to student involvement, demographic change, population growth, and needs over the last twenty years. In this initial section, then, we first explore the impact of the leadership of Michael "Mick" Ferrari as the ninth chancellor of the university and of Victor J. Boschini, Jr., as the tenth chancellor of TCU in responding to student voices.

Chancellor Michael "Mick" Ferrari,
who served as ninth chancellor of TCU.
*Photo courtesy of TCU Marketing
and Communications.*

Michael "Mick" Ferrari (1998–2003)

Mick Ferrari led TCU as chancellor from 1998 to 2003. Ferrari was the first chancellor to be appointed who did not have an affiliation with the Disciples of Christ,[142] which is a longstanding connection with TCU, given that TCU's founders, Randolph and Addison Clark, were ministers of this denomination.[143] Under Ferrari's leadership, TCU demonstrated a new focus on inclusivity and diversity. Ferrari is also remembered for increasing the overall student enrollment from 7,395 in 1998 to 8,275 in 2003, at that time the largest student population in the university's history.

Ferrari's bold vision for TCU included the establishment of a Diversity Council, spearheaded by Cornell Thomas.[144] Thomas, who served as the special assistant to the chancellor for diversity and community, collaborated with a team of fifteen faculty, staff, students, alumni, and campus community members who were nominated or chosen based on recommendations made to Ferrari.[145] Ferrari charged the Diversity Council with a plethora of responsibilities to support efforts to diversify the campus community racially and culturally. Responsibilities included establishing programs to support and improve diversity as it pertains to the recruitment and retention of faculty, staff, and students of color; recommending policies pertaining to curriculum, student life, and university governance; managing or curtailing diversity flashpoints; measuring progress and providing annual written reports to Ferrari and the university community on increased intercultural and diversity development; sponsoring programming, workshops, and speakers on diversity topics; and working in close partnership with faculty, staff, and student groups as well as advisory boards on increased diversity efforts.[146] Key accomplishments fulfilled by the council include a two percent increase of the undergraduate minority student population, from 12 percent in 1998 to 14 percent in 2003; establishing an annual Conference on Inclusiveness for students, faculty, and staff in 1999; and creating the Community Scholars Program in 2000. Each of these concrete accomplishments prompted new challenges, which will be highlighted in the student involvement, academics, and athletics sections respectively.

Ferrari is remembered for his tenacious leadership during his tenure on our campus. As chancellor, Ferrari established an intentional partnership between the university and Fort Worth to "enrich the city's intellectual, economic, and cultural development," bridging the gap between the university and the broader Fort Worth community.[147] Under his leadership, TCU athletics rose in prominence and increased its number of athletes of color because of the shift in conference affiliations.[148]

Chancellor Victor J. Boschini, Jr., standing outside of the Dee J. Kelly Alumni Center, 2020. *Photo courtesy of TCU Marketing and Communications.*

Victor J. Boschini, Jr. (2003–2025)

Victor Boschini stepped into his role as the tenth chancellor of TCU in 2003 and is today chancellor emeritus. Having led TCU for five times as long as Ferrari, Boschini has inspired dynamic transformations in student involvement, academics, athletics, and infrastructure. The most significant changes that have impacted TCU under his leadership include greater emphasis on the student experience, academic excellence, and athletic strength.[149] Boschini is also responsible for increasing TCU's endowment to support a dramatic enhancement and expansion in TCU's infrastructure and increased scholarship funds, two significant improvements that have positively contributed to TCU's national reputation.[150] In addition to increasing TCU's presence nationally, Boschini has ensured that the university has thrived through a period of growth, global economic uncertainties, and an unprecedented pandemic.[151]

Over the last twenty years, under Boschini's leadership, TCU has expanded its footprint and its student, faculty, and staff population. Acting on the university's strategic plan "Together," which was adopted in 2017, TCU focused more intensively on diversity and inclusion initiatives that foster a greater sense of belonging among faculty, staff, and students. To nurture a student-driven campus community, Boschini strengthened TCU's endowment, which is currently over $2.5 billion, invested in over thirty new building and renovation projects, and supported the athletic shift to the Big 12 Conference, the highest level of NCAA Division I sports.[152] Over the years of Boschini's leadership, TCU faculty revised the core curriculum twice and voted to include an essential competency overlay that focuses on diversity, equity, and inclusion (DEI); this new requirement has yet to be implemented, however.

The latter years of Boschini's leadership also included 2016 student demands made by Black students and their allies and the 2020 student demands made by the Coalition for University Justice and Equity (CUJE). Further, TCU's campus was marked by an increase in political unrest in response to the number of murdered Black people at the hands of police nationwide. The murder of George Floyd in the summer of 2020 at the start of the coronavirus pandemic was one of the key factors that led to the establishment of the Race & Reconciliation Initiative at TCU. Hence, during Boschini's tenure, diversity, equity, and inclusion as well as the RRI became important facets to TCU's brand.

Under Boschini's leadership, TCU has undergone remarkable change in the number and demographics of students. In 2003, the total student population was 8,300, with 14 percent students of color.[153] In 2020, the year that the RRI was established, the total student population increased to 11,379, with students of color 28 percent.[154] Such changes have, at times, elicited racial tensions on campus. In an interview for the Race & Reconciliation Initiative's Oral History Project, when asked about his assessment of TCU's race relations, Boschini explained, "I always say it like this, it's like world peace; you may never reach it, but you better damn well be working towards it every day of your life."[155] Student activists echoed Boschini's sense of urgency that TCU must work continuously to confront systemic challenges to foster necessary change.

Student Involvement

As scholars of higher education have noted, student involvement in their college or university is necessary for their holistic development in attaining the necessary skillsets that support students as learners and citizens both in their personal and professional lives. Such involvement fosters a sense of belonging, enhances academic performance, and cultivates leadership skills. Through day to day and extracurricular activities, students sharpen their engagement in teamwork, time management, and communication, all of which are essential for their future careers. Involvement in coursework and curriculum, clubs, sports, and community service promote social integration and cultural understanding, fostering a diverse and inclusive environment. In addressing the significance of student involvement from 1998 to 2020, we examine TCU's history of student activism, student-led organizations, and the collective student voice, all of which played a vital role in shaping the university and broader campus community.

History of Student Activism at TCU

Over the last twenty years, TCU student activism has served as a catalyst for positive and progressive change. Historically, student movements have sparked significant societal transformations, such as the broadening of civil rights for Black, Indigenous, Latinx, Asian Pacific American, or LGBT people, or forcing the U.S. military to conclude an unpopular war in Vietnam. Such movements have had the potential to cultivate leadership skills, foster empathy, and empower future generations to confront injustice.[156] Through ongoing activism, students have challenged norms, demanded accountability, and advocated for change on issues ranging from civil rights to environmental sustainability.[157] Consistently, students from various marginalized and underrepresented backgrounds have been at the forefront of TCU student activism, calling for greater diversity and cultural change on campus and beyond.

A university's racial climate profoundly influences students, shaping their sense of belonging, academic performance, and overall well-being. Negative racial tensions can create feelings of isolation, fear, and insecurity among marginalized groups, hindering their academic and social experiences. Over the last twenty years, with greater intensification in the last decade, an epidemic of anti-Muslim, anti-Black, anti-Asian, and anti-immigrant violence spread across the U.S. During and following the 2016 U.S. presidential campaign, an escalation in racist political rhetoric intensified the isolation, fear, and insecurity felt by historically underrepresented students across the nation, who often faced biases, microaggressions, and discrimination on and off campus.[158] These various challenges were felt by TCU students too. In response to the unjust killing of Black teenager Trayvon Martin in 2012, TCU students, faculty, and members of the TCU's National Association for the Advancement of Colored People (NAACP) organized a silent march, "Walking Colors," to raise awareness regarding anti-Black hatred and violence and to advocate for justice.[159] This was the beginning of a new era of social and political unrest at TCU, as students, faculty, and staff from historically marginalized racial and religious groups advocated for equity, accountability, and inclusion at the institution.

Shortly following the murder of Trayvon Martin, the 2016 U.S. presidential election was marked by significant social and political unrest. Both major party candidates, Donald Trump and Hillary Clinton, elicited strong reactions from the public. Trump's controversial rhetoric, particularly regarding immigrants, race, and gender, fueled protests and demonstrations across the country. Issues such as income inequality, healthcare, and foreign policy also sparked intense debate.[160] Social media played a pivotal role in disseminating information and shaping public opinion, often intensifying this political polarization. The election outcome, with Trump winning the presidency despite losing the popular vote, further deepened divisions and prompted ongoing activism in response to Trump administration policies.[161]

Students, faculty, and staff at many U.S. colleges and universities, TCU included, protested the Trump administration's harmful and racist rhetoric, especially as it targeted students of Latinx origin. Mayra Guardiola, a graduate student in TCU's English department, organized a "Defend DACA" protest on campus in response to President Trump's decision to issue a deadline of six months for the Deferred Action for Childhood Arrivals (DACA). Although Boschini sent a campus-wide email in response, stating the DACA decision "created a great deal of uncertainty," many campus community members were frustrated over the lack of a stronger response to support DACA.[162]

Building upon the DACA protests, TCU students from marginalized groups were making their voices heard by the administration through organizing a silent protest at a TCU football game and posting public letters that highlighted the struggles of students of color and the need for cultural and policy changes. Over the summer of 2016, during the preseason, Colin Kaepernick, quarterback for the San Francisco 49ers, began a silent protest aimed at raising awareness of racial injustice and police brutality against Black people in the United States. Rather than standing during the national anthem before games, Kaepernick chose to kneel silently instead.[163] This action was highly visible, drawing attention from fans, media, fellow players, as well as students of color at TCU. Soon after, in September 2016, TCU students organized a silent protest at TCU's football game against Iowa State to stand in solidarity with Colin Kaepernick.

Following the silent protest at TCU's football game, in December 2016, a letter titled "Letter from Black Students and Allies of TCU" was sent to TCU administrators with over fourteen demands to enhance diversity, inclusion, and accountability on campus.[164] The students called for a zero-tolerance policy for racially insensitive speech, an increase in faculty of color (at the time, only 14.5 percent of faculty were BIPOC, an increase of .5 percent since 2003), sensitivity training for all members of the TCU community, and accurate reporting on diversity progress. Additionally, students highlighted the need for a multicultural center, housing for multicultural Greek organizations, and required cultural sensitivity training for Greek life. Other requests included creating ethnic studies courses, hiring a chief officer of diversity and inclusion, and lowering the flag in honor of victims of racial violence. The demands stressed the importance of systemic and cultural change while ensuring protection from retaliation for those involved in the process.[165]

While the TCU administration got to work in implementing changes in response to some of the 2016 demands, TCU's challenges with race and racism could not be fixed overnight. In November 2017, a letter titled "Letter from Black Students to TCU Department Heads" expressed students'

November 20, 2017

— who else received ?

Dear TCU Department Heads,

As you know, TCU has a diversity problem. This problem, as it pertains to race, culture, religion, socio-economic status, immigration status, sexual orientation, and gender, is pervasive. Our mission statement clearly identifies our role "to educate individuals to think and act as ethical leaders and responsible citizens in the global community." The constant covering up of diversity issues completely contradicts our mission statement. This is evidenced when we, as students, attempt to voice concerns to move the University toward ethical leadership and we are silenced. Based on the October 2016 meetings with Chancellor Boschini, Provost Donovan, Vice Chancellor Cavins-Tull, Dr. Turner, and others, we feel that only the surface was scratched about the change that we want to see on campus. Due to political manners in which TCU is run, no action plan was put in place to address our demands and joint concerns, which were released prior.

We ask, "Why does TCU not strive 'to educate individuals to think and act as ethical leaders and responsible citizens in the global community' in regards to social justice methodologies?" Our isolated TCU environment hinders students' overall growth by using dismissive phrases like, "We are all one Horned Frog family," and "We all bleed purple." These phrases can be directly compared to the "colorblind" rhetoric, which is detrimental to society, because it dismisses the presence of the cultures that diversify America. As we know, our "Horned Frog family" is 69.4% White. Because of the structures of power and privilege in direct relation to hierarchies of race, this majority never walks around campus with the notion that they do not belong, nor do they feel as though they are outsiders. This lack of diversity makes Students of Color and our White allies constantly feel unwelcome. This is evidenced in the ways that certain institutional resources are allotted toward some and not others, as demonstrated in SGA programming, TCU curricula, housing, and Greek life.

According to our core values, "TCU values academic achievement, personal freedom and integrity, the dignity and respect of the individual, and a heritage of inclusiveness, tolerance and service." Besides the mention of "academic achievement," all other values must be questioned.

If we truly value "personal freedom," why must we ask permission to speak openly and freely?

If we truly value "dignity and respect," why must we be the targets of racially stereotyped preconceived ideas of who we are by TCU students, faculty, and staff in classrooms and on campus?

If we truly value "a heritage of inclusiveness," why is there a diversity problem at TCU? Why does the majority feel like 90% instead of 69.4%?

Institutions of higher learning should be places at which we explore, debate, and think critically about important historical and contemporary issues. TCU has an urgent matter at hand. The students are being silenced, there is a lack of diversity, and our mission statement and core values simply do not hold weight. Let's deal with it.

We must lead on, TCU. We must lead on.

Black students at TCU send a letter to department heads addressing issues of diversity in 2017. *Photo courtesy of Karen Steele.*

ongoing discontent with the university. The letter addressed the pervasive lack of diversity at TCU, which highlighted issues of race, culture, religion, socioeconomic status, immigration status, sexual orientation, and gender. The letter criticized the university's failure to address these issues despite TCU's mission emphasizing ethical leadership and responsible citizenship. Further, the letter expressed frustration with the lack of action following discussions with university leaders in October 2016 and accused TCU of silencing student concerns. The letter questioned the university's commitment to inclusion, tolerance, and service, citing examples of discrimination and unequal resource allocations. The letter concluded by urging TCU to confront these issues and uphold its core values by fostering open dialogue to redress systemic inequalities.

By 2016, a newly established DEI Committee was pushing for systemic changes in TCU's diversity, equity, and inclusion efforts, and later, by 2018, the newly created Office of Diversity and Inclusion had greater oversight to support many of the changes that students, faculty, and staff had identified; yet in 2019 and 2020 three lawsuits filed against the university—alleging physical intimidation, verbal harassment, and microaggressions against students of color—revealed ongoing problems. While officially TCU stated that it was committed to providing a safe and respectful environment for all students and would be investigating the allegations,[166] the lawsuits would catalyze further change at TCU. The student-led alliance Coalition for University Justice and Equity (CUJE) led the charge as students spoke out on social media and issued another list of demands to TCU administration to address the various forms of persistent discrimination that students from minoritized and marginalized identities face at TCU.[167] The objective of the coalition was to ensure that TCU upheld its pledge to promote diversity, equity, and inclusion. In response to the lawsuit, CUJE called for the termination of several administrators at the heart of the 2019 lawsuit, the disbandment of an academic unit, and a written assurance from TCU's Board of Trustees to establish an on-campus cross-cultural center within the next three years. Inspired by students who called for change at TCU in 2016, CUJE illustrates the importance of student activism at TCU that pushed for an equitable sense of belonging and inclusion on our campus.

Student-Led Organizations

Student-led organizations that highlight affinity to students' racial or ethnic identities play a crucial role at colleges and universities for several reasons. First and foremost, organizations tied to students' affinities or most salient identities can provide a supportive community for students from diverse backgrounds, fostering a sense of belonging, inclusivity, and empowerment. These student-led organizations offer spaces where students can freely express their cultural heritage, share experiences, and celebrate traditions, enriching campus life.[168] Also, student-led organizations that center racial and ethnic identities serve as platforms for advocacy and activism, addressing systemic issues such as discrimination, inequality, and cultural insensitivity on campus. Through educational initiatives, events, and campaigns, student-led organizations raise awareness and promote social justice, contributing to a more inclusive and equitable university campus environment. Moreover, these organizations that largely comprise students from historically marginalized racial and ethnic backgrounds aim to enhance diversity and inclusion through bringing a sense of awareness and understanding of students from these cultural backgrounds within and across the broader TCU campus community.[169]

One of TCU's first student-led racial or ethnic organizations, the Black Student Caucus (BSC), which was active from 1982 to 1997, focused on ensuring the voices and needs of Black students across TCU's campus were being heard. From hosting events such as the "Black Student Caucus Lecture Series" to partnering up with various departments and other student-led organizations on campus to promote and amplify issues that Black students were facing at TCU and beyond, the Black student population was making their presence known. In 1997, the Black Student Caucus was sunsetted. Darron Turner, at the time the Director of Minority Affairs, cited low attendance and lack of engagement as reasons for the disbandment.[170] An important legacy of the BSC was creating a list of Black student alumni, which would help to establish, in 1999, the first alumni group focused on racial or ethnic identity, the Black Alumni Alliance, which offers its members a culturally supportive environment through programming, community service, and social events.

Like Black student-led organizations, the first of many Latin American and Latinx student-led organizations was established decades ago, in the 1980s. Among the first were the Organization of Latin American Students (1988–2006), the Hispanic Alumni Association (2004–), the League of United Latin American Citizens (2006–2010), the United Latino Association (2010–2022), and currently the United Latinx Association, whose motto is "Unifying the diverse Latinx students at TCU with a desire to promote academic excellence in our community."[171] Throughout the years, the Latinx student population and campus community members have put on various events and initiatives to promote and uplift the greater Latinx community at TCU.

In the 1990s, Asian Pacific American students, like other TCU students of color, were working to be seen and heard at TCU. Through student-led organizations such as the United Asian Community, Students for Asian Indian Cultural Awareness, and Asian Student Association, students hosted a number of social events and educational sessions that highlighted the diverse cultures and experiences of Asian students at TCU. In 1999, TCU's Asian Pacific American community came together to host TCU's first "Asian Festival."[172] Michael Ly, president of the Asian Student Association, explained to the *Daily Skiff* that the purpose of the festival was to expose students to different Asian cultures through food, dance, and education.[173] Such events at TCU highlighted the ever-growing population of Asian Pacific Americans who were settling in the Dallas-Fort Worth Metroplex.

In the late 2010s, TCU saw an increase in its international student population, which at the time was only five percent of TCU's overall student body.[174] Many TCU international students during this time came from Vietnam. With this increase in international students from Vietnam, Vietnamese students on campus came together in 2013 to form the student-led organization known as the Vietnamese Student Association (VSA) with the goal to spread awareness about Vietnamese culture, represent Vietnamese students' voices on campus, and enhance TCU's student unity.[175]

One of the most underrepresented student ethnicities (and nationalities) at TCU and indeed across the United States is Indigenous. Because the land that became the TCU campus has been the home for Indigenous peoples for millennia, TCU holds a special obligation to supporting and amplifying Indigenous voices as a step towards rectifying this historical injustice. In the 1990s, four Indigenous students—Kathleen Whitekiller (Cherokee), Robyn Mitchell (Diné), Tabitha Tan (Diné), and Mike Charlie (Navajo)— established TCU's first Native American student organization.[176] By 2000, the student-led organization Native and Indigenous Students Association (NISA) was founded and now works both independently and in concert with the Native American and Indigenous Peoples Initiative at TCU.

Just as student activism has enacted change and inclusion on campus, so too have student-led organizations made their mark. One recent and effective tool that student-led organizations have been able to utilize to amplify their collective voices is social media. The collective student voice at TCU encompasses the engagement of student activism as well as student-led organizations to facilitate change across the university to ensure that students' identification of their needs are heard and responded to. The last twenty years have illustrated, repeatedly, what positive change can occur when students are on the front lines of creating and implementing such transformations.

Academics

TCU's academics have changed dramatically over the last twenty years, as TCU's students, faculty, staff, and administration have sought to diversify the campus and promote a more inclusive space for all. With the addition of now standing initiatives to recruit and support highly talented students of color, such as the Community Scholars and STEM Scholars programs, building on existing TRIO programs such as the Upward Bound and Mc-Nair Programs, TCU faculty twice revised the core curriculum, began to develop new courses, and established new interdisciplinary programs in ethnic or area studies to provide all TCU students with the knowledge and skills to live and thrive in diverse communities.

In 1989, the U.S. Department of Education created the Ronald E. Mc-Nair Post-Baccalaureate Achievement Program. A TRIO program (that is, a federal outreach and student services program designed to identify and provide services for individuals from historically marginalized backgrounds), the McNair Program was designed to prepare undergraduates from underrepresented backgrounds for doctoral studies.[177] In 1991, TCU joined this program; the U.S. Department of Education granted the university $400,000 for the next three years to help serve marginalized communities from low-income and first-generation backgrounds. During the first year of the program, the university was able to fund twenty students, ten of whom were freshmen and sophomores, and ten of whom were juniors and seniors.[178] TCU's McNair Program built on the existing Upward Bound Program, established at TCU in 1970, which served academically disadvantaged high school students in the area to encourage these individuals to attend universities through tutoring, mentorship, and attending summer programs on the TCU campus.[179] Adding to these two distinctive TRIO programs, TCU established the Student Support Services in 1997, an attempt to retain undergraduates, boost their grade point averages, support on-time graduation, and encourage these individuals to pursue post-graduate degrees.[180]

Despite some preliminary attempts to address the lack of diversity on the TCU campus in the 1990s, many people argued—recalling the Black student demands of 1971—that the university could do more by recruiting talented local students from predominantly non-white high schools to TCU.[181] In 2000, TCU created the Community Scholars Program to actively recruit and aid in the retention of highly skilled and talented students of color through providing full tuition, fees, housing, and books for underrepresented high school students who did not have the financial resources to attend TCU on their own. Students who received this scholarship had to maintain rigorous standards as they had to be active in Student Support Services, complete community service, meet with monthly program advisors, attend intercultural meetings, participate in the Leadership Council, and attend four monthly workshops.[182] By 2020, the Community Scholars Program had expanded to support, cumulatively, 500 students from across thirteen majority-minority Dallas-Fort Worth high schools.[183] In 2017, TCU established the STEM Scholars program, which similarly provides a four-year comprehensive scholarship, academic support, and leadership development to increase the number of the best and brightest students who show a commitment to diversity and inclusion in STEM fields.

As the student section noted, a recurrent theme in student protests since 2016 has been the call for more diverse curriculum, which has galvanized a number of TCU faculty to establish a range of interdisciplinary ethnic or area studies programs where students could pursue a minor; most of these programs are housed in the AddRan College of Liberal Arts. Over thirty years ago, Asian Studies—the first ethnic or areas studies program at TCU—was established in 1993, in response to students seeking a more comprehensive academic course of study about Asia. Andrew Fort, professor of religion, was its first director, followed by Carrie Liu Currier, associate professor of political science, who directed the thriving program until 2018. Like Asian Studies, Latino/a (now Latinx) Studies built on a campus history of celebrating Hispanic heritage. After over a year of organizing by liberal arts faculty with expertise in Latino/a history and culture, it was first offered as a minor in 2009, with anthropology senior instructor Miguel Leatham as the inaugural director.

Whereas the first ethnic studies programs emerged from heritage months and student-led organizations celebrating distinctive ethnic cultures, students' demands in reaction to rising national, state, and campus racial tensions catalyzed other academic changes to curriculum and campus practices. In 2015, the Native American and Indigenous Peoples Initiative began, a collaboration between TCU faculty, such as instructor of religion Scott Langston and professor of English Theresa Gaul, and Indigenous leaders, such as Chebon Kernell, a citizen of the Seminole Nation of Oklahoma, and Terri Parton, president of the Wichita and Affiliated Tribes, that focuses less on research or curriculum building than on modeling mutual understanding and respect between our campus and Indigenous communities. The same year, Jewish Studies (now only offered in the Brite Divinity School) was launched; the program has struggled to thrive at TCU due to an inadequate number of TCU faculty teaching courses to sustain the minor. Students advocated for the need to study the history, politics, culture, and religions in the Middle East, prompting Hanan Hammad, professor of history, to launch Middle East Studies, a thriving program she has continued to direct for over ten years. African American and Africana Studies (AAAS) and Comparative Race and Ethnic Studies (CRES), on the other hand, were established in direct response to student protests and demands in 2016. Like the Native American and Indigenous Peoples Initiative, CRES relies on collaborations among faculty, staff, and community members to fulfill its mission. Indeed, CRES expresses ambitions that go beyond course offerings and programming: its motto, "More than a Major, a Movement," promises to help decolonize the curriculum and higher education overall. [184] CRES, which now houses Latinx and AAA studies as well, was elevated to a department in 2018 and offers students the opportunity to major or minor in this area of study.

Athletics

While academics and athletics pursue different, and sometimes competing, goals in U.S. higher education, at TCU they work in concert to recruit and retain students, including students of color. Indeed, TCU student athletes are the most racially and ethnically diverse student population on campus. When combined, race and athletics are two forces that frequently drive societal, political, and cultural tensions in the United States. The rising national prominence of TCU football and women's and men's basketball has highlighted the need for inclusive practices across the university and an end to the exploitation of athletic talent for university gain. As the culture of athletics has changed dramatically at TCU from 1998 to 2020, this section addresses several key athletic developments due to conference changes and realignments, the Rose Bowl effect, social justice protests, and the growth of student-athlete activism at TCU.

From 1998 to 2020, TCU's athletics expanded and underwent several conference changes from the Western Athletic Conference (1996) to Conference USA (2001) to the Mountain West Conference (2005) and to the Big 12 Conference (2011), where they remain to this day.[185] TCU's rapid transition to ever more prominent conferences enhanced the national stature of TCU athletics, most prominently in football and men's and women's basketball. The hiring of Gary Patterson in 2000 as the head football coach built on the successful revitalization of the football team under Dennis Franchione, who was head coach from 1997 to 2000. By the end of the 2000s, Patterson had guided the football team to five ten-win seasons, four straight postseason bowl wins from 2004 to 2008, and frequent appearances in the Associated Press's top twenty-five polls throughout the season.[186] TCU alumnus Jamie Dixon returned to coach the men's basketball team in 2016 and has led the team to several Big 12 victories since his arrival, which is a significant turnaround, having had a record of 2 to 16 the season prior to him becoming head coach.[187] Like TCU men's basketball, the women's basketball team has enjoyed a winning streak, having secured several conference titles, even if the media visibility of women's basketball cannot match that of men's basketball.[188] Since joining the Big 12, TCU's athletics has contributed to enhancing TCU's national visibility while also increasing the number of athletes of color on campus.

Athletics and Social Justice

As athletics became a critical component of TCU's growing visibility in the 2010s, student athletes began to take a more active role in using their platform to advocate for social changes on their campus. At the same time, as the discussion above detailed, other students began to see athletic venues as a strategic location to promote a more socially inclusive and conscious student body. In 2016, Caylin Moore, a junior quarterback on the TCU football team, created an organization called Strong Players Are Reaching Kids (SPARK), alongside teammates Aaron Curry and Michael Carroll. The main goal of the organization was for the football players to travel around the Fort Worth area to "encourage children to reach their dreams." The organization sought to cultivate leadership among student athletes while also bridging the divide between the university and the broader Fort Worth community.[189] These leadership programs spurred on greater involvement from alumnus and NFL Hall of Famer LaDainian Tomlinson, who helped create the Tomlinson Student-Athlete Development Endowment Fund to help student-athletes develop skills in leadership and citizenship. Founded as a way for Tomlinson to give back to the university and its student-athletes and with the backing of Jeremiah Donati, TCU's director of intercollegiate athletics, the former Horned Frog running back expressed his ambition that student-athletes from all twenty-one of TCU's sports could use these funds to prepare, on and off the field, to be responsible university and community leaders.[190]

Infrastructure

Perhaps one of the most visible changes to TCU over the last twenty years is its built environment. The addition and renovation of dorms, classrooms, a student union, and athletic facilities has been so extensive to earn TCU the weary nickname "Texas Construction University." While TCU's campus improvements have enhanced the utility and beauty of its infrastructure, this built environment also communicates to its community who is welcomed and included. Indeed, for years, students with minoritized identities have called for changes to TCU's infrastructure that communicates that they be-

View of TCU's Native American Monument.
Photo courtesy of TCU Marketing and Communications.

long. This final section, then, highlights several important changes to TCU's infrastructure that focus on belonging and have benefitted from student advocacy: the Native American Monument, the Divine Nine Pillars, the Intercultural Center, the Portrait Project, and the Sesquicentennial Plaza.

TCU's campus is situated on the home of the original inhabitants of the Wichita and Affiliated Tribes. At the university, we acknowledge the many benefits we have of being in this place, which we share with all living beings, human and non-human. To pay homage to the Wichita and Affiliated Tribes, in 2018, the university erected the Native American Monument.[191] The monument encompasses a bronze, circular plaque mounted in rustic mahogany granite. On the monument, there are two statements, along with the seals of TCU and the Wichita and Affiliated Tribes. This monument honors individuals of the Wichita and Affiliated Tribes and is a reminder that students who identify with these backgrounds hold sacred their ethnic identities.

Another inclusive change to TCU's built environment is the Divine Nine Pillars, which is located in the Greek Village on the west side of campus.

TCU's Divine Nine Pillars are the first pillars on a U.S. university campus to represent the historically Black Greek organizations.
Photo courtesy of Amiso George.

Entrance to TCU's Intercultural Center, featuring mural
The World is Ours by Brian Dickson, Jr., '21, and Kristin Gaytan.
Photo courtesy of TCU Marketing and Communications.

As TCU was redesigning the Greek Village in 2016, students petitioned to increase the visibility of Black Greeks on campus, specifically those affiliated with the Divine Nine. TCU became the first university in the country to create pillars to represent the National Panhellenic Council (NPHC), often referred to as the Divine Nine.[192] The Divine Nine encompasses a total of nine historically Black fraternities and sororities: Alpha Phi Alpha Fraternity; Alpha Kappa Alpha Sorority; Kappa Alpha Psi Fraternity; Omega Psi Phi Fraternity; Delta Sigma Theta Sorority; Phi Beta Sigma Fraternity; Zeta Phi Beta Sorority; Sigma Gamma Rho Sorority; and Iota Phi Theta Fraternity.[193] On TCU's campus, six of the nine organizations are currently active: Alpha Phi Alpha, Alpha Kappa Alpha, Kappa Alpha Psi, Omega Psi Phi, Delta Sigma Theta, and Sigma Gamma Rho. As situated on TCU's campus, the Divine Nine Pillars are placed in the order in which they were chartered at the university with Alpha Phi Alpha being the first in 1971.

Since 2016, TCU students of color have identified the need for a space of their own. In 2021, TCU fulfilled this demand in establishing the Intercultural Center in the Brown Lupton Student Union to cultivate a campus community that celebrates underrepresented students' identities, cultures, and experiences.[194] This diverse and inclusive space on campus provides co-curricular opportunities and support to students of color, international students, LGBTQ+ students, and TCU's Student Government Association. Since its opening, the space has hosted mariachi performances, ballet folk-

Allene Parks Jones, '63, senior photo from the 1963 Horned Frog Yearbook. Her portait is featured in the triptych *Among the Firsts*, on the first floor of The Harrison. *Photo courtesy of TCU Library.*

The Sesquicentennial Plaza will embody the continuous work of race and reconciliation.
Photo courtesy of Office of Connected Culture.

lorico dances, NAACP meetings, Heritage Month events, Greek life fundraisers, and a drag show celebrating Selena, the "Queen of Tejano music."

Another effort to diversify the campus has been via the Portrait Project, an initiative that grew out of courses taught by Jacqueline Lambiase in Strategic Communication and Nino Testa in Women and Gender Studies, whose students catalogued the way TCU's portraits persistently excluded women and people of color. This project, which was overseen by Marcellis Perkins, when he served as the graduate assistant in the Office of the President and Chancellor, was established to diversify portraiture around campus and commemorate historically marginalized and underrepresented members of the TCU community.[195] Some of these portraits that are hung across campus include a portrait of Allene Jones ('63), TCU's first Black faculty member, which hangs prominently in Annie Richardson Bass building, and "Among the Firsts," which honors some of TCU's first Black graduates: Ann McBride, Allene Park Jones, and Patsy Brown, which hangs in The Harrison.[196] Additional portraits include "Based on Quanah Parker" and "Based on Mrs. Jack Treetop-Standing Rock 1908," two stunning paintings by the contemporary Comanche and Kiowa artist J. NiCole Hatfield, commissioned to reflect TCU's relationship with Indigenous Peoples.[194] The project committee continuously works to incorporate future honorees in the Portrait Project, all of which bring awareness to individuals who are or were a part of the TCU campus community and identify with historically marginalized racial or ethnic backgrounds.[197]

As a way to center the needs of students and to combat racist ideologies, TCU's infrastructure contributes towards TCU's efforts of moving toward a multicultural, anti-racist community. For example, in response to one of the recommendations of the Race & Reconciliation Initiative regarding the university's built environment, TCU has embarked upon the redesign of a major artery on the east side of campus to commemorate the diversity of achievements throughout the history of TCU.[198] The walkway linking University Drive to Dan Rogers Hall, Sesquicentennial Plaza will serve as a major campus gateway that reflects the university's past, present, and future in the continuous commitment to race and reconciliation.

Part One Notes

1. Qtd. in Erica L. Green and Abbie VanSicke, "A Call in Birmingham For a Nation to Recall Ugly Truths of the Past," *New York Times*, September 15, 2023, 18.

2. Randolph Clark manuscript draft, Joseph Lynn Clark Papers, 14. Special Collections, Mary Couts Burnett Library, Texas Christian University.

3. Andrés Reséndez, *A Land So Strange: The Epic Journey of Cabeza de Vaca* (New York: Basic Books, 2007); Juliana Barr, *Peace Came in the Form of a Woman: Indians and Spaniards in the Texas Borderlands* (Chapel Hill: University of North Carolina Press, 2007).

4. Mark Allen Goldberg, "Comanche Captivity, Black Chattel Slavery, and Empire in Antebellum Central Texas," *Linking the Histories of Slavery: North America and its Borderlands* (Santa Fe: SAR, 2015), 197–222.

5. Goldberg, "Comanche Captivity," 197–222.

6. Paul Barba, *Country of the Cursed and the Driven: Slavery and the Texas Borderlands* (Lincoln: University of Nebraska Press, 2021). Slavery was illegal in most of Mexico but still practiced well into the nineteenth century.

7. Richard B. McCaslin, "Wheat Growers in the Cotton Confederacy: The Suppression of Dissent in Collin County, Texas during the Civil War." *Southwestern Historical Quarterly* 96.4 (April 1993), 526–39.

8. Andrew J. Torget, *Seeds of Empire: Cotton, Slavery, and the Transformation of the Texas Borderlands, 1800-1850* (Chapel Hill: University of North Carolina Press, 2015).

9. Figures calculated from the 1860 U.S. Census.

10. William Dean Carrigan, "Slavery on the Frontier: The Peculiar Institution in Central Texas," *Slavery and Abolition* 20.2 (1999), 64–96.

11. Richard B. McCaslin, "Wheat Growers in the Cotton Confederacy: The Suppression of Dissent in Collin County, Texas during the Civil War." *Southwestern Historical Quarterly* 96.4 (April 1993), 526–39.

12. See McCaslin, "Wheat Growers"; Joseph Lynn Clark, *Thank God, We Made It!* (Austin: University of Texas Press, 1969), 233–34; and Graham Landrum, *Grayson County: An Illustrated History of Grayson County* (Fort Worth, TX: University Supply & Equipment, 1960).

13. Joseph Lynn Clark, *Thank God, We Made It!*, 233–34. For a profile of Joseph Lynn Clark (1881–1969), see the Texas State Historical Association's Handbook of Texas: https://www.tshaonline.org/handbook/entries/clark-joseph-lynn.

14. Randolph Clark, *Reminiscences: Biographical and Historical* (Wichita Falls, TX: Lee Clark, 1919), 25.

15. Joseph Lynn Clark Papers, Box 19, Randolph Clark undated manuscript draft of *Reminiscences*, transcription page 2. Special Collections, Mary Couts Burnett Library, Texas Christian University.

16. Ibid.

17. Clark, *Thank God*, 293–94.

18. Randolph Clark, *Reminiscences*, 25.

19. Clark, *Thank God*, 293–94.

20. Clark, *Thank God*, passim.

21. For the character of frontier religion in Texas, see Carter E. Boren, *Religion on the Texas Frontier* (San Antonio: Naylor Company, 1968).

22. Joseph Clark, *Thank God, We Made It*, 233–34. For context on the decision-making process on whether to fight, see David Charles Grear, *Why Texans Fought in the Civil War* (College Station: Texas A&M University Press, 2012) and Carl H Moneyhon, *Texas after the Civil War: The Struggle of Reconstruction* (College Station: Texas A&M University Press, 2004).

23. Barbara Thorp Wilkins, "High Hopes & Human Frailties: The Story of a Pioneer's Dream and a Town that Almost Was," *Granbury! Magazine* (summer 1986). Online at http://www.granburydepot.org/z/biog2/ThorpSpringHistory.htm

24. Clark, *Thank God*, 331–32.

25. Clark, *Thank God*, 350.

26. Clark, *Thank God*, 345.

27. Clark, *Thank God*, 383–84.

28. Clark, *Thank God*, 391.

29. Eighth Census of the United States, 1860, Slave Schedule, Johnson County, Texas; Charley Thorp Death Certificate, State of New Mexico, Aug. 21, 1927; US Census, Dallas County, Texas (Lancaster), 1900, ED 137, Sheet 9. We do not know whether Pleasant Thorp purchased or fathered Charley because slave schedules were published in 1850 and 1860; Charley was born between these years.

30. Clark, *Thank God*, 361–63; Randolph Clark, "Charles Thorp," clipping from *Christian Courier*, 1927, in Joseph Lynn Clark Papers, Box 22, folder titled "Charley Thorp."

31. Ibid.

32. *Granbury News*, June 7, 1894, 8, March 8, 1894, 5.

33. Clark, *Thank God*, 361–63; Randolph Clark, "Charles Thorp," clipping from *Christian Courier*, 1927, in Joseph Lynn Clark Papers, Box 22, folder titled "Charley Thorp."

34. U.S. Census, 1870, Fannin County, Texas (Bonham), 12; Clark, *Thank God*, 364.

35. Clark, *Thank God*, 264.

36. After AddRan's departure for Waco, the school's former campus was home to a succession of other short-lived schools, including Jarvis Institute, Add-Ran Jarvis College, and Thorp Spring Christian College. Charley Thorp may have continued to work at the first of these schools, which hired Randolph Clark as its president. By 1900, Thorp was living in Lancaster, probably still working for Randolph, who had become president of another short-lived school there, Randolph College. See Rhonda L. Callaway, "Thorp Spring Christian College," *Handbook of Texas Online*, https://www.tshaonline.org/handbook/entries/thorp-spring-christian-college; Burris, "Higher Calling," 256–59; 1900 U.S. Census, E.D. 134, Sheet 9, Lancaster, Dallas County, Texas.

37. Waco, Texas, City Directory, 1900, 96; Waco, Texas, City Directory, 1902–1903, 133, both in https://www.ancestry.com/search/collections/2469/; U.S. Census of 1900.

38. *Proceedings of the Eighth Annual Convention of the Texas Division of the United Daughters of the Confederacy* (Fort Worth: Speer Printing Co., 1904), 34, 85; *Skiff*, Nov. 28, 1903. The officers included Mary Taliaferro, president; Bess Coffman, first vice president; Cassie Holloway, second vice president; I.V. Purcell, third vice president; Ginnie Miller Ree, secretary; Alma Hood, historian; Louise Andrews, registrar; and Le Noir Dimmitt, treasurer.

39. Johnson scrapbook: Scrapbook of Olive McClintic Johnson, who attended TCU 1898–1901 and taught 1901–1906. Box 32, Record Unit 8, TCU Scrapbook Collection, https://repository.tcu.edu/handle/116099117/4609 Link for online version, 73; *Waco Semi Weekly Tribune*, Nov. 29, 1905.

40. *Skiff*, March 25, 1905.

41. *Skiff*, Sept. 26, 1903.

42. *Skiff*, October 31, 1903. Easley's "colonel" title appears to have been honorific; we have found no evidence that he was a military veteran.

43. *Skiff*, April 11, 1903.

44. *Thirteenth Census of the United States*, Vol. 1, Population (Washington: Government Printing Office, 1913), 120; 244.

45. Richard Selcer, "Fort Worth, Texas, Where the West and the South Meet: A Brief History of the City's African American Community, 1849–2012, in BlackPast, https://www.blackpast.org/african-american- history/fort-worth-texas-where-west-and-south-meet-brief-history-citys-african-american-communi/; President's Annual Report

of the Texas Christian University, 1930, TCU Digital Repository, Mary Couts Burnett Library, https://repository.tcu.edu/handle/116099117/7075; Detail from "Aerial view includes Clark Field behind Library," 1930, TCU Digital Repository, Mary Couts Burnett Library, https://repository.tcu.edu/handle/116099117/2798. The servant house sat approximately where the southwestern corner of Scharbauer Hall sits today.; President's Annual Report of the Texas Christian University, 1930, TCU Digital Repository, Mary Couts Burnett Library, https://repository.tcu.edu/handle/116099117/7075; Detail from "Aerial view includes Clark Field behind Library," 1930, TCU Digital Repository, Mary Couts Burnett Library, https://repository.tcu.edu/handle/116099117/2798.

46. *Skiff,* Sep. 28, 1917; *Skiff,* Jan. 11, 1919; *Horned Frog,* 1919 [in the "College Year" section]; Fort Worth City Directories, 1918, 1920, 1926, 1927, 1930, 1936; "Briscoe's a Granddad Now!," *Skiff,* Oct. 2, 1929; *Horned Frog,* 1928, 325; U.S., City Directories, Fort Worth, Texas, City Directory, 1926, Ancestry.com, https://www.ancestry.com/search/collections/2469/; *Skiff,* Nov. 14, 1913.

47. *Skiff,* May 25, 1911; *Skiff,* Oct. 31, 1913; *Skiff,* Jan. 15, 1915; *Skiff,* Oct. 12, 1918; *Skiff,* Oct. 5, 1919; *Skiff,* Feb. 21, 1921; *Horned Frog,* 1923, p. 218; *Skiff,* Oct. 16, 1923.

48. *Skiff,* Oct. 30, 1914; *Horned Frog,* 1919, tenth page of "College Year" section.

49. *Skiff,* Oct. 30, 1914. Newspaper database searches reveal many dozens of accounts of the game being played at Texas fairs and carnivals, including two in Fort Worth: a 1926 Rotary Club picnic and a 1926 "Boys Day in Industry" banquet, both of which used eggs and a live target; see *Fort Worth Star- Telegram,* July 15, 1922; and *Fort Worth Star-Telegram, May* 5, 1926. For other Texas examples, see *Corpus Christi Caller-Times,* July 12, 1914; *San Angelo Evening Standard,* Nov. 13, 1915; *Hamlin Herald,* Oct. 3, 1930; *Austin American-Statesman,* Oct. 23, 1932; *El Paso Times,* May 10, 1933; *San Angelo Morning Times,* Nov. 15, 1935; *Canyon News,* Oct. 27, 1938; *El Paso Herald,* April 2, 1941; *Pampa Daily News,* Dec. 3, 1944. Several of these explicitly note the use of human targets. A 1918 classified ad in El Paso actually advertised for workers to be targets in the game, promising "Good salary or percentage to good worker"; see *El Paso Times,* July 8, 1918. For New York's ban, see *New York Age,* May 17, 1917.

50. Harold Rich, *Fort Worth Between the World Wars* (College Station: Texas A&M University Press, 2020), 61–70.

51. *Skiff,* Nov. 3, 1916.

52. *Skiff,* May 5, 1919.

53. *Skiff,* Mar. 20, 1922.

54. *Skiff,* Mar. 27, 1922; *Horned Frog,* 1923, p. 264.

55. Kenneth N. Hopkins, "The Early Development of the Hispanic Community in Fort Worth and Tarrant County, Texas, 1849–1949," *East Texas Historical Journal* 38 (2000), 57–58.

56. *Horned Frog,* 1916, seventh page of "College Year" section.

57. *Skiff,* May 2, 1903.

58. *Skiff,* Jan. 16, 1913.

59. *Skiff,* Oct. 21, 1921. The *Skiff* republished Clark's article from the *Christian Courier.*

60. On Jarvis Christian College, see Rachel Jenkins, "Jarvis Christian College," Handbook of Texas Online, accessed May 31, 2022, https://www.tshaonline.org/handbook/entries/jarvis-christian-college.

61. *Skiff*, Dec. 14, 1911.

62. Clipping from Dura Louise Cockrell Scrapbook, 1923, TCU Special Collections. According to the *Fort Worth Star-Telegram* (November 22, 1921), it was a mixed-race audience at the North Side Coliseum.

63. *Skiff*, Feb. 25, 1921.

64. *Skiff*, Jan. 23, Feb. 6, 1922.

65. Skiff, Oct. 30, 1923.

66. *Skiff*, Feb. 19, 1915; *Skiff*, Feb. 4, April 16, 1916.

67. *Skiff*, Oct. 8, 1915, p. 3, Oct. 22, 1914, p. 3; *Horned Frog*, 1916; *Texas Christian University Bulletin*, 1916, 167.

68. *Skiff*, May 29, 1914.

69. *Skiff*, July 21, 1916.

70. *Skiff*, July 24, 1913.

71. *Skiff*, Apr. 4, 1912.

72. *Skiff*, Oct. 29, 1920.

73. *Skiff*, Jan. 22, 1924.

74. Statement by J. M. Moudy, June 7, 1963a, fol. RU16, series 1, box 3, Records of James M Moudy, "Correspondence 1960–1964," Special Collections/TCU Archives, Fort Worth, TX.

Ordinance 2401, 1947, Record Group 2, series I, box 3, Fort Worth Public Library Digital Archive, "Ridglea Wall Records." http://www.fortworthtexasarchives.org/digital/collection/p16084coll37/id/17/rec/19

75. Blake Gandy, "'Trouble Up the Road:' Desegregation, Busing, and the National Politics of Resistance in Fort Worth, Texas, 1954–1971" (Master's thesis, Texas State University, 2020).

76. Gandy, "Trouble Up the Road," 76.

77. Christian Argueta Soto, "'The City Don't Care, Man:' Como Residents Offer Views of Fort Worth's Plans to Upgrade Water, Sewer Mains," *Fort Worth Report*, April 16, 2022. https://fortworthreport.org/2022/04/16/the-cityhttps://fortworthreport.org/2022/04/16/the-city-dont-care-man-como-residents-offer-views-of-fort-worths-plans-to-upgrade-water-sewer-mains/dont-care-man-como-residents-offer-views-of-fort-worths-plans-to-upgrade-water-sewer-mains/.

78. Estrus Tucker, "Como, Fort Worth, Texas," Civil Rights in Black and Brown Interview Database, June 12, 2015. https://crbb.tcu.edu/clips/410/como-fort-worth-texas.

79. National Civil League. https://www.nationalcivilleague.org/america-city-award/.

80. "Prestigious Country Club Admits First Black Members," *United Press International* Archives, April 27, 1991. https://www.upi.com/Archives/1991/04/27/Prestigious-country-club-admits-first-black-members/6456672724800/

81. Augusta National did not admit Blacks until 1990 and women unti. 2012.

82. Peter Martínez, "Colonia Mexicana: Mexicans Subject to Modern Empire in Fort Worth, Texas." *Journal of South Texas* 33, no. 1 (Spring 2019): 56–72. Porterfield would then become an official research consultant for Fort Worth Federal Housing Authority in 1939. See Leonard D. Cain, *A Man's Grasp Should Exceed His Reach: A Biography of Sociologist Austin Larimore Porterfield* (United Kingdom: University Press of America, 2005).

83. Floyd Armand Leggett, "Social Antecedents and Consequences of Slum Clearance in Fort Worth, Texas" (Master's thesis, Texas Christian University, 1940); Robert Eugene Baker, "Areas of Social Disorganization and Personal Demoralization in Fort Worth, Texas" (Master's thesis, Texas Christian University, 1938). Leggett and Baker, among others, were graduate students at TCU's Sociology Department working under the direction of Professor Porterfield. Note that Leggett's report also recommended the eradication of Chambers Hill, a Black neighborhood adjacent to I.M. Terrell High School, because of its abundant moral and social pathologies.

84. In 1939, the Fort Worth Housing Authority also created a separate housing complex for Black residents called Butler Place. While the location of the complex was chosen for its proximity to I.M. Terrell High School, it has since been enclosed by three major highways. Ripley Arnold was later demolished and became the site of Radio Shack Headquarters and later the Tarrant County College Trinity River Campus. Lili Zheng, "Fort Worth's Butler Place Redevelopment Plan Moving Forward," *NBCDFW* (August 31. 2022). https://www.nbcdfw.com/news/local/fort-worths-butler-place-redevelopment-plan-moving-forward/3061620/

85. Leggett, "Social Antecedents," 92.

86. The Historians of Latino Americans (HOLA) of Tarrant County is an organization of historians, educators, journalists, activists, librarians, archivists, and active community members who critically examine and document the racial and ethnic experience of the Hispanic community in the Fort Worth area.

87. Tina Nicole Cannon, "Cowtown and the Colorline: Desegregating Fort Worth's Public Schools" (PhD diss., Texas Christian University, 2009).

88. The school district's desegregation plan was approved by the court, but it had to remain under court supervision until the plan was complete. The board would declare the plan "complete" in 1967, but the NAACP, with the help of future Supreme Court decisions, notably *Swann v. Charlotte-Mecklenberg*, would successfully argue in court that the district remained segregated, forcing the district to draft a series of new plans, which necessitated them remaining under court supervision.

89. Suzanne Sprague, "Integration Still a Challenge in Fort Worth," *KERA-Radio,* Dallas, TX, September 7, 2001. https://www.keranews.org/archive/2001-09-07/integration-still-a-challenge-in-fort-worth

90. Charles Ess, "Packaged People," *Skiff,* November 21, 1969. https://repository.tcu.edu/handle/116099117/15289

91. *Runyon v. McCrary*, the landmark case by the U.S. Supreme Court which outlawed racial discrimination and segregation in private schools occurred in 1976.

92. Dwonna Goldstone, *Integrating the 40 Acres: The Fifty-Year Struggle for Racial Equality at the University of Texas* (Athens, GA: University of Georgia Press, 2012).

93. Richard Morehead, "College Students Favor Gradual Integration," Dallas *Morning News,* December 12, 1958, 4; Morehead, "35 Schools Lower Ban," Dallas *Morning News,* March 23, 1958; Morehead, "Three Dallas Institutions Accepting Few Negroes," *Dallas Morning News,* January 7, 1959; Morehead, "Integration Now the Rule in Most Colleges," *Dallas Morning News,* July 7, 1960.

94. M. E. Sadler, "Chancellor's Report to the Board of Trustees, 1963–64," Special Collections/TCU Archives, Fort Worth, TX.

95. "Pictorial Presentation of Texas Christian University with Biographical Sketches of its Faculty," *Texas Christian University Bulletin,* 1903. https://repository.tcu.edu/handle/116099117/42190

96. Frederick W. Gooding, Jr., Sylviane Ngandu-Kalenga Greensword, and Marcellis Perkins. *A History to Remember: TCU in Purple, White, and Black* (Fort Worth, Texas: TCU Press, 2023), 51–52.

97. The *Horned Frog,* 1943, 77. https://repository.tcu.edu/handle/116099117/11069; National Archives at St. Louis; St. Louis, Missouri; *WWII Draft Registration Cards For Texas, 10/16/1940-03/31/1947*; Record Group: *Records of the Selective Service System,* 147; Box: 1121; "N. T. A. C. Game Heads Chores For '44 Squad," *Skiff,* September 20, 1940, https://repository.tcu.edu/handle/116099117/13534; Year: *1930*; Census Place: *Precinct 1, Kaufman, Texas*; Page: *20A*; Enumeration District: *0002*; FHL microfilm: *2342100.*

98. *Horned Frog,* 1941. 287; "SA Fact," *Skiff,* March 21, 1941. https://repository.tcu.edu/handle/116099117/13558

99. "Names 'n Notes," *Skiff,* June 18, 1948.

100. Betty Wilke Pederson, "Letter to the Student Office," Records of M. E. Sadler, Box 10, Archives and Special Collections, TCU Mary Couts Burnett Library. Letter reads: "Gentlemen: I'm very sorry this has had to happen, but I'm giving you the reason you won't receive numerous contributions! To quite a large amount of "exes" there is no reason whatsoever for negroes to attend T.C.U. as long as they have schools that can offer the same courses. I assure you (along with quite a few of my friends who are also "exes") that I will never contribute to anything our ex-school needs and will never let my children attend a school with negroes! I might add that we are all terribly sorry this has had to happen."

101. M. E. Sadler, "Letter to Mrs. Betty Wilke Pederson," Records of M. E. Sadler, Box 10, Archives and Special Collections, Records of M. E. Sadler, Mary Couts Burnett Library.

102. "Teacher Relates Blacks' Rise," *Skiff,* February 15, 1977.

103. Brite only offers graduate programs.

104. TCU, "Press Release: At Will," *TCU News Service,* January 24, 1964. Special Collections, TCU Mary Couts Burnett Library. https://repository.tcu.edu/handle/116099117/21233.

105. James M. Moudy, "Photocopy of Statement by Moudy on Race," 1963. Special Collections, TCU Mary Couts Burnett Library. https://repository.tcu.edu/handle/116099117/21231

106. Mark Wassenich, interview by Sylviane Ngandu-Kalenga Greensword, Race & Reconciliation Initiative Oral History Project, Texas Christian University, March 16, 2021. https://repository.tcu.edu/handle/116099117/52346.

107. Brittany Britto, "Rice's Reckoning: University to Launch Task Force to Address its Segregationist History," *Houston Chronicle,* June 14, 2019. https://www.houston-chronicle.com/news/houstonhttps://www.houstonchronicle.com/news/houston-texas/education/article/Rice-s-reckoning-University-to-launch-task-14061581.phptexas/education/article/Rice-s-reckoning-University-to-launch-task-14061581.php#

108. TCU Board of Trustees Minutes. 1964. Special Collections. TCU Mary Couts Burnett Library. https://repository.tcu.edu/handle/116099117/21232.

109. M. E. Sadler, Texas Christian University, *The Chancellor's Report,* 1965–1973, 10–13, Records of James E. Moudy, TCU Special Collections. TCU Mary Couts Burnett Library

110. Marian Brooks Bryant, interview by Sylviane Ngandu-Kalenga Greensword, Race & Reconciliation Initiative Oral History Project, Texas Christian University, August 11, 2021. https://repository.tcu.edu/handle/116099117/52346

111. M. E. Sadler, "Letter to Mr. Calvin Cumbie, Registrar," January 28, 1964, Records of M. E. Sadler, Record Unit 14. Box 10, TCU Special Collections.

112. Amos Melton, "Letter to Dr. M. E. Sadler," January 29, 1964. Records of M. E. Sadler. Record Unit 14. Box 10, TCU Special Collections.

113. This summary is based on a survey of contemporaneous campus publications, oral histories collected through the Race & Reconciliation Initiative Oral History Project, Civil Rights in Black and Brown, and other academic projects such as Professor Dan Williams's Honors Special Project: Vision and Leadership.

114. *Texas Christian University Catalog,* 1940. https://repository.tcu.edu/handle/116099117/48397.

115. *Texas Christian University Catalog,* 1945. https://repository.tcu.edu/handle/116099117/48409

116. "Dr. Emert to Lecture, Show Indian Handcraft," *Skiff,* November 16, 1951; "Dr. Emert Will Discuss Indian Culture in Class," *Skiff,* November 14, 1952.

117. "Hammond in California," *Skiff,* March 12, 1954; "Many Departments List Courses for First Time Next Semester," *Skiff,* January 15, 1954; "Fine Arts Faculty Displays Abstract, Realistic in Show," *Skiff,* January 22, 1954; "3 History Courses Added," *Skiff,* September 1, 1959; "Dr. Worcester Writes Article On Sioux Chief," *Skiff,* November 20, 1964; "Ancient Cultures Studied," *Skiff,* November 5, 1965; "Prof Digs Baja," *Skiff,* May 24, 1966.

118. "Indian Art is Specialty of New Faculty Member," *Skiff,* September 17, 1974.

119. Arnoldo DeLeón is a first-generation high-school, college, and graduate school alumnus.

120. Arnoldo De León, interview by Civil Rights in Black and Brown Oral History Project, Texas Christian University, 2016. https://crbb.tcu.edu/clips/7028/biographical-information-early-life-and-education.

121. Arnoldo De León, "Mexicans and Mexican-Americans in Texas, 1910–1920" (Master's thesis, Texas Christian University, 1971).

122. Arnoldo De León, "White Racial Attitudes Toward Mexicanos in Texas, 1821–1900" (PhD. diss, Texas Christian University, 1974).

123. "Asian Studies Program Mulled; Relevance, Experts Needed," *Skiff*, February 29, 1972. https://repository.tcu.edu/handle/116099117/15455

124. "AddRan Looks to Hire Faculty Member to Teach Chinese," *Skiff*, February 22, 2007. https://repository.tcu.edu/handle/116099117/45869

125. "First Series Talk: Negro not Black," *Skiff*, October 15, 1968.

126. TCU Race & Reconciliation Initiatives Committee, *First Year Report*, April 21, 2021. https://repository.tcu.edu/handle/116099117/52380

127. For example, Ivory Dansby, who transferred from Jarvis in 1965, reported being called "my favorite colored girl," and hearing the word "nigra" as her professor routinely and nonchalantly used this term to refer to her. Dansby also shared that TCU history professors used textbooks with derogatory, racist content. *Wake: The Skiff Magazine*, "On Breaking the Negro Cycle," May 1968, 9. https://repository.tcu.edu/handle/116099117/21235.

128. Jones was also the first Black professor with a Ph.D. to obtain tenure at TCU.

129. TCU hired a part-time Upward Bound Black instructor in the early 1970s, but this instructor left soon after.

130. TCU officially apologized in 2003, after LeVias was inducted in the College Football Hall of Fame, "Busting Through the Line," *Skiff*, September 21, 2007.

131. "Busting Through the Line," *Skiff*, September 21, 2007.

132. James I. Cash, interview by Sylviane Ngandu-Kalenga Greensword and Frederick Gooding, Jr., Race & Reconciliation Initiative Oral History Project, Texas Christian University, May 14, 2021. https://repository.tcu.edu/handle/116099117/52346.

133. Ronald Hurdle, interview by Sylviane Ngandu-Kalenga Greensword, Race & Reconciliation Initiative Oral History Project, Texas Christian University, April 19, 2021. https://repository.tcu.edu/handle/116099117/52346.

134. L. Michelle Smith, interview by Sylviane Ngandu-Kalenga Greensword, Race & Reconciliation Initiative Oral History Project, Texas Christian University, March 23, 2022. https://repository.tcu.edu/handle/116099117/52346.

135. SMU Jones Film, "WFAA February 3-4, 1971 Part 2," https://www.youtube.com/watch?v=80v1iY55qhE&t=428s

136. Three years earlier, a similar controversy had arisen—this time among mostly white students—as the Chancellor Moudy and Dean of Men John Murray stated that faculty retained the right to deny classroom access to students whose hairstyle did not convey "clear differentiation of the sexes" or whose facial hair "made one look like Buffalo Bill." "Faculty Retains Right To Make Hairy Decisions," *Skiff*, October 18, 1968.

137. "Walkout Spurs Black Outcry," *Skiff*, February 5, 1971.

138. "Black Man Must Serve Whites Too," *Skiff*, April 2, 1971. https://repository.tcu.edu/handle/116099117/15369

139. Louise Ferrie, "Black Minor Pass Next Fall," *Skiff*, April 2, 1971. https://repository.tcu.edu/handle/116099117/15369. Jon Shipley, "New Attitudes Crumble Racism," *Skiff*, March 20, 1973. https://repository.tcu.edu/handle/116099117/15571

140. "Jarvis College Students Differ In Views of Visit, McKissick," *Skiff*, October 25, 1968.

141. Trish Spence, "Jarvis Christian Student Swap Broadened Perspectives," *TCU Magazine*, Spring 2021. https://magazine.tcu.edu/spring-2021/jarvis-christian-college-exchange/

142. "Remembering Former TCU Chancellor Michael Ferrari," *TCU 360*, May 19, 2015, https://tcu360.com/2015/05/19/34390remembering-former-tcu-chancellor-michael-ferrari/

143. Ibid.

144. David Van Meter, "Diversity: Amid All Our Differences are Opportunities to Work Together," *TCU Magazine*, Fall 1999. http://www.magarchive.tcu.edu/articles/1999-01-F04.asp?issue

145. Cornell Thomas, interview by Frederick Gooding, Jr., and Sylviane Ngandu-Kalenga Greensword, Oral History Project Interview, TCU Race & Reconciliation Initiative, August 31, 2021, https://repository.tcu.edu/handle/116099117/63628

146. Karen Kassebeer, "Diversity Council Forms," *Skiff*, March 9, 1999.

147. Rick Waters, "A Man on a Mission: Chancellor Michael R. Ferrari," *TCU Magazine*, Spring 2003. https://magazine.tcu.edu/spring-2003/man-mission-chancellor-michael-r-ferrari/

148. Rick Waters, "A Man on a Mission: Chancellor Michael R. Ferrari," *TCU Magazine*, Spring 2003. https://magazine.tcu.edu/spring-2003/man-mission-chancellor-michael-r-ferrari/

149. "Victor J. Boschini," Office of the Chancellor and President, accessed May 30, 2024, https://chancellor.tcu.edu/the-chancellor/biography/

150. Ibid.

151. Ibid.

152. Jacque Nguyen, "Ferrari, Boschini Match up in Funding, Spending," *Skiff*, February 12, 2003. https://repository.tcu.edu/bitstream/handle/116099117/18866/20030212.pdf?sequence=1&isAllowed=y

153. Office of Institutional Research, "Texas Christian University Facts and Data," 2003, accessed 31 May 2024, https://ir.tcu.edu/wp-content/uploads/2021/05/TCU-FactBook2003.pdf

154. Office of Institutional Research, "Texas Christian University Facts and Data," 2020, accessed 31 May 2024, https://ir.tcu.edu/wp-content/uploads/2022/01/Fall2020.pdf

155. Victor Boschini, interview by Sylviane Ngandu-Kalenga Greensword, Oral History Project Interview, TCU Race & Reconciliation Initiative, March 2, 2021, https://repository.tcu.edu/handle/116099117/63665

156. R. A. Rhoads, "Student Activism, Diversity, and the Struggle for a Just Society," *Journal of Diversity in Higher Education* 9, no. 3 (2016), 189.

157. B. Eatch, B and J. Iannacone, "The Importance of Students and their Use of Power through Student Activism," *Journal of Student Affairs* 5 (1996), 17–29.

158. L. D. Reid and P. Radhakrishnan, "Race Matters: The Relation between Race and General Campus Climate," *Cultural Diversity and Ethnic Minority Psychology* 9, no. 3 (2003), 263.

159. "TCU NAACP to Host March for Trayvon Martin," *TCU 360*, April 2, 2012, https://tcu360.com/2012/04/02/15001tcu-naacp-host-march-trayvon-martin/.

160. L. Trimbur, "Taking a Knee, Making a Stand: Social Justice, Trump America, and the Politics of Sport," *Quest* 71, no. 2 (2019), 252–265.

161. Kristina Clement, "More than Free Speech: Politics, Higher Education, and the First Amendment," Dissertation Thesis, Georgia State University, 2020.

162. "Move to End DACA Is Met with Protest," *TCU 360*, September 6, 2017, https://tcu360.com/2017/09/06/move-to-end-daca-is-met-with-protest/.

163. K. Foltz, "Research Note: The (Re)-Education of Colin Kaepernick, the Social Protest He Led, and His Quest to Work in the National Football League," *Journal of Higher Education Athletics & Innovation* 1, no. 10 (2022), 58–67.

164. "Black Students and Allies at TCU." TCU Race & Reconciliation Initiative, December 1, 2016, https://www.tcu.edu/race-reconciliation-initiative/conversations/posts/black-students-allies-tcu-2016.php

165. Ibid.

166. Robbie Vaglio, "Honors Student Says Washington D.C. Trip Was 'Miserable'; Chancellor Calls for Faculty Training," *TCU 360*, February 3, 2020, https://tcu360.com/2020/02/03/honors-student-says-washington-d-c-trip-was-miserable-chancellor-calls-for-faculty-training/.

167. "CUJE List of Demands, January 2020." TCU Race & Reconciliation Initiative, January 12, 2020, https://www.tcu.edu/race-reconciliation-initiative/conversations/posts/cuje-list-of-demands-january-2020.php

168. S. D. Museus, "The Role of Ethnic Student Organizations in Fostering African American and Asian American students' Cultural Adjustment and Membership at Predominantly White Institutions," *Journal of College Student Development* 49, no. 6 (2008), 568–586.

169. N. A. Bowman, J. J. Park, and N. Denson, "Student Involvement in Ethnic Student Organizations: Examining Civic Outcomes Six years after Graduation," *Research in Higher Education* 56 (2015), 127–145.

170. "Black Student Caucus," Mary Couts Burnett Library. Accessed May 31, 2024. https://naming.tcu.edu/authorities/9161/black-student-caucus

171. "TCU United Latinx Association (@tcuula) • Instagram photos and videos." *Instagram.* Accessed May 3, 2024. https://www.instagram.com/tcuula?utm_source=ig_web_button_share_sheet&igshid=ZDNlZDc0MzIxNw.

172. M. Korte, "Asian Festival," *Skiff,* April 21, 1999.

173. Ibid.

174. Office of Institutional Research, "Texas Christian University Facts and Data," 2014, accessed 31 May 2024, https://ir.tcu.edu/wp-content/uploads/2022/01/Fall2014.pdf

175. "Vietnamese Student Association Seeks to Bring Cultural Diversity to Campus." *TCU 360*, November 9, 2015.

176. Tabitha Tan, "Resilience Kicks In: An Interview with Tabitha Tan," *Being in Relation: Indigenous Peoples, the Land, and Texas Christian University,* co-edited by C. Annette Anderson, Theresa Strouth Gaul, and Scott Langston, forthcoming by TCU Press, 2025.

177. Lisa Silver, "Grant Encourages Minorities to Get TCU Education," *Skiff,* October 8, 1992. https://repository.tcu.edu/handle/116099117/45708.

178. Greg Weed, "Grant Ready for Minorities, Under-represented Students," *Skiff*, October 24, 1991. https://repository.tcu.edu/handle/116099117/17364. Cindy Rugeley, "High School Students Aided by Program," *Skiff,* April 6, 1977. https://repository.tcu.edu/handle/116099117/15973.

179. Kristina D'Aun Bosquez, "TRIO helps expand students' resources," *Skiff,* October 24, 1997. https://repository.tcu.edu/handle/116099117/17967.

180. Ibid.

181. Joaquin Herrera, "Focus on Diversity: Students Question TCU's Minority Enrollment, Committee to Discuss Answer," *Skiff,* November 18, 1999. https://repository.tcu.edu/handle/116099117/18518. Diana Munro. "Students speak out," *Skiff,* March 30, 1999. https://repository.tcu.edu/handle/116099117/18134.

182. Emily Ward, "New Program Attracts Area Students," *Skiff,* December 1, 2000. https://repository.tcu.edu/handle/116099117/18134.

183. Rachel McDaniel, "Program Works to Counter Low Hispanic Attendance," *Skiff*, November 15, 2007. https://repository.tcu.edu/handle/116099117/45951. "Community Scholars," TCU Community Scholars. Accessed May 31, 2024. https://communityscholars.tcu.edu/

184. "Comparative Race and Ethnic Studies," TCU Comparative Race & Ethnic Studies. Accessed May 31, 2024. https://www.tcu.edu/academics/programs/comparative-race-ethnic-studies.php#:~:text=CRES%20is%20more%20than%20a,engagement%2C%20inquiry%20and%20academic%20excellence.

185. "Timeline of TCU Conference Changes," *TCU 360*, October 6, 2011, https://tcu360.com/2011/10/06/13622tcu-football-takes-another-step-history/. "Patterson Signs Contract Extension," *TCU 360*, December 5, 2008, https://tcu360.com/2008/12/05/patterson-signs-contract-extension-12286878/

186. "Patterson on Verge of 100 Games Coached," *TCU 360*, December 5, 2008, https://tcu360.com/2008/12/05/patterson-on-verge-of-100-games-coached-12286883/

"Gary Patterson," TCU Athletics. Gofrogs.com, 2003. https://gofrogs.com/sports/football/roster/coaches/gary-patterson/548

Joel Anderson. "Mobile Bowl officials extend invitation to TCU," *Daily Skiff*, November 30, 1999. https://repository.tcu.edu/handle/116099117/18522.

187. "Jamie Dixon: Head Coach," TCU Men's Basketball. Accessed May 31, 2024. https://gofrogs.com/sports/mens-basketball/roster/coaches/jamie-dixon/1334#:~:text=Dixon%2C%20a%202007%20TCU%20Athletics,at%20the%20University%20of%20Pittsburgh.

188. Killer Frog Forum, "TCU 360: Women's Basketball Attendance is Still Not Where it Needs to Be," Accessed May 31, 2024. https://forum.killerfrogs.com/index.php?threads/tcu-360-women%E2%80%99s-basketball-attendance-is-still-%E2%80%9Cnot-where-it-needs-to-be%E2%80%9D.208439/#post-2389786

189. "TCU Athletes are "SPARK-ing" an Interest in Fort Worth Area Students," *TCU 360*, April 18, 2016, https://tcu360.com/2016/04/18/tcu-athletes-are-spark-ing-an-interest-in-fort-worth-area-students/.

190. Benton McDonald, "Tomlinson, Athletics Announce Endowment Fund Geared towards Student-Athlete Development," *TCU 360*, March 18, 2019. https://tcu360.com/2019/03/18/tomlinson-athletics-announce-endowment-fund-geared-towards-student-athlete-development/.

191. For the following information, we are indebted to RRI's Heritage Tour, accessible here: https://maps.tcu.edu/index.html

192. Ibid.

193. "National PanHellenic Council," The Divine Nine. Accessed May 30, 2024. https://www.nphchq.com/

194. For the following information, we are indebted to RRI's Heritage Tour, accessible here: https://maps.tcu.edu/index.html

195. Ibid.

196. Ibid.

197. Ibid.

198. Ibid.

Additionl Images

Hand holding a sticker with the Race & Reconciliation logo. *Photo by James Anger, TCU Marketing and Communication.*

During RRI week in spring 2022, RRI team members created a heritage trail (now permanently accessible on TCU's interactive map as "Race & Reconciliation Initiative Heritage Trail"). *Photo by James Anger, TCU Marketing and Communication.*

TCU's second annual Reconciliation Day was held in the BLUU Auditorium and included performances by African drummers. *Photo by Amy Peterson, TCU Marketing and Communication.*

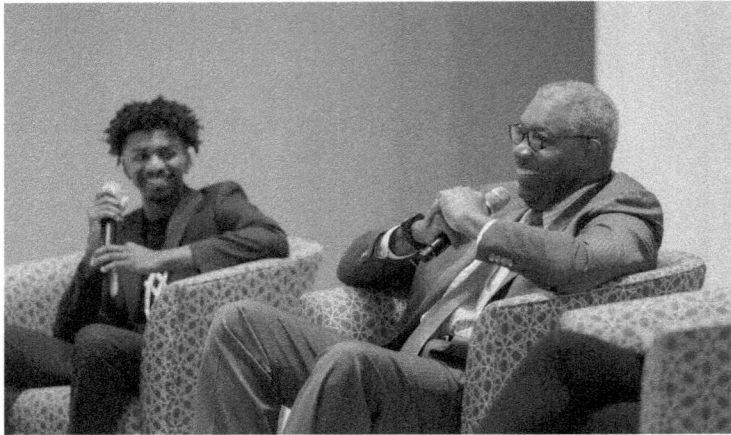

Detail from RRI panel discussion with James Cash, moderated by TCU student athletes Darius Ford (pictured) and Tomi Taiwo, November 2022. *Photo by Leo Wesson, TCU Marketing and Communication*

TCU's third annual Reconciliation Day was held in the BLUU Ballroom and featured Indigenous drummers and recognized the founders of the Native American and Indigenous Peoples Initiative with the Plume Award. *Photo by Amy Peterson, TCU Marketing and Communication.*

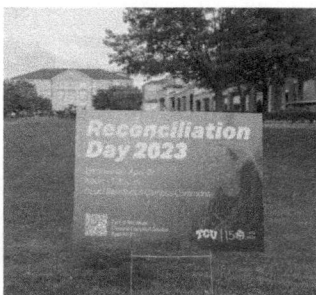

TCU's third annual Reconciliation Day was held in the BLUU Ballroom and outside in the Campus Commons. *Photo by James Anger, TCU Marketing and Communication*

During Reconciliation Day in 2024, RRI recognized faculty who helped to found and nurture ethic and area studies programs at TCU with the Plume Award. Shown (left to right), Amiso George, Carrie Liu Currier, Miguel Leatham, Ariel Feldman, Hanan Hammad, Claire Sanders, Karen Steele. *Photo by Amy Peterson, TCU Marketing and Communication.*

During Black History month in February 2024, RRI honored TCU alumnus Ronald Hurdle with the Plume Award. Shown (left to right) Marcela Molina, Jenay Willis, Karen Steele, Ronald Hurdle, Amiso George, Kelly Phommachanh, and Tiffany Hoang. *Photo by Amy Peterson, TCU Marketing and Communication.*

TCU's fourth annual Reconciliation Day was held in the BLUU Auditorium and included performances by student artist Claudia Tiffany Rodriguez. *Photo by Amy Peterson, TCU Marketing and Communication.*

Part Two

Ubuntu as a Tool for Reconciliation

Frederick Gooding, Jr.

***

OTHER THAN A LESSENING of the intensity of the gusts themselves, nothing better prevents and protects a tree from being completely extracted in the face of strong headwinds than its *roots*.

When I was named the inaugural chair of TCU's Race & Reconciliation Initiative (RRI) in late July 2020, there were several headwinds with which to contend. Earlier in the year, in January 2020, an explosive lawsuit alleging racial discrimination rocked the campus. While the case was ultimately not litigated in court, a number of critical and necessary conversations surrounding race relations nonetheless developed as a result. Yet the momentum behind this dialogue was tampered significantly when, in March of 2020, the whole world had to reckon with the unsettling global pandemic we now know as COVID-19. Racial tensions nationwide were inflamed by the senseless killing of George Floyd on May 25, 2020. The excruciating nature of Floyd's death spurred a national reckoning with race—one that was steadily brewing with the controversial nature of similarly tragic deaths of unarmed Black American (and Texan) citizens like Botham Jean, Sandra Bland, and Atatiana Jefferson, all of whom were innocently caught between the unforgiving crosshairs of race, class, and history.

TCU's Board of Trustees charged RRI with the task of studying TCU's relationship with slavery, racism, and the Confederacy. TCU was not alone in its proactive response as numerous other corporate entities and educational institutions made it known that they were working to dismantle the damaging pillars of racial discrimination that stood unchallenged for far too long. For example, after 131 years, PepsiCo decided to alter the infamous brand

The Race & Reconciliation Sign, installed next to the Founders Statue in August 2020. *Photo courtesy of TCU Marketing and Communications.*

name and image for "Aunt Jemima" pancakes and syrup products to Pearl Milling Company "to make progress toward racial equality" in the aftermath of George Floyd.[1] While TCU was not undergoing a wholesale alteration of its brand, for many on our campus, it was nonetheless nerve-racking to anticipate what would come from our study and, understandably, we were equally uncertain about how the task would be executed.

There were also additional headwinds to consider as tackling the topic of race is hardly a capricious one, given its personal and political implications. So, in knowing that strong roots prevent a tree from being ripped up in the face of strong headwinds, I as an African American male elected to tap into the best leadership practices that I believed would lead to larger organizational success. Thus, here I share here with you, the reader, the culture-specific leadership principles that kept me grounded.

Ubuntu, Largely and
Loosely Defined

Ubuntu is the powerful, unique principle that a person is a person because of other people. While the concept is a South African (i.e., Nguni Bantu) ethical ideology focusing exclusively upon people's relationships with and to one another, the concept is universal in application and manifests itself in a myriad of creative ways.[2] For instance, Nelson Mandela refers to the proverb "Umuntu ngumuntu ngabantu," which may be translated as "a person is a person because of other people."[3] While Ubuntu is noble, its philosophical underpinnings may initially appear to pose a challenge within a capitalistic economic framework for leadership, where the individual named "in charge" of a particular project or enterprise is prized and measured and, in many cases, benefits from acting in one's own self-interest. With respect to the principles of Ubuntu, however, the leader can draw the strength necessary to lead only by agreeing to be led by others.

In my first two years as chair of the RRI, I learned—and hopefully we demonstrated —that the concept of Ubuntu allows for a shared space and place where principles of idea sharing flow freely without sacrificing an individual's claim for personal gain. If anything, if a leader is successful in leveraging their energies for the benefits of a shared group experience, the collective community directly reinvests in this individual as a reflection of a larger symbol of possibility.[4]

While Ubuntu is a principle that can be translated into many different variations, a version that resonates with me most is "I am, because we are," the epitome of collective community ideals, as implicit in this definition is the unspoken prerequisite of a relationship being created, nurtured, and sustained. This simple but profound recognition of human relationships is the fire that ignites one's awareness of self-consciousness. Thus, in the phrase "I am, because we are," the "we are" recognizes the holistic picture. The "I am" recognizes the individual grain of sand that helps form the desert, just as the single droplet of water helps form the sea, just as the solitary, shining star in the appearance of darkness helps form an indelible part of a larger constellation seen and appreciated by imaginations from afar.

Equally intellectually delicious is the parallel interpretation of Ubuntu as "a person is a person because of other people." This idea also respects the ability of an individual to connect with others. In other words, the community of which one *feels a part* expresses the positive and redeeming qualities of each individual who comprises the whole. For me, these principles of belonging were obvious choices with which to foreground the efforts to start (and sustain) a positive and productive conversation about race and reconciliation. I knew it would not be easy, but I calculated that it would be worth it.

As Ubuntu was a principle with which I was fortunate to be familiar due to my cultural background and experience, I thought it was only right to share. The Ubuntu style of leadership recognizes individual voices as important parts of the whole. We simply *had* to operate as a team in order to accomplish all that we did: one cannot do everything by oneself. Yet we learned (and hopefully modeled and demonstrated) that while nobody can do everything, everybody can do something! Success would have been impossible without me listening to others under the principles of Ubuntu, from fellow faculty to staff and administration, to alumni, to members of our community, and of course, my dear wife, who reminded me to keep doing the best I can with what I have.

The 3Es as the Three Keys to Creating Community

I propose that we can reconcile past and existing tensions occluding our efforts to embrace rather than erase our true histories by employing what I call the 3Es framework when it comes to race relations. The 3Es are a helpful rubric that I find to be quite effective in promoting participation by larger numbers of people who mean well but may inhibit themselves from jumping into difficult dialogues concerning race relations stemming from the fear of not wanting to "say or do the wrong thing." Quite simply, the 3Es holds that most people in the world are indeed good people (although conceivably, Dallas Cowboys football fans are likely one of the most glaring exceptions to this premise), but that they are limited by the 3Es: a lack of education, exposure, and experience.[5]

Education broadly represents the acquisition of information. Most especially within the liberal arts on a university campus, of course, we guide students not just on the rote memorization and accumulation of facts, but also on how to leverage said facts and data as tools for critical inquiry and continued exploration. Hence, factual information acquired by way of primary and secondary sources is a solid foundation with which to start. Yet political skirmishes in populous states such as Texas and Florida over critical race theory (CRT) and Advanced Placement (AP) classes in African American history demonstrate that deciding which facts to educate the youth with are still in contention.[6]

For example, education comprises learning tangible facts and information that are materially new or different than existing datasets, such as discovering that musician Babatunde Olatunji is a renowned Nigerian percussionist who is credited with popularizing African music in the west during the early 1960s, with his debut album, *Drums of Passion*, going quintuple platinum while introducing "new" drums such as *iya ilu* and *omele*. After knowing such new information, *one may think differently*, or have the insight about simple drums also serving as bridges of complex cultural understanding. In other words, from an institutional standpoint learners should ask themselves, "What have I formally learned that puts me in a better position to understand another experience?" Typically, the answer is that new information leads to new insights.

With respect to how the first step of education applies to RRI, Sylviane Ngandu-Kalenga Greensword, the inaugural postdoctoral fellow for the Race & Reconciliation Initiative, hit the ground running as she educated herself on how to single-handedly become a film producer and chief architect of the RRI Oral History Project. While I sheepishly may claim credit for orchestrating our oral history and videography training by consulting with colleague Max Krochmal and TCU graduate student Moises Gurrola, who collaborated on TCU's *Civil Rights in Black and Brown* oral history project, it was Greensword who through trial and error conducted a bevy of oral history interviews of key TCU historical figures that can now be found in the online repository at the university's Mary Couts Burnett library.[7] Similarly, initially serving as the RRI graduate research assistant, Marcellis Perkins educated himself about how best to reach broader audiences and spearheaded the creation of the RRI-based podcast, *Reconcile This!* which has reached over thirty countries internationally. The podcast highlighted the good work that good people were doing both on and off campus in the name of reconciliation. As a member of Team RRI, Karen Steele educated both herself and me on the best practices employed by peer member institutions of the international consortium Universities Studying Slavery (USS). All the foregoing examples of early education were critical to our later successes.

The second step in the 3Es' progression is exposure, which is the next level of understanding. While the exposure step shares many similarities with education, it is nuanced by requiring more engagement from the learner to build upon facts and data one acquires through active exploration. Exposure can therefore mean extended conversations, additional readings, the digestion of related musical and artistic works, associated cuisine samplings, or any other specific opportunity to deepen one's connection to the material. More importantly, as learners grow more comfortable exploring the finer details of the subject matter, one is now in a better position to convert such information into knowledge.

Exposure represents the opportunity to see and hear. Thus, in returning to the Olatunji example, exposure may consist of listening to his "Akiwowo" track for 4 minutes and 42 seconds, sung in his native tongue of Yoruba, which deftly employs call and response techniques to tell the story of a passenger asking the conductor to take the entire group home. Learners should ask, "What have I seen or heard outside of 'my normal' that has put me in a position to be more receptive to another perspective?" Typically, the answer is that new insights lead to new beliefs.

To cultivate community on campus and to promote greater exposure to the work of RRI, Team RRI was proactive in creating multiple touch points to expose our TCU community to both the RRI brand and the concept of reconciliation. In our first year, we conducted over ninety programs in efforts to be inclusive of the varied perspectives that constitute our "many shades of purple." Off campus, we visited community businesses such as Black Coffee to hold open discussions, while on campus we collaborated with fraternity and sorority life to create a Campus Quest, where students ran around campus to identify historical sites all in the name of fun! All this exposure was crucial to cultivating a receptive community that would continue to embrace the concept of reconciliation.

The third and final step is experience, arguably the most difficult but most meaningful step of the 3Es, for a meaningful experience requires that one relinquish control, humbly acknowledge that there are gaps in one's learning, and immerse oneself in a live scenario that allows one to internalize what one

Mural created as part of TCU's first Reconciliation Day in April 2021. The artwork on the west side of the wall (shown) was created by Fine Arts students Lauren Fieniken, Quin Frazier, Faith Glass, Micah Matherne, and Katalina Watson. *Photo courtesy of TCU Marketing and Communications.*

knows to be true. Take for example study abroad experiences, which help cultivate learner qualities such as "adaptability, self-awareness, tolerance for ambiguity, teamwork, leadership, work ethic, and problem-solving and intercultural skills."[8] In fact, such experiences are so beneficial, they are linked to improving the graduation rates for all students—and especially non-white students.[9] Study abroad epitomizes the third step of experience insofar as learners are able to take advantage of structured, substantive opportunities to apply what they learn about others outside of their originating identity framework. Often, through shared experiences, one's knowledge is converted to budding wisdom. The hope is that one will grow wise enough not just to respect another's culture—as in, refraining from adjudging whether it is superior or inferior—but to thrive and appreciate the manifold benefits of working constructively across difference.[10]

Experience broadly represents the opportunity to feel. For example, beyond listening to Olatunji, a learner may actively participate in a live African drum circle and literally feel the vibrations of the open interplay between the mother drum, or *iya ilu*, and the baby drum, or *omele*. Hence, learners can ask, "What opportunities have I had that have pushed me beyond the superficial to a substantive appreciation of another way of being?" Typically, the answer is new beliefs lead to new behaviors.

In the case of applying the experience step to RRI, the creation of the first Reconciliation Day on April 21, 2021, was an opportunity to create a shared experience that would become part of each person who attended. In turn, attendees could become part of a larger community amenable to the concept of healing in the name of reconciliation. Not only was Reconciliation Day an attempt to institutionalize a long-standing commitment to growth and change beyond reactionary measures that fizzle out after a couple of years, but also Reconciliation Day was a dynamic opportunity for people to experience for themselves the "art of the possible" when it comes to positive progress. Of course, we did not solve all the world's problems that day, but we did demonstrate that many of us are willing to make the noble effort to try. A shared experience truly underscores the pronoun "we," as our collective humanity is shared and experienced through the specific, purple-tinted lens of TCU.

Walking the Path of Reconciliation

What I appreciate about the concept of reconciliation is that it makes no promises of specific progress in the future but rather pledges to continue down the path in the name of progression. While the distinction is subtle, it is nonetheless significant as it is important to communicate that the concept of reconciliation can be engaged at any point in time. Just as the iconic four plumes of Frog Fountain are encased by a circle, our efforts for reconciliation must also come full circle and be holistic in telling a fuller truth if we are to proceed with the healing process. The good news is that while nobody can do everything, everybody can do something! There is *always* room for inclusion in keeping with the mathematical principle that once the circle is formed, it can be *infinitely* expanded and still keep its shape. Everyone who dares to wear the purple is part of the process since every voice counts. I find the principles of Ubuntu to be a helpful and inclusive leadership tool. When Ubuntu principles reaffirm that "I am, because we are," this statement

The RRI logo pays subtle homage to the iconic symbol Frog Fountain.
Photo courtesy of TCU Marketing and Communications.

cogently reminds us how *each of us* has to remain diligent in creating a truly effective and inclusive "we."

In addressing our university's racial tensions, TCU's Race & Reconciliation Initiative represents not necessarily "progress" but rather "progression." Part of the healing process is listening patiently and empathetically understanding that often the more we learn, the more we have to do. While many of our racial tensions cannot be solved so easily, it is not that complicated to try to make a sincere effort to grow. Hopefully, the continuing efforts of RRI evidence the principle that only when we come together will we realize our ever-present capacity to move forward together.

As the Ubuntu principles worked for us, they may work for others. Who knows where exactly the path of reconciliation may lead? So long as every voice counts and individuals are still able to add infinitely to our ever-expanding circle, then we stand to remain rooted within a truly inclusive community willing and able to wrestle with the 3Es: education, exposure, and experience.

May we continue to do the best we can with what we have…

Notes

1. Tiffany Hsu, "Aunt Jemima Brand to Change Name and Image Over 'Racial Stereotype,'" *New York Times,* February 10, 2021, https://www.nytimes.com/2020/06/17/business/media/aunt-jemima-racial-stereotype.html

2. Mohamed Chérif Diarra, "Ubuntu as Humanistic Education: Challenges and Perspectives for Africa?" in *Re-Visioning Education in Africa: Ubuntu-Inspired Education for Humanity,* eds. Emefa J. Takyi-Amoako, N'Dri Thérèse Assié-Lumumba (London, UK: Palgrave MacMillan, 2018), 120.

3. Mark Watson, Mary McMahon, Nhlanhla Mkhize, Robert D. Schweitzer, and Elias Mpofu, "Career Counseling People of African Ancestry" in *Counseling People of African Ancestry,* ed. Elias Mpofu (New York, NY: Cambridge University Press, 2011), 282.

4. Frederick Gooding, Jr., *The Griot Tradition as Remixed through Hip Hop: Straight Outta Africa* (New York, NY: Rowman & Littlefield, 2023), 36.

5. Frederick Gooding, Jr., Sylviane Ngandu-Kalenga Greensword, Marcellis Perkins, *A History to Remember: TCU in Purple, White and Black* (Fort Worth, TX: Texas Christian University Press, 2023).

6. Megan Zahneis, Beckie Supiano, "Fear and Confusion in the Classroom," *Chronicle of Higher Education,* June 9, 2023, https://www.chronicle.com/article/fear-and-confusion-in-the -classroom.

7. "Oral History Project," *Mary Couts Burnett Library,* n.d., https://exhibits.tcu.edu/s/race-reconciliation-initiative/page/introduction.

8. "In an IIE [Institute of International Education] research study involving 4,500 college alumni who studied abroad between the 1999–2000 and 2016–2017 academic years, about 90 percent of respondents said their overseas experience cultivated these qualities in them." Miki Tanikawa, "How Study Abroad Can Benefit College Students," *U.S. News & World Report,* September 8, 2023, https://www.usnews.com/education/articles/how-study-abroad-can-benefit-college-students.

9. Karin Fischer, "Latitudes: Study Abroad's Impact on College Education," *The Chronicle of Higher Education,* May 4, 2022, https://www.chronicle.com/newsletter/latitudes/2022-05-04.

10. Frederick Gooding, Jr., *Race and Media Literacy, Explained (or Why Does the Black Guy Die First?)* (New York, NY: Teachers College Press, 2024), 35–36.

Take It Easy While We Reconcile This!

Marcellis R. Perkins

IN THE PREVIOUS CHAPTER, Frederick Gooding (Dr. G) explained how the Race & Reconciliation Initiative conceived of actionable research to help TCU confront its racial history. As inaugural chair, Dr. G presented a broad plan for us to expose, educate, and engage. At the same time, we felt a balance of excitement and uncertainty around the work that we were to undertake in how we would ultimately empower our community and audience. Thus, looming around our academic endeavor of researching the University's relationship with slavery and racism was a bit of concern of being seen as a "performative" parade of pseudo racial reckoning and disingenuous intellectual inquiry.

It is not uncommon for institutions or corporations to prioritize diversity efforts when external pressures or tragic events bring about communal displeasure of how racial issues have been previously mishandled in the eyes of disenfranchised communities. Additionally, we understood that attempting to do this kind of emotionally taxing and deep research during a global pandemic brought about an unprecedented uncertainty of when or how things would return to normal.

When asked to join the initiative as the inaugural graduate research assistant, I too wondered, while honoring my own positionality, about the sincerity of TCU's desire to be transparent about its racial histories, especially during this time. As a Black male who attends a predominately white institution and whose identity is often misrepresented in media and academia, I wanted to contribute to RRI in a genuine, authentic manner, one that centered storytelling and facilitated community connection. I knew that if I were to be a part of the RRI team, I would need the opportunity to show up in a way that did not compromise my values of truth, justice, and joy. Luckily, working under a leadership team that saw my potential and championed my ideas, I was able to help co-construct one of RRI's marquee additions: a podcast.

In truth, the work that we were expected to do for the university, our campus community, colleagues, and even ourselves was widely unknown as this academic venture came with no real *blueprint*. TCU's chancellor and board of trustees stipulated that we were to study TCU's relationship with slavery, racism, and the Confederacy to better understand the present-day realities of race relations at TCU and to broaden our institutional memory regarding matters of race. The charge given to RRI was a broad and vague desire for the institution to be transparent and forthcoming about its history. However, what also laid underneath the thick layers of skepticism, concerns, uncertainty, and even confusion was a prime opportunity to explore new avenues to produce research, to explore innovative ways to collaborate with other institutions, spark dialogue, to provide a place for historically excluded narratives to be included into the university's identity, and most importantly for communal healing and understanding.

Although we were equipped with accomplished scholars and bold leaders from across campus, we adopted a "build as we climb" attitude. We possessed an outline of what we wanted to do; *how* we wanted to get there would rely on the intellectual and creative minds that were assembled to think strategically and collaboratively. Many universities that are a part of the Universities Studying Slavery consortium prioritized producing peer-reviewed scholarly

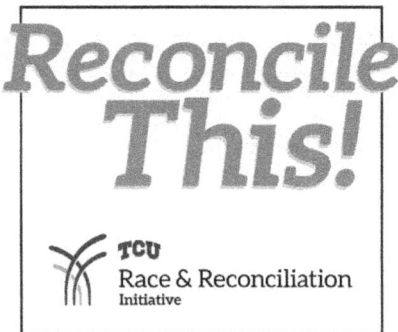

Reconcile This!
TCU
Race & Reconciliation
Initiative

Reconcile This! logo.
Photo courtesy of TCU Marketing and Communications.

articles, monographs, and collections and posted regular updates on their university-sponsored websites. In understanding that each university was unique in its institutional structure, support, desired outcome, and research capacity, those who had committed to serve RRI knew that we would be able to borrow ideas and approaches but would ultimately have to address the direct needs of our own community.

While our campus was slowly returning to in-person classes, we decided that our primary community engagement approach would consist of virtual town halls that would be hosted on Zoom. These panel discussions would feature members of the research team, students, TCU faculty and staff members, as well as community members to discuss their work and their own research attempts on working towards racial reconciliation and understanding. Although Zoom severely limited our ability to engage in personal environments, our goal was to reach the widest possible audience in our goal of bringing our campus together and keeping the campus community informed. In studying our peer institutions, which were also attempting to navigate difficult conversations regarding race during the COVID-19 pandemic, we knew that finding ways to continue connecting with the community to gain support would be an important factor and indicator in the success of the initiative. Broadening our output beyond what is typically valued in the academy, RRI would diversify its research methods and output through oral history, informal roundtables, workshops, murals, portraiture, multi-dimensional presentations, and a podcast that would emerge as a useful supplementary and complementary research production platform.

By evaluating the low attendance of students at our events, I thought through how we might better engage our students and invite them into the conversation and the work of reconciliation. As someone who had previously hosted a college-run radio show in Massachusetts, I knew that students enjoy flexible and alternative ways to learn outside of reading and writing. Therefore, I approached Dr. G with an idea of cohosting a podcast where we added an additional touch point and avenue for our campus community to engage in the work of RRI. In combining our love for hip-hop, conversation, and intellectual thought, the podcast *Reconcile This!* was born.

An academic podcast that presented candid conversations that centered healing and research, *Reconcile This!* would go on to be the sound of the Race & Reconciliation Initiative for three seasons. Covering topics from curriculum development, research findings, book releases, and socio-political commentary, Dr. G and I would go on to record forty episodes; the first episode, named after Jay-Z's 2001 album *The Blueprint,* was released January 25, 2021.

With a shared love for learning and music, we offered a pedagogical approach to academic discourse using the genius of hip-hop. Reflected in the episode titles, which shared the names of beloved hip-hop albums or tracks, each podcast showcased how we used formal and informal dialogue, lived experiences, critical observation, creative storytelling, and formal analysis to remix podcasting so that we could sustain both formal and informal learning spaces. We did not expect how the sounds of *Reconcile This!* would travel air waves outside of our campus community and be enjoyed both nationally and globally.

Aside from reaching a broader audience, we also intentionally provided an avenue in which conversations that were typically held in siloed spaces within the academy could be accessed and heard outside of the college campus to bridge communities. As a graduate student, I know how academic research tends to use specialist or jargonistic language and is written for those who are in the academy. This academic style further excludes the local community from being a part of the institutional research beyond as subjects. We wanted the local community to be equal collaborators of thought and practice. *Reconcile This!* as a podcast and a platform allowed all listeners to engage with academic research and to obtain tangible tools to implement the work in their own personal and professional lives.

During the first season, we primarily highlighted RRI research: we interviewed TCU faculty, staff, and students to highlight the impactful work that everyday Horned Frogs were already doing. Edited and produced by student worker Kai Grady (duties I assumed in years two and three), the podcast communicated that despite TCU being virtual, there were still countless members on our campus who were dedicated to making the campus a better place. With over fifteen individual interviews, the first season set the precedent for what *Reconcile This!* could do and ultimately what RRI would represent. We covered a range of topics, from the mental health of Black men with Brandon Dixon, insights of student Greek life with Jordan Carter and Cassie Trosino, and the misconceptions of Women and Gender Studies with Randa Tawil. The growing success of *Reconcile This!* started to attract

Frederick Gooding, Jr., and Marcellis Perkins interview Rhondda Thomas of Clemson University. *Photo courtesy of Karen Steele.*

Frederick Gooding, Jr., and Marcellis Perkins welcome Rhonda V. Magee for their first live recording of *Reconcile This! Photo courtesy of TCU Marketing and Communications.*

listeners outside of the state of Texas and even beyond the United States with countries such as Azerbaijan, Australia, Chile, Croatia, Guatemala, Iran, Italy, Jamaica, Mauritius, Panama, New Zealand, Senegal, United Kingdom, and Qatar tuning in.

Whereas the first season highlighted RRI and TCU's campus community, the second season focused on the work and research of our colleagues across the country. Dr. G and I maintained our commentary on national news regarding race and provided updates about RRI events and research. Some of our most popular episodes featured RRI postdoctoral fellow Sylviane

Greensword, graduate student Cecilia Hill, and NFL Hall of Famer and TCU trustee LaDainian "LT" Tomlinson, each of whom explained the work they were doing on campus to elevate thought and work with local communities to drive healing and understanding. The biggest highlight of the second season came by way of a research trip to Clemson University, featuring Rhondda Thomas, the Calhoun Professor of Literature and founder of the *Call My Name* project. Dr. G, Karen Steele, and I were invited to South Carolina to learn more about the research process in documenting Clemson's institutional relationship with slavery and the Confederacy. Thomas would also become our first guest from outside of TCU; this episode, titled after the 1996 Nas album *It Was Written*, was our first live podcast.

Seeing the momentum and popularity of the podcast, Dr. G and I soon began to receive emails from colleagues outside of TCU wanting to join as a guest for *Reconcile This!* Jay Augustine from Duke University joined us to discuss his book *Called to Reconciliation: How the Church Can Model Justice, Diversity, and Inclusion.* Conversations featuring Thomas and Augustine showcased the possibility of communal conversation and what may be possible at different institutions.

Our third season was our most action packed as it elevated *Reconcile This!* as a leading podcast platform engaging in critical conversation regarding individuals and their relationship and process of understanding race relations. We charted listeners in all fifty states and nearly twenty-five countries outside of the U.S. We featured guests such as Reverend Wheeler Parker, Jr., the last surviving cousin of Emmitt Till, who was with him the night of his kidnapping, and Kirt von Daacke, co-chair of the University of Virginia's President's Commission on Slavery and the University. In our third season, we hosted another live podcast, this time with Rhonda V. Magee, the director of the Center for Contemplative Law and Ethics at the University of San Francisco, in the Van Cliburn Concert Hall.

In my opinion, one of the most touching episodes featured Frederick Rouse III, grandson of Mr. Fred Rouse, a Fort Worth Black man who was lynched in 1921. Episode 3.12 "HIStory" delved into how Frederick Rouse III shouldered the work of healing generational and communal trauma by elevating his grandfather's story and reminding us all on the connectivity of history.

Something about that episode, I felt, captured the essence of what *Reconcile This!* stood for. The conversation was raw, vivid, and emotionally pulling while being intellectually inspiring. Rouse's conversation illuminated how TCU's desire to study its relationship with slavery and the Confederacy was connected to the development of local histories. Clearly, Rouse didn't need a Ph.D. in history to talk about his community work and the impact that it had, nor did he need to be a TCU community member to have access or impact on the work that was being done on campus by RRI or TCU. Rouse was an everyday person who dared to do extraordinary work to discuss and explore the possibilities of racial reckoning.

Our last episode, recorded in the fall of 2023, was another live recording that featured Sylviane Ngandu-Kalenga Greensword, Dr. G, and I celebrating the publication of the first RRI-related book, *A History to Remember: TCU in Purple, White, and Black*, and our experiences as co-authors. The episode included both the book launch and a panel discussion with notable Black TCU alumni Ronald Hurdle, Zoranna Jones, Aundrea Matthews, Leon Reed, and LaDainian Tomlinson.

Undoubtedly, *Reconcile This!* humanized our research through featuring researchers willing to have difficult and open conversations while allowing for the personalities of the cohosts and guests to be authentically present. Too often when reading research, we miss the opportunity to hear the voice and tone of the scholar. Instead, we interpret what we are reading through the lens of our own capacities and understanding, which can lead to misunderstanding and disconnection. This is why a podcast—or a YouTube series or other social media—is increasingly used by academics as a resource that allows for broader access.

Reconcile This! has already proven useful for classroom instruction and scholarly presentations. In her TCU course Exploring Diversity, Whitnee Boyd played episodes from the first season of *Reconcile This!* for her students to analyze and discuss. These first-year students learned about TCU's history and discovered narratives about TCU that are often excluded from the traditional institutional account. I later joined the class to participate in a panel discussion on how podcasting fits into academic research and can enhance dialogue by modeling how to have difficult conversations around taboo topics like race. Even outside of the realm of the TCU campus, our podcast has prompted other ways to engage with others academically. Pablo Montes in

Frederick Gooding and Marcellis Perkins, cohosts of *Reconcile This!*
Photo courtesy of TCU Marketing and Communications.

the College of Education invited me and fellow graduate students to record a podcast episode on concepts learned in his Indigenous and decolonization curriculum course. Led by graduate student Nicole Weinberg, the episode featured dialogue and journal entries from TCU graduate students Blake Lentz, Kelcia Righton, Kelly Phommachanh, and Lea Lester. Ultimately, the podcast would be transcribed, submitted, and accepted to one of the largest higher education networks globally, the American Education Research Association (AERA), and would be published in 2024. This publication led the participants to present at the AERA national conference in Philadelphia in 2024 for a roundtable on "Decolonize That! Podcasting a Graduate-level Seminar about Decolonization in Higher Education."

Reconcile This! has facilitated other kinds of connections, such as through invitations to collaborate with other academics to build community in the Dallas-Fort Worth metroplex. In the Spring of 2023, Dr. G and I were inducted into the Maladjusted Cohort on behalf of the Dallas Truth, Racial Healing and Transformation. This opportunity allowed us to participate in communal dialogues, attend workshops to elevate our production, and engage in other scholarly communal work being done in the DFW area. *Rec-*

oncile This! was featured in numerous newspaper and magazine articles and prompted an interview by Shaun Rabb of KDFW Fox News.

With a range of special guests who are college professors, museum curators, students and community leaders, research directors, scholarly authors, and more, *Reconcile This!* created a necessary space that communicated about RRI's academic research with a modern flare. We intended to find a creative way to connect with the campus and local community during a global pandemic. What resulted, after forty episodes and three years, was an intentional podcast that not only connected with community but also supplied a space of healing and reflection. *Reconcile This!* served as a reminder that research can utilize various methods and modes to mobilize collectives towards a common goal. The journey of *Reconcile This!* was indeed an impactful aspect of the Race & Reconciliation Initiative. With a pair of mics, two of RRI's core team members modeled the endless possibilities of collaborative and intentional efforts.

Perkins Notes

1. Frederick Gooding, Jr., and Marcellis Perkins, Episode 1: The Blueprint. *Reconcile This!* Podcast Audio. January 25, 2021. https://podcasts.apple.com/us/podcast/episode-1-the-blueprint/id1549430350?i=1000506530732; Jay-Z. *The Blueprint.* Roc-A-Fella Records, 2001.

2. Frederick Gooding, Jr., and Marcellis Perkins, Episode 2: Black on Both Sides/ Healing at the Crossroads with Dr. Brandon Dixon, Dr. Alan Gallay, Dr. Eric Wood. *Reconcile This!* Podcast Audio. February 8, 2021. https://podcasts.apple.com/us/podcast/episode-2-black-on-both-sides-healing-at-the-crossroads/id15494303 50?i=1000508237286. Episode 6: The Miseducation with Dr. Jacque Lambiase, Ms. Jordan Carter, Ms. Cassie Trosino. *Reconcile This!* Podcast Audio. April 12, 2021. https://podcasts.apple.com/us/podcast/episode-6-the-miseducation/id1549430350?i=1000516848012 Episode 3: The Dreamer, The Believer with Dr. Randa Tawil, Dr. Sue Anderson, Assistant Vice Chancellor Mr. Adrian Andrews. *Reconcile This!* Podcast Audio. February 22, 2021. https://podcasts.apple.com/us/podcast/episode-3-the-dreamer-the-believer/id1549430350?i=1000510242367

3. Frederick Gooding, Jr., and Marcellis Perkins, *Reconcile This!* Analytic Reports. Spotify. May 1, 2024. https://open.spotify.com/show/7kSKCkQXxjPZrWZva5Kg9i

4. Frederick Gooding, Jr., and Marcellis Perkins, Episode S2.5: It Was Written with Dr. Rhhonda Thomas. *Reconcile This!* Podcast Audio. December 20, 2021. https://podcasts.apple.com/us/podcast/episode-s2-5-it-was-written-ft-dr-rhondda-thomas-part-1-2/id1549430350?i=1000545523785; Nas. *It Was Written.* Columbia Records, 1996.

5. Frederick Gooding, Jr., and Marcellis Perkins, Episode S2.8: Be with Dr. Jay Augustine. *Reconcile This!* Podcast Audio. February 17, 2022. https://podcasts.apple.com/us/podcast/episode-s2-8-be-ft-dr-jay-augustine/id1549430350?i=1000551432968; Augustine, Jonathan C. *Called to Reconciliation: How the Church Can Model Justice, Diversity, and Inclusion.* Grand Rapids, MI: Baker Academic, a division of Baker Publishing Group, 2022

6. Frederick Gooding, Jr., and Marcellis Perkins, Episode S3:13: A Written Testimony with Reverend Wheeler Parker Jr. *Reconcile This!* Podcast Audio. May 5, 2022. https://podcasts.apple.com/us/podcast/episode-s2-13-a-written-testimony-ft-rev-wheeler-parker-jr/id1549430350?i=1000559780096; Frederick Gooding, Jr., and Marcellis Perkins. Episode S3.4: Train of Thought with Dr. Kirt von Daacke *Reconcile This!* Podcast Audio. December 14, 2022. https://podcasts.apple.com/us/podcast/episode-s2-13-a-written-testimony-ft-rev-wheeler-parker-jr/id1549430350?i=1000559780096

7. Frederick Gooding, Jr., and Marcellis Perkins, Episode S3.11: (Live) A Beautiful Revolution with Professor Rhonda Magee *Reconcile This!* Podcast Audio. May 1, 2023. https://podcasts.apple.com/us/podcast/live-episode-s3-11-a-beautiful-revolution-ft/id1549430350?i=1000611342691

8. Frederick Gooding, Jr., and Marcellis Perkins, Episode S3.12: HIStory with Mr. Frederick Rouse III *Reconcile This!* Podcast Audio. May 10, 2023. https://podcasts.apple.com/us/podcast/episode-s3-12-history-ft-frederick-rouse-iii/id1549430350?i=1000612537157

9. Frederick Gooding, Jr., and Marcellis Perkins, Episode S3.13: A History To Remember: TCU Purple, White & Black with Dr. Sylviane Ngandu-Kalenga Greensword *Reconcile This!* Podcast Audio. May 25, 2023. https://podcasts.apple.com/us/podcast/episode-s3-13-a-history-to-remember-tcu-purple/id1549430350?i=1000614506878; Frederick Gooding, Sylviane Ngandu-Kalenga Greensword, and Marcellis R. Perkins. *A History to Remember: TCU in Purple, White, and Black (*Fort Worth, TX: Texas Christian University Press, 2023).

10. Frederick Gooding, Jr., B. Lentz, L. Lester, Pablo Montes, Marcellis Perkins, Kelly Phommachanh, K. Righton, Nicole Weinberg, "Decolonize That! Podcasting a Graduate-level Seminar about Decolonization in Higher Education." Roundtable, Philadelphia Convention Center. Philadelphia, April 12, 2024.

11. Frederick Gooding, Jr., and Marcellis Perkins, "Here & Now: "Reconcile This! Podcast Race Relations at TCU," interview by Shaun Rabb, April 1, 2021, video 3:29.

Finding Charley

Sylviane Ngandu-Kalenga Greensword

ON APRIL 22, 2022, at TCU's second annual Reconciliation Day, I experienced history coming to life as I saw the animated bodies of people who had previously resided in my imagination. Reconciliation Day, a TCU tradition launched by the Race & Reconciliation Initiative (RRI), constitutes an opportunity for the university to assess its progress toward a campus where everyone is respected and valued. In line with the principles of Ubuntu detailed in Chapter 1 of Part Two, this day allows the TCU community to meditate on how putatively everyone's contributions collectively and continuously shape our flagship institution's culture.

As RRI's inaugural postdoctoral fellow, I supervised archival research and directed the RRI's Oral History Project (OHP). Because TCU was founded after Emancipation in 1873, I initially found it difficult to "reconcile" these two assignments under the thematic umbrella of slavery. While early trustees like the Clarks and the Jarvises came from slave-owning families, the wealth they accumulated from slave labor only benefitted TCU indirectly. The name Charley Thorp would bridge this gap.

Initial Curiosity and Inquiry

As Part One details, Charley Thorp was formerly enslaved by Col. Pleasant Thorp, who founded the town of Thorp Spring and owned AddRan/TCU's first building. I came across Charley's name while perusing the literature of our institution's first years, notably *Thank God, We Made It!*, a memoir by

Joseph Lynn Clark that details the Clark family's journey to Hood County and their investment in higher education during Reconstruction.[1]

Charley was the son of an unknown white father and a Black woman, whom the colonel had purchased before Charley's birth. After Emancipation, Charley remained in Thorp Spring. He worked for TCU from its founding in 1873 until the university's relocation to Waco in 1891. His wife, Kate Lee Thorp, was formerly enslaved by Col. Roswell Lee, TCU co-founder Randolph Clark's father-in-law. Kate tended to laundry on the TCU campus. According to Clark, she and Charley provided "indispensable" services to the university: virtually everything except teaching.[2] Among his official titles, Charley was the campus's lead security guard, handyman, and landscapist. He and Kate were beloved members of the Thorp Spring community.

The Rubric

On December 8, 2020, Frederick Gooding, the inaugural RRI Chair, sent me a succinct email:

SG,
Peep game attached; please scan/skim and provide a summary report
about key ideas you believe we should emulate in orienting/orchestrating
our Oral History Project by the time of our last check in for the year.
-Dr. G

The attachment consisted of a "Rubric of Best Practices for Descendant Engagement in the Interpretation of Slavery at Museums and Historic Sites," created in 2018 by the committee of descendants of enslaved workers from Montpelier, the historic Virginia home of James Madison, ahead of the inaugural National Summit on Teaching Slavery. I spent the next five days working tirelessly to create a seven-page pre-evaluation of TCU as "historic site" and how the RRI's OHP could help tell the story of these descendants. I sent Dr. G my findings, as always worried that my work would not be up to par. In my assessment, our data was deficient: we cannot base our OHP on descendants whose existence and location we have not determined. During our meeting, Dr. G inspected my report for what seemed an endless thirty seconds, then said: "Well, this is stellar. Find these descendants and get started."

I supervised the archival team, which was comprised of undergraduate history majors with archival training—Lauren Laphen, Katie Conzonire, Mary Michael Williams—and one M.A. student in history, Briana Salas. These students also worked under the guidance of Mary Saffell from TCU Library's Special Collections, looking for race-related content. With this team's assistance, I was determined to assemble the Thorp story puzzle. Despite the striking dearth of information, I quickly resolved to document their existence based on official data; use these official documents to paint them as human beings with complexities and sensitivities, including their experience as Black individuals in North Texas at the turn of the century; understand how TCU affected these experiences; and trace and find their descendants. As I discovered more about the Thorp descendants, I was determined to bring them to campus to honor their ancestors' memory and spread knowledge of their existence.

Documenting Charley
and Kate's existence

Ubuntu's principles of education, exposure, and experience are highly rooted in our ties to our communities' folkloric histories. When I consider non-canonical historical narratives, I generally operate under the rule: trust *and* verify. Memoirs and oral history, which are too often discounted and disregarded as unsubstantiated testimony, are genuine sources of historical knowledge.[2] In the Thorps' case, most testimonials actually checked out. Slavery schedules show that Col. Pleasant Thorp owned at least three biracial boys (including Charley) and one Black woman. Charley's death certificate showed that his mother's name was Jude, and that he had been born enslaved. The memoirs of the Lee family, as documented in *Iron Guns, Bronze Arrows & Brass Scales* and supplemented in *Thank God, We Made It!*, detail that Kate and her brother Louis were also enslaved biracial children born in the household of Col. Roswell Lee. Kate, Louis, their mother, and their grandmother had all belonged to this family by way of the colonel's soon to be ex-wife. After Emancipation, they remained under Mrs. Lee's legal guardianship, and Kate remained close to Randolph's wife-to-be, Ella Lee. An 1870 census confirms Kate's residence with the white Lees.

Charley and Kate's story

Ella married Randolph Clark in 1870, and they settled in Thorp Spring. Her stepsister Kate tagged along, as well as her young son Lee Williams from a previous brief marriage. There, she met Charley, who already had at least two children: Kitty with Mollie Ruffins (a biracial woman who, according to census information, was the white Thorps' neighbor), and Colonel with Leona Hightower. The latter was the daughter of Simon Hightower who, according to oral history, may have been the former slave of a man named Hightower who taught at AddRan for a brief period.

In January 2021, I organized a field trip to Thorp Spring to visualize the landscape where the Thorps resided. I was joined by Dr. G, RRI graduate assistant Marcellis Perkins, RRI taskforce member Sue Anderson, and TCU alumnus Mark Wassenich. Karen Nace, a local historian, was our tour guide. Before viewing TCU's founding site, we started our visit at the Hood County Jail Museum. This museum features artifacts, documents, and even limestone and nails from the original AddRan building and from the Colony, a Black settlement founded by the Hightower family after Emancipation.[3] At TCU's founding in 1873, and for decades afterwards, the Colony supported the only local Black school, which ended at grade eight.[4] I visited the settlement's ruins after leaving the old AddRan location. While Thorp Spring is now only a twenty-minute drive, 150 years ago, it would have taken hours on horseback, and even longer by foot, given the state of the roads. Since Charley and Kate lived beside the AddRan building, Black education—not to mention white education—remained out of reach for their children.

I also paid several visits to the Granbury Depot and the Hood County Courthouse, where I was able to find notes from the county judges, copies of deeds, and court records. I found out that Charley and Kate had purchased their land from Charley's former master's son, Henry Pleasant Thorp, but the latter had then sued him for non-payment of mortgage. I remain unsure as to how this dispute was resolved, but I can imagine that Henry P. was eventually compensated. Indeed, later records indicate that Charley owned cattle and horses and had registered his trademark at the courthouse. In his eulogy-like article, Randolph Clark wrote that despite Charley's superior intellect, "his acquaintances did not amount to great aims."[5]

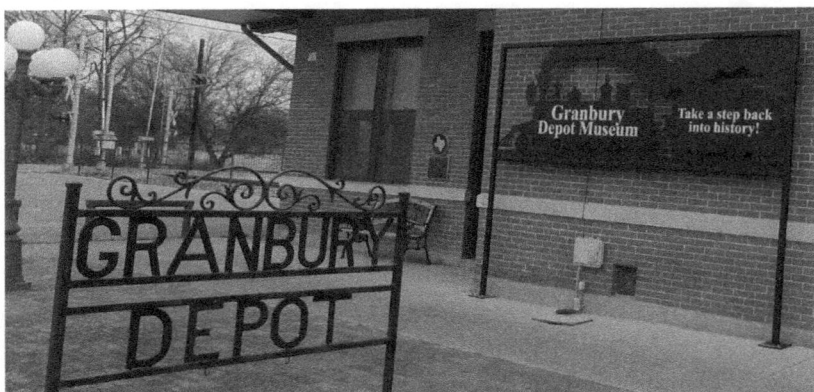

The Depot houses a plethora of official administrative county records.
Photo courtesy of Sylviane Ngandu-Kalenga Greensword.

Again, court records confirm this assumption: on numerous occasions, Charley, his sons, and their friends were arrested for brawling, petty theft, public cursing, and drunkenness. After TCU moved to Waco, the Black Thorps remained in Thorp Spring for less than a decade, then relocated to Dallas. Moreover, Charley had a complicated love life. He fathered children with multiple women, before and during his marriage to Kate. As he had done after the death of his first wife, he attached himself to a white household after Kate's passing in 1915. A 1920 census reports that he was a servant for the family of Witt Sears, an affluent man from Thorp Spring who then moved to New Mexico.[6] While Randolph Clark attributed Charley's unchristian behavior to a birth in bondage and increased postbellum hardships for emancipated Blacks, I was pleased to uncover the numerous success stories among his descendants' lives.

The Thorp Legacy

Death records are extremely informative. For instance, Charley's listed informant on his death certificate was his employer, Witt Sears. This means that Charley likely died on the job, as a servant. In the case of his grandson Colonel Thorpe, Jr., his informant was Julia Thorpe. Ancestry.com reveals that Julia was his daughter, and there were records of her high school yearbook and college education. Because Colonel Jr. passed away in 2001, I figured that I could complete a simple Google search and find some information about either Julia or him. Sure enough, Julia was on social media! From what was available in the public domain, I tried to locate her "Friends" who shared her last name, as a strong probability of their connection with Charley. I contacted Michael, who turned out to be her son, and he confirmed the connection, but deferred to his mother to get involved in this research project.

I then found that Charley and Kate's granddaughter Daisy Thorp had died in 1991, and it led me to her daughter, Dorothy Chiles. I entered her name in my browser. I saw that she was married to Dock Duncan and lived in Lancaster, Texas, the final resting place of Charley and Kate. The website also listed her relatives, among whom is Debra Duncan Holmes. Why did this name sound familiar? I quickly resorted to Ancestry.com. Debra had been working on an online family tree. It was a work in progress. She had hit dead ends and followed rabbit trails. Nevertheless, too many of my discoveries were matching hers for it to be a coincidence. After some more Facebook search time, I found an entire group of Duncans from Dallas and Lancaster. I relaunched my callouts first to Debra, then to her sister Damita. They both called me back within a few days. We spoke for close to an hour. Damita designated Debra as our main contact, given her extensive work with genealogy. In the meantime, Julia had returned my call and confirmed her interest in her family's history.

In a similar fashion, following the lineage of Charley Thorp and Leona Hightower's daughter Kitty Thorp led me to the obituary of their great-great-great-great-grandson, Royce Schells. His 2014 obituary listed all his siblings and children. This document was recent. Surely, some of his relatives had to be on social media! And indeed they were. I zeroed in on Loriessa, Royce's sister, because her wife had created a family tree on Ancestry as well. After an emotionally charged phone call, we agreed to stay in contact.

Through a series of virtual meetings, I introduced Julia, Debra, and Damita and her daughter Dyneshia to several members of Loriessa's family. This is when I hatched the idea to bring the Thorp descendants to campus, to welcome them formally, and to honor the memory and legacy of Charley and Kate Thorp. My goal was to reconcile TCU with its history by including the stories that had been forgotten from the institutional narrative for way too long.

Reconciliation Day 2022

After a year and a half of searching for Black descendants, Team RRI hosted the Thorps on Reconciliation Day 2022 for a poignant reunion. At the end of a luncheon to honor the family, Chancellor Victor Boschini announced that he would provide a full scholarship for one of the descendants to attend TCU starting in the fall of 2022. I was ecstatic for him. TCU's Associate Director of Communications Holly Ellmann and Loriessa took me to the side and had to remind me: "Sylviane, you made it happen. If you hadn't found him and brought him here, this wouldn't have happened."

We also formally interviewed Loriessa for the OHP during her visit, where she expressed how central the RRI's discovery was for her family:

> I can't tell you how important that is, for me personally, and a lot of folks in my family [...] I am blown away by that. I am grateful! You know, we had found about Charley Thorp at some point [...] and then when you brought your details [...] it helped to clarify a lot of things for us.[7]

As a result of Reconciliation Day's success, *TCU Magazine* writer Tim Madigan also reached out to Julia, Debra, and Loriessa, and the magazine published an article on the day's events and the Thorp legacy.[8]

Debra Duncan Holmes and Loriessa Taylor-Randle received the Plume Award on Reconciliation Day 2022. Left to right: Chancellor Victor Boschini, Loriessa Taylor-Randle, Sylviane Ngandu-Kalenga Greensword, Debra Duncan Holmes, Frederick W. Gooding, Jr. *Photo by Leo Wesson, Courtesy of TCU Marketing and Communications.*

During Reconciliation Day 2022, TCU commemorated the legacy of Charley and Kate Thorp. TCU extended a special welcome to many of this couple's descendants (shown). *Photo courtesy of TCU Marketing and Communications.*

Reflections and insights

My quest to "find" Charley allowed me to see history come alive. While I knew about the Confederacy, as a French native, I never fully appreciated what the Confederacy meant for people who look like me until I investigated a former hub for the Confederate Twentieth Battalion, a group of men fighting and risking their lives for the right to keep people who look like me in chattel enslavement and servitude. As I was visiting the museum, I stared at the Confederate currency, identical to what the Clarks and the Thorps used for daily transactions, to buy bread, clothing, and other items of fancy or sustenance.

I knew about the Emancipation Proclamation and I personally witnessed the grandmother of Juneteenth, Opal Lee, receive an honorary doctorate from TCU. Not until I visited the Colony, however, could I visualize Simon and Hettie Hightower, with their forty acres of farming land and their mule, preparing to host the newly formed community of freed Blacks to celebrate the first Juneteenth.[8] I could also picture the continuation of Black people's subaltern position in the social hierarchy, which seems paradoxical given their emancipated status. Unlike the Hightowers, numerous freed Blacks remained members of the households that had enslaved them, like Charley, who stayed close to Col. Pleasant Thorp and named his first-born son Colonel. Or like Kate, who resided with Ella Lee Clark (and her mother Big Kate, who resided with Ella's mother Susannah) and named her first-born son Lee.

I knew about the numerous contributions of Black soldiers who enlisted in the military to defend the freedoms that we now enjoy. In contrast with Pleasant Thorp and the Clarks' involvement with the Confederacy, I have, for the past three years, accumulated registration and deployment records of Charley and Kate's descendants. After World War One, the U.S. sent army men to Europe, such as Company 342, the service battalion for Colored soldiers. The couple's son Fred Thorp was among these men. After enlisting in 1917, he fulfilled his postbellum military duties in France, the country where I was born. The Thorps also count several World War Two veterans, like Charlie Thorp, who was 5'2" and 150 pounds and actively served at age 55. Anthony C. Thorp was also a World War II veteran. After the war, he settled in Dallas with his wife Catherine, where he was a mechanic and she a beautician. Upon his death in 1951, Catherine reached out to his Thorp Spring community and applied for a veteran headstone at Hightower Village Cemetery in the Colony. She made special arrangements with Hattie Hightower, whose name is reminiscent of Hettie Hightower, the grandmother of Anthony's aunt Kitty Thorp Smith.

Randolph Clark, co-founder of TCU, as well as an elementary and secondary school, deplored his beloved friend Charley's lack of education despite his superior intellect. Census data confirms that Charley could neither read nor write. Nevertheless, Randolph was proud to drive Charley and his daughter (probably Mary) to the Jarvis Christian Institute when she expressed interest in higher education. Charley's grandson Colonel Jr. would go on to be a highly successful student in a predominantly white high school. He was on several teams: football, baseball, and wrestling, where he was also the team's secretary and treasurer. Likewise, Charley's great-great-great-great-granddaughter Regina Schells is now an electrical engineer and STEM educator with scholarly publications. Randolph Clark's daughter "Sook" would reprimand Charley when he questioned his own faith. However, Charley's great-great-grandson David Duncan, who shared his ancestor's love of hats, was the Chaplain of the VFW Post 1836, and a deacon at the Church of the Living God P.G.T. in Dallas.

Charley and Kate Thorp's life stories tell us more than remarkable individual achievements: they teach us about Hood County's Black community. While I still have stacks of unread files from the Granbury Depot and state and county archives, I am proud of the growing awareness of Charley and Kate's existence: four episodes of the RRI's internationally renowned podcast *Reconcile This!* discuss Charley's contributions and accomplishments; the public radio station KERA released a story in June 2022; the book *A History to Remember: TCU in Purple, White, and Black* covers several aspects of the couple's life at AddRan; and TCU's Portrait Project, led by Marcellis Perkins, which unveiled two stunning silhouette portraits of these two instrumental members of the TCU community. The portraits now hang in The Harrison on TCU's campus.[9] Since we do not have any known photograph of the couple, the award-winning artist Letitia Huckaby modeled her portraits after two Thorp descendants, whose location was determined thanks to my research. Through my research on this couple, I gained a peculiar appreciation for TCU as a ubiquitous space. Indeed, AddRan is the very reason why these two met in the first place. Through the concept of Ubuntu, we can see that Charley and Kate's story is interwoven with the very fabric of our university, contributing to its collective identity. This interconnectedness now challenges us to honor and remember their contributions, embodying the belief that "we are, because they were."

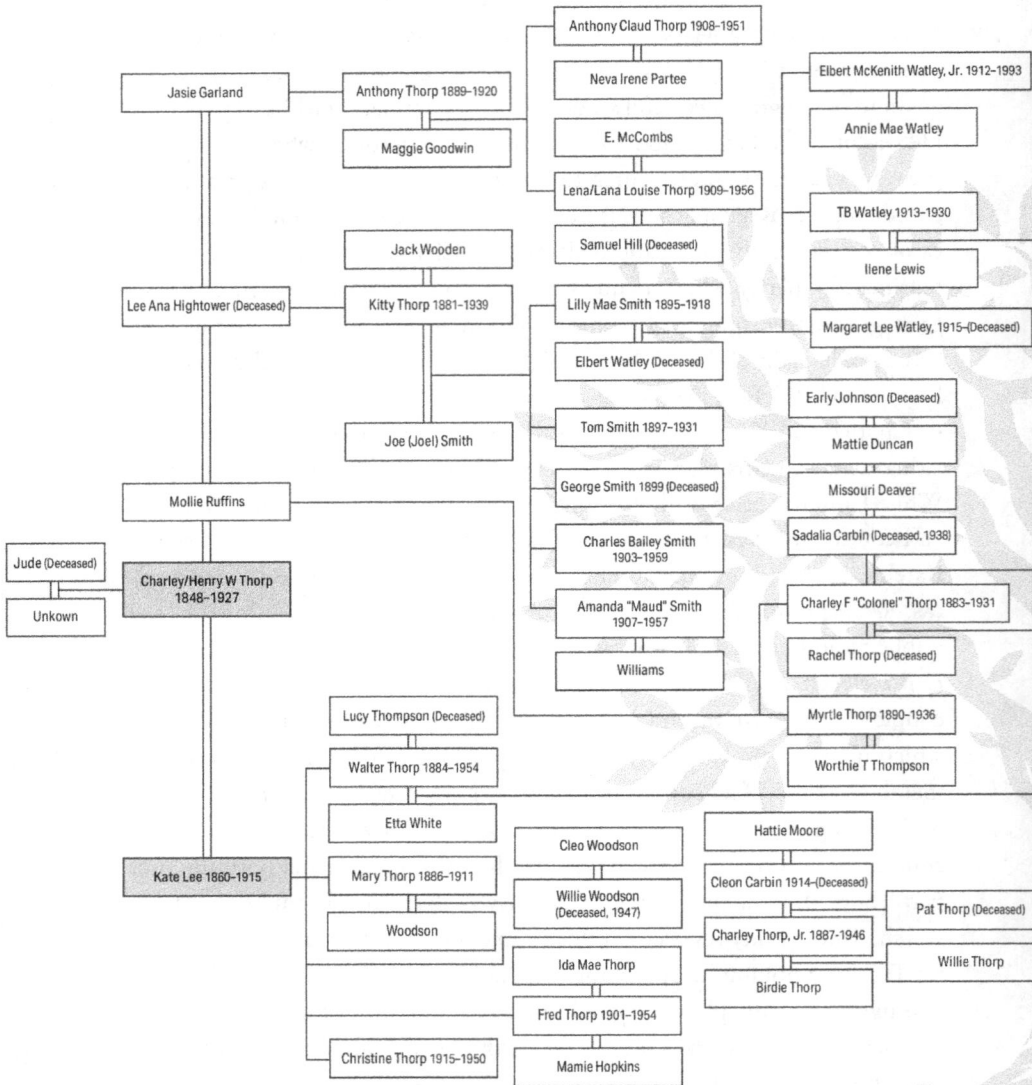

Anthony Claud Thorp 1908–1951

Jasie Garland

Anthony Thorp 1889–1920

Neva Irene Partee

Elbert McKenith Watley, Jr. 1912–1993

Annie Mae Watley

Maggie Goodwin

E. McCombs

Lena/Lana Louise Thorp 1909–1956

TB Watley 1913–1930

Jack Wooden

Samuel Hill (Deceased)

Ilene Lewis

Lee Ana Hightower (Deceased)

Kitty Thorp 1881–1939

Lilly Mae Smith 1895–1918

Margaret Lee Watley, 1915–(Deceased)

Elbert Watley (Deceased)

Early Johnson (Deceased)

Joe (Joel) Smith

Tom Smith 1897–1931

Mattie Duncan

George Smith 1899 (Deceased)

Missouri Deaver

Mollie Ruffins

Charles Bailey Smith 1903–1959

Sadalia Carbin (Deceased, 1938)

Jude (Deceased)

Charley/Henry W Thorp 1848–1927

Amanda "Maud" Smith 1907–1957

Charley F "Colonel" Thorp 1883–1931

Unkown

Williams

Rachel Thorp (Deceased)

Myrtle Thorp 1890–1936

Lucy Thompson (Deceased)

Worthie T Thompson

Walter Thorp 1884–1954

Etta White

Cleo Woodson

Hattie Moore

Kate Lee 1860–1915

Mary Thorp 1886–1911

Willie Woodson (Deceased, 1947)

Cleon Carbin 1914–(Deceased)

Pat Thorp (Deceased)

Woodson

Charley Thorp, Jr. 1887–1946

Ida Mae Thorp

Willie Thorp

Birdie Thorp

Fred Thorp 1901–1954

Christine Thorp 1915–1950

Mamie Hopkins

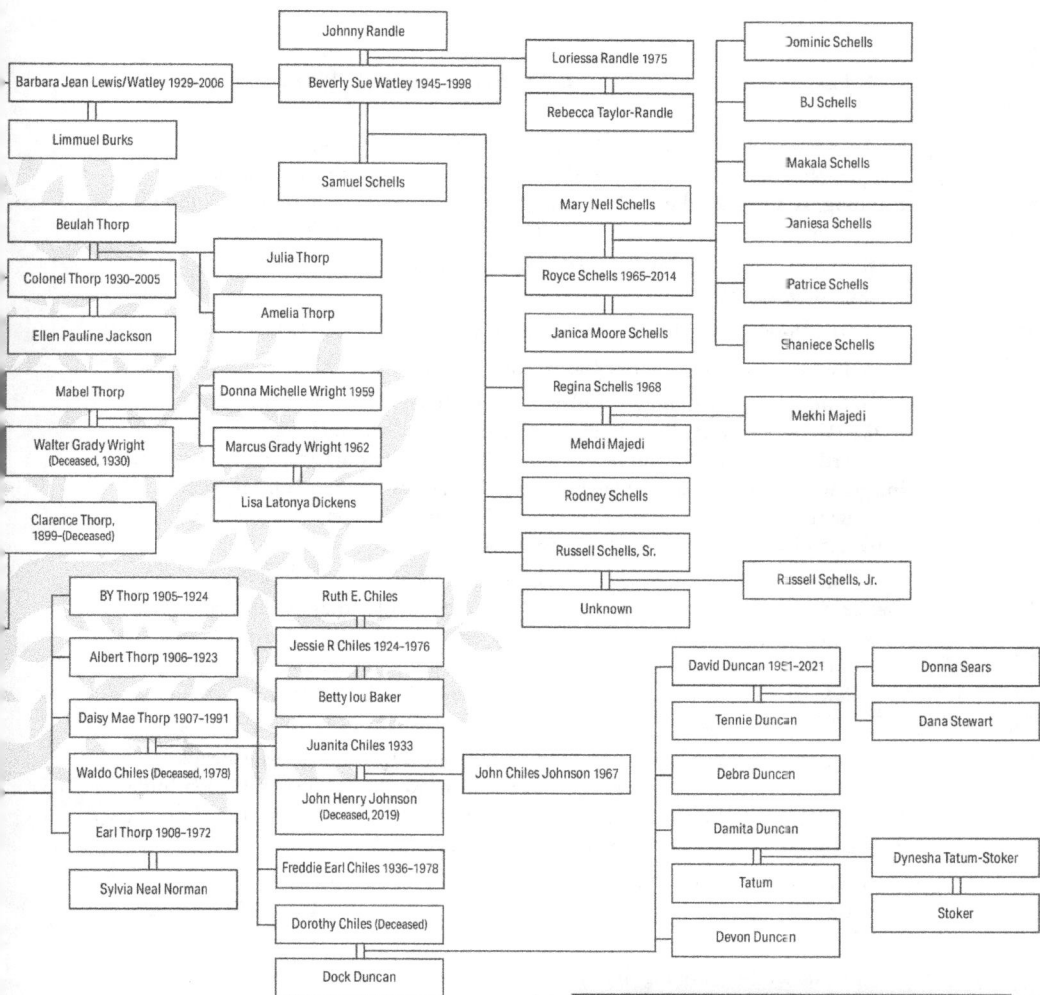

Johnny Randle

Barbara Jean Lewis/Watley 1929–2006

Beverly Sue Watley 1945–1998

Limmuel Burks

Samuel Schells

Loriessa Randle 1975

Rebecca Taylor-Randle

Dominic Schells

BJ Schells

Makala Schells

Daniesa Schells

Beulah Thorp

Julia Thorp

Colonel Thorp 1930–2005

Amelia Thorp

Ellen Pauline Jackson

Mary Nell Schells

Royce Schells 1965–2014

Patrice Schells

Mabel Thorp

Donna Michelle Wright 1959

Janica Moore Schells

Shaniece Schells

Walter Grady Wright (Deceased, 1930)

Marcus Grady Wright 1962

Regina Schells 1968

Mekhi Majedi

Lisa Latonya Dickens

Mehdi Majedi

Clarence Thorp, 1899–(Deceased)

Rodney Schells

Russell Schells, Sr.

Russell Schells, Jr.

Unknown

BY Thorp 1905–1924

Ruth E. Chiles

Albert Thorp 1906–1923

Jessie R Chiles 1924–1976

David Duncan 1951–2021

Donna Sears

Betty lou Baker

Tennie Duncan

Dana Stewart

Daisy Mae Thorp 1907–1991

Juanita Chiles 1933

John Chiles Johnson 1967

Debra Duncan

Waldo Chiles (Deceased, 1978)

John Henry Johnson (Deceased, 2019)

Damita Duncan

Earl Thorp 1908–1972

Dynesha Tatum-Stoker

Freddie Earl Chiles 1936–1978

Tatum

Sylvia Neal Norman

Dorothy Chiles (Deceased)

Devon Duncan

Stoker

Dock Duncan

Charley & Kate Thorp Family Tree

Family tree of Charley Thorp and
his descendants: a work in progress.
*Image courtesy of Sylviane Ngandu-
Kalenga Greensword.*

Greensword Notes

1. Joseph Lynn Clark. *Thank God, We Made It!: A Family Affair with Education.* University of Texas, 1969.

2. To put things into perspective, Charley's important position would be comparable to that of an Associate Vice Chancellor for Facilities and Campus Planning, as he reported directly to the university leadership and was given substantial decision-making power on campus infrastructure planning and improvements.

3. Mary Estelle Gott Salterelli. *Historic Hood County: An Illustrated History.* HPN Books, 2009. 23–24.

4. The closest high schools for Black students were located in Fort Worth.

5. Randolph Clark, "Charles Thorp," *Christian Courier.* (1927).

6. *United States Federal Census* [database on-line]. Year: *1920*; Census Place: *Justice Precinct 6, Hood, Texas*; Roll: *T625_1819*; Page: *1A*; Enumeration District: *30*. Retrieved from Ancestry.com. Provo, UT, USA: Ancestry.com Operations, Inc., 2010. Images reproduced by FamilySearch. https://www.ancestrylibrary.com/discovery-ui-content/view/36571721:6061?tid=&pid=&queryId=fe703b4c-cea2-4fc4-bf35-5b021fe54d2c&_phsrc=QWa25&_phstart=successSource.

United States Federal Census [database on-line]. Year: *1930*; Census Place: *Precinct 9, Lincoln, New Mexico*; Page: *4B*; Enumeration District: *0010*; FHL microfilm: *2341130*. *Retrieved from* Ancestry.com. Provo, UT, USA: Ancestry. com Operations Inc, 2002. https://www.ancestrylibrary.com/discoveryui-content/view/108121708:6224?tid=&pid=&queryId=9bb68542-341b-4be7-a3cb-2e55398165d7&_phsrc=QWa27&_phstart=successSource.

7. Loriessa Taylor-Randle. "Oral History Interview with Loriessa Taylor-Randle." Interviewed by Sylviane Ngandu-Kalenga Greensword, Race & Reconciliation Initiative. (2022). https://repository.tcu.edu/bitstream/handle/116099117/57844/Interview_Transcription_Loriessa_Taylor-Randle.pdf?sequence=3.

8. Tim Madigan. "FORGOTTEN NO MORE: TCU's Race & Reconciliation Initiative Shows the Promise of the future through a Face from the Past." *TCU Magazine.* (Fall 2023).

9. Frederick W. Gooding, Jr., Sylviane Ngandu-Kalenga Greensword, and Marcellis Perkins. *A History to Remember: TCU in Purple, White, and Black.* TCU Press, 2023.

Speaking the Truth:
Telling Y[Our] TCU Story

Jenay Willis

AS THE FINAL DIRECTOR of RRI's Oral History Project (OHP) and a scholar with a background in the history and practices of higher education, I brought a distinctive lens to my work at TCU. A predominantly white institution (PWI), TCU has perpetuated systems of oppression, such as racism, sexism, and classism, that have long impacted the lives of individuals from historically marginalized racial and ethnic backgrounds, inclusive of Black, Indigenous, Latinx, and Asian Pacific American identities. Through the OHP, I had the privilege and honor of being in conversation with members of the TCU community—students, faculty, staff, and alumni who are Black, Indigenous, and People of Color, as well as white—who willingly shared their stories navigating race relations and racism with the university. While many of these stories highlight experiences of pain or trauma, participants who shared their stories recognized the OHP as a place of individual and collective healing. Offering such a sacred space supports individuals from historically marginalized racial and ethnic backgrounds in being the drivers of their own healing journeys. Additionally, the OHP allows those from privileged backgrounds, namely white individuals, to acknowledge their power held in having white privilege while honoring how the university aims to achieve collective healing for all through reconciling the past to renew a progressive future.

The Oral History Project exists as a part of the Race & Reconciliation Initiative (RRI), a university-wide academic endeavor that relies upon archival research. Established in the fall semester of 2020, the Oral History Project was initially envisioned by the inaugural chair of the Initiative,

Frederick Gooding, Jr., and Sylviane Ngandu-Kalenga Greensword, the inaugural postdoctoral fellow, who designed and implemented the project with Gooding's support. Through the Oral History Project, RRI created a platform to shed light on individual's experiences with race and racism while at TCU. The narratives captured through the Oral History Project include stories that enlarge our understanding of two key periods in TCU's history: the transition to integration (1941–1971) and recent and related histories (1998–2020).[1]

TCU's Oral History Project is significant for many reasons. It honors the humanity in living research. Hearing directly from individuals who can speak to their experiences tied to race relations and racism at TCU is powerful and engages in truth telling. Individuals sharing their narratives are speaking from firsthand experience. Also, as the director of the OHP, I can directly engage in the research project using my own lens, lending itself to key takeaways and lessons learned in my role. Given this, I begin by addressing the necessity of humanizing history. Then, I examine the ways in which oral history exists as rich history. I also address oral history as a research methodology to highlight the stories of individuals who were willing to share their experiences tied to race and racism. Through vignettes, I offer examples that showcase and address the different approaches I employed to record their narratives, and I conclude with some lessons learned.

Humanizing History through Oral Narratives

Hearing the stories of TCU affiliates and campus community members involves creating and sustaining spaces rooted in communal healing, care, and compassion, which humanizes their experiences. To achieve communal healing, I first honored the individual healing of each community member who shares their story before attending to the collective healing fostered between each of these individuals and the university, with myself included as the director of the project. My own care as researcher elicits the stories of all community members who willingly share, allowing their narratives to be heard uninterrupted. This approach requires that I bring my whole self to the work, transforming silences or dehumanizing narratives into humanizing experiences, which honors what each of the individuals lived through and experienced. To demonstrate compassion, I worked to connect communal healing and care, which together drive a progressive change between all who have chosen to share their story and the TCU community at large. The Oral History Project provides space for hearing from those people whose experiences are underrepresented or absent in our university narrative.[2] Creating the space to actively listen to each of the narratives shared by individuals is necessary to create and sustain change while honoring as well as acknowledging the past experiences of all who dare to share.

Oral History as Rich History

Well before scholars adopted oral history as a research method, oral history was stories passed down by family and community members; as such, oral history is rich history that has been transferred from one generation to the next.[3] As a significant part of the RRI at TCU, the Oral History Project has been able to preserve the experiences of many community members through their own oral histories. Providing the space for these individuals to share their stories offers a greater depth and richness to the history of TCU while studying the university's history of slavery, racism, and the Confederacy. Further, providing such a space honors the university's past while honoring the present in hearing their stories to forge a brighter future for the university and broader Fort Worth community. Highlighting their stories and housing them in the library's archives, which are publicly accessible, the Oral History Project allows these individual journeys to be studied and incorporated into a fuller story of TCU. The OHP often uncovers and reveals hurtful experiences at TCU that have, perhaps counterintuitively, catalyzed lifelong resilience. As individuals reflect on their experiences at and with the university, they often share that they feel no regrets because their experiences and stories contribute to their strength as well as their overall sense of who they are today. RRI's OHP enables all community members who participate to reflect on their past experiences and acknowledge how these experiences built their character and contribute to who they are presently. Allowing oral history to be understood as rich history thus humanizes our research and equips us to pass on new stories for generations to come.

Oral History as Method

To record the stories of affiliates and community members at TCU, the OHP engages in multiple methods to ensure that diverse stories are heard and shared from the subject's perspectives. I built on the work of my predecessor, Sylviane Ngandu-Kalenga Greensword, who interviewed over thirty individuals in her three years directing the OHP. Upon taking leadership, I approached the Oral History Project by employing two methods: (1) the "Telling Y[Our] Story" series and (2) Oral History Project interviews. The latter is an extension of the former, both of which will be addressed below.

The first method by which I captured oral histories was through a pop-up event that I call "Telling Y[Our] Story," which I began during the start of my tenure as director. Much briefer and simpler than typical oral histories, "Telling Y[Our] Story" enabled me to capture brief memories from alumni and community members who came to TCU for an event sponsored by RRI. Setting up near but not at the center of the RRI event, I recruited before and after the formal program and conducted my brief recordings mostly after the main event had concluded. After verbally securing the interviewee's consent, I captured their response to a single question, "If you could tell your TCU story in two minutes, what would it be and why?" Through this series, I recorded the equivalent of elevator speeches. Such an approach offered me the opportunity to recruit individuals in a low-stakes manner to tell one story. Engaging in this way allowed those who were interested to tell their stories on a first come, first served basis. Additionally, in telling their stories in approximately two minutes, participants were encouraged to sit for a future, longer interview, so I could elicit a fuller story of their TCU experiences.

The second methodology that I employed builds upon the first. To recruit campus community members for the OHP, I followed up with subjects from the "Telling Y[Our] Story" series by asking them if they would like to provide an extended version of their story. I also recruited individuals through email by sharing a recruitment letter with the details of the Oral History Project. Oftentimes potential subjects emerged organically through our RRI research; other times, an interviewee mentioned other individuals whose stories could enhance what we were already uncovering about TCU's past. Once they confirmed their willingness and interest in participating in the Oral History Project, participants were asked to sign consent forms to record audio and video as well as use their narratives for the purposes of our research, a standard practice required by TCU's Institutional Research Board (IRB). Such logistical communication paradoxically enabled me to build connections to a growing community of interviewees and campus community members willing to share their stories.

For the OHP, I worked diligently to construct questions based upon the pre-existing knowledge I gathered in researching each individual whom I planned to interview. After drafting questions, I emailed them to the interviewees for approval and feedback; I also invited them to include additional questions that they would like to answer. This process helped support me and the interviewee as we built comfort with one another and shared in mutual vulnerability. Such a process allowed participants to comfortably convey private stories while maintaining agency in the telling, which provides them with fuller autonomy in their narrative.

No matter the method in recording the experiences and stories of TCU community members, it is vital to note that the interview process is entirely voluntary. For the "Telling Y[Our] Story" series, I secured verbal consent from the interviewees in the sharing of their stories. For the OHP, I employed the more rigorous standard required by the Institutional Review Board of ensuring written informed consent before conducting the interview. Each format offers a distinctive approach to recording the stories of campus and community members of TCU who identify with historically marginalized racial and ethnic backgrounds and share their experiences with race relations and racism at TCU.

Oral History Project in Action

As the former director of the OHP, I engage deeply in heart work, which stems from my compassion and care for those with whom I am in community and conversation. This project elicits a range of emotions from sadness, happiness, and anger to joy and peace. Experiencing a roller coaster of emotions is worthwhile in that I travel back down memory lane with the interviewees who graciously give their time in sharing their stories. In taking that trip with me, they are often reminded of how far they have come and how much further we as a university must go in reconciling the past to rebuild genuine relationships and remain committed to a brighter future. In drawing out and then unpacking these individual histories, the Oral History Project remains a place of vulnerability, healing, and safety, rooted in authenticity and truth telling.

To illustrate the heart work of the OHP, I share a vignette of Aundrea Matthews, Leon Reed, Jr., and me, while engaged in the "Telling Y[Our] Story" series at the *TCU in Purple, White, and Black* book launch event held in October 2023. The conversation allowed Matthews and Reed to revisit some memories of the past and relish in the laughter and joy of how far they have come as esteemed Black alumni of TCU.

> Jenay: Thank you for joining me today. So, if you would, could you please start by sharing your affiliations with TCU?
>
> Aundrea: Aundrea Matthews, Class of '92, 2000, and I went to Brite and graduated from there in 2006.
>
> Leon: Leon Reed, Jr., I was here from '94 to '99 and, well, let's rumble!
>
> Jenay: Let's go! If you could tell your story in two minutes as it relates to race and reconciliation, what would it be and why, collectively?
>
> Aundrea: Hmmm, in two minutes, what race and reconciliation means for me? Race and reconciliation for me means the work that we did becomes known and that our stories can educate, empower, and inspire future generations. I personally don't need [them] to say anything. I don't need their apologies. I need their resources, their access, their opportunities … a place where they make real change to remove the barriers.
>
> Leon: When I think of race and reconciliation, I look at reconciliation as harmonizing. When you reconcile and you bring something that's disconnected and get it to where it's connected. I at least enjoy the spirit that the university is trying because a lot of places won't even try, and so when I was here one thing I was gonna do was be involved. If you had it, I want it, if it's a benefit you have, I want that benefit too.
>
> Jenay: I love that y'all both said that! If we want it, we can have it.

Upon sharing her ideas about race and reconciliation, Aundrea Matthews expressed interest in highlighting her experiences as a Black woman and student leader on campus. The following dialogue reflects her experiences at TCU tied to race and racism and how she overcame experiences of harm:

Aundrea: Let's take the time to celebrate and talk about how powerful, connected, inspired, enlightened, and empowered and creative and determined and just phenomenal we are. When do we get the time to celebrate how we got over?

Jenay: We've gone through all of the adversity and everything. but let's now celebrate the moment!

Aundrea: The moment! That's why I appreciate this project, 'cause we don't often get the opportunity to say, "I stand on the shoulders of Dr. Matthews and others 'cause they went here when I could've never imagined going to TCU." They did, and we did it 'cause we created our own spaces and bonded together. We brought people into the fold and built community […] We hugged one another, cooked for one another, cried together, and were just there for each other.

Jenay: That's how your spirit was fed and continued to be fed while at TCU.

Aundrea: Absolutely! That is how we got over!

From the bonds created to the knowledge shared through sisterly and brotherly relations, the vignettes above highlight how TCU alumni Aundrea Matthews and Leon Reed, Jr., "got over": that is, they overcame tremendous obstacles during their time at TCU. It was not merely about the adversity faced in the darkest of times, however; equally important, they dwelt on how they built their character through moments of laughter, joy, and sorrow. Such stories relayed how they overcame barriers, conquered adversity, and accumulated many accomplishments along the way. Through the continuous heart work of the Oral History Project, I hold space for individuals from historically marginalized racial and ethnic backgrounds to share how they too "got over." These individuals share how their experiences at TCU ignite a light in them to illuminate and guide the generations to come.

Lessons Learned

Oral history is both a cultural practice and a research method to collect powerful stories that can be shared and passed down from one generation to the next. At TCU, the RRI's Oral History Project allows us to gather and synthesize multiple truths about our past. Such an approach acknowledges that a single truth is experienced by one individual; multiple truths, in contrast, allow us to understand a fuller history of our campus. As a method, oral history is both timeless and timely in studying our university's history with slavery, racism, and the Confederacy.

As I have worked to tell a fuller history of TCU's past, I consider my own positionality in leading the Oral History Project as well. As a Southern rural Black woman who serves as the director of the OHP, I often reflect on the shared identities I hold with many individuals that I am in conversation with through this project, specifically Black and Brown people. Acknowledging the power and privilege of my role as director, I cultivate a sacred space for TCU community members to feel safe and vulnerable in sharing their truths. I often challenge the power dynamics in the space to engage in a shared power approach that acknowledges everyone sharing their narratives as the knowledge holders of their very own experiences. Such an approach supports the TCU community members who take part in the OHP and centers their individual and collective healing.

Willis notes

1. TCU's Race & Reconciliation Initiative Oral History Project is housed in the Mary Couts Burnett Library and is publicly accessible here: https://www.tcu.edu/race-reconciliation-initiative/findings/oral-history-project.php

2. D. G. Solórzano and T. J. Yosso, "Critical Race Methodology: Counter-Sorytelling as an Analytical Framework for Education Research," *Qualitative Inquiry* 8, no. 1 (2002), 23–44. https://doi.org/10.1177/107780040200800103

3. "Oral History: Defined," Oral History Association, accessed June 2, 2024, https://oralhistory.org/about/do-oral-history/

Taking a New Route: Creating TCU's Indigenous Campus Tour

Theresa Strouth Gaul, Jessica Mundy, Lori Salazar, Shafiq M. Said, Victoria M. Washington

Introduction
Theresa Strouth Gaul

Like all universities sitting on Indigenous lands and especially as a university with the word "Christian" in its name, Texas Christian University (TCU) is implicated in and has benefited from the histories of colonization, dispossession, removal, and genocide enacted on Native peoples throughout U.S. history and in this region of North Texas.[1] The words of TCU's Land Acknowledgment require the TCU community to recognize and foster the "responsibilities" and "relationships" we exist within with "all living beings, human and non-human." In fall 2023, graduate students in a course I taught in the English department called Seminar in American Literature before 1900: Cultural Encounters in the Archive worked to actualize the commitment of TCU's Land Acknowledgement by considering the land on which the campus sits and the built campus as an archive of Indigenous perspectives and history. In consultation and collaboration with Native community members, the students and I created the first draft of a self-guided TCU Indigenous Campus Tour.

The idea for the tour emerged within TCU's Native American and Indigenous Peoples Initiative (NAIPI), which began around 2015. Centering Native people and knowledge, NAIPI hosts an annual Native and Indigenous Peoples Day Symposium; erected a monument to the Wichita and Affiliated Tribes, upon whose ancestral homeland TCU is located; developed a land acknowledgment; created a Native American Advisory Circle for the university; sponsors a wide array of programming; offers pedagogical workshops; and has worked with the university to establish scholarships for Native students and better recruit and support Indigenous faculty, staff, and students. Since 2020, NAIPI has existed alongside TCU's Race & Reconciliation Initiative (RRI). While the idea of the tour and the course project were independent from RRI, they were inevitably shaped by the environment RRI has fostered by encouraging academic, research-based campus-wide conversations on campus about how to acknowledge TCU's histories of racial exclusion, recognize the contributions of marginalized groups to TCU, actively work to repair past harms, and create a culture of belonging, equality, and respect for everyone at TCU. Knowledge of instructors' and students' work on the TCU Portrait Project, which began as a grassroots initiative and is now housed in the Chancellor's office, and the RRI Heritage Trail Tour, which mentions Indigenous peoples at two of thirteen campus sites, also informed our conception of the need for and potential of this project.

Given TCU's status as a predominately white institution (PWI) with a very low number of students who indicate that they identify as American Indian, it is unsurprising that all of the participants in the project are non-Native, had no prior relationships with Indigenous communities, and identify variously as Black (1), Latinx (2), Palestinian-American (1), and white (5 plus professor). Students had varying responses to and concerns with the idea of undertaking this project when it was first introduced to them at the beginning of the semester. It was important to all of us to only move forward with this project if it would be beneficial and positive for Native people at TCU and in broader communities. In preparation for our work on the campus tour, we read and discussed scholarship on how to respectfully work in Indigenous studies and with Native communities, studied examples of Indigenous campus tours created on other campuses, and learned about the histories of Native peoples in North Texas.[2]

We also shared meals with Native community members, who gave us guidance in undertaking this project. These guests included TCU professors Wendi Sierra (Oneida) and Pablo Montes (Chichimeca Guamares and P'urhépecha), alumnus Albert Nungaray (Tewa), student Haylee Chiariello

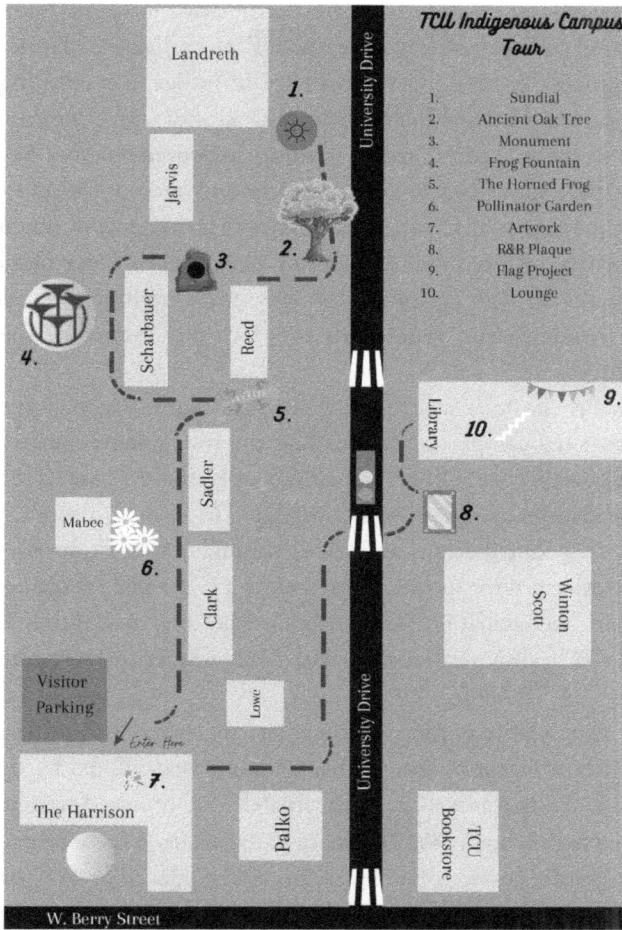

TCU's Indigenous Campus Tour route. *Image courtesy of Theresa Strouth Gaul.*

(Cherokee), and community member C. Annette Anderson (Cherokee and Chickasaw), who speaks to her experience with the project in another essay in this book. TCU's Office of Leadership and Student Involvement provided a service-learning grant to support costs associated with the project.

We conceptualized the tour as a gesture of reciprocity for Indigenous peoples within the TCU community or those who visit our campus, since they often ask to see and learn about features of campus that demonstrate Native presence and resilience when they visit our courses or programs to share their wisdom, knowledge, experience, or expertise with us. Non-Native people were a second audience we hoped to reach. Each audience had unique needs. The first group may hope to see evidence of Indigenous contributions on campus, an accurate depiction of their past histories with the university, and a lasting and genuine commitment to future improved relations between the university and Native communities. The second audience would primarily encounter the tour as an experiential activity to learn new information about Native peoples' histories and worldviews, a chance to re-see familiar campus landmarks through an Indigenous lens, and a prompt to consider what "being in relation" with Indigenous peoples really means for the campus community.

Ultimately, the tour incorporates ten sites. Some are well-known, human-constructed campus landmarks that the tour re-envisions through an Indigenous perspective. Others are natural aspects of the land or recent projects or installations specifically acknowledging Indigenous peoples' presence, resilience, and contributions at TCU. Throughout, the tour presents histories of Native groups in the region and at TCU while reflecting on what steps toward "reconciliation" TCU needs to take as an institution to develop respectful and healthy relationships with Native American communities and peoples.

At the time of the writing of this essay, the tour has been shared with around thirty Indigenous community members and piloted by students in several TCU courses as well as approximately one hundred students from a local public high school. With feedback gathered from these sources, TCU's Native American Advisory Circle will provide guidance on how or whether to move forward with the tour in a bigger, more broadly accessible way, for example through digital, audio, or guided versions.

In the following sections of the essay, four graduate students who wrote content for stops on the tour describe the learning they encountered in the process of participating in the course project.

Celestial Bodies: Embodiment as a Tool for Liberation in Re-Membering Histories
Victoria M. Washington

Damage has been done. Without feeding into the subliminal and prurient taste for Othered trauma that the academy maintains, I pause to acknowledge that so much unspeakable, real harm has been endured by Indigenous peoples throughout the world. As European colonization spread, it adopted academia as an institutional purveyor of intellectual colonial activity. Research is its weapon of choice. TCU, like many U.S. academic institutions, has a troubled history, marred by bloody land grabs from Indigenous folx and the enslavement of Black people. At first, I was against participating in TCU's Indigenous Tour. I did not want to contribute to further harm. I was approaching the project the only way I knew how, from my perspective. From my position, I knew the danger of allowing institutions of power to have access to your stories. Such institutions have a tendency to co-op and bend narratives for their own benefit and to cast themselves in the most optimal light. It was my first semester at a PWI, and I did not want to be part of that legacy. It was not until I spoke with several members of varied Indigenous communities that I felt comfortable working on the project.

As I worked on the project, I was keenly aware of my identity and perspective as an outsider from another marginalized community. I am a Black woman with roots in the Mississippi Delta. Although there is a history of

TCU's Campus sundial, the first stop on the Indigenous Campus Tour where participants reflect on the Wichita creation story. *Photo courtesy of TCU Marketing and Communications.*

interaction and cultural exchange between Black folx from that region and the Choctaw and Chickasaw peoples, I knew I could never create something in an Indigenous way. However, I respected the "Native intellectual tradition that insists on Native peoples' centrality and humanity."[3] This meant setting the creation narrative of the Wichita and Affiliated Tribes, whose land TCU occupies, as a starting point for the tour and presenting it in a way that did not Other it. Beginning with the Wichita creation narrative disrupts white temporality. It offers an alternative starting point to reality and civilization. It wrests time and history from Eurocentric origins and thus insists on the humanity and cultural value of the Wichita people. I was careful not to refer to the narrative as a myth or to say, "the Wichita believe." White scholarship uses such terms to mark non-White epistemologies as invalid or unreliable.

Even with all these good intentions, I still fell short. In my emphasis on nature and the seasons, I invoked a Western valuation of the seasons that does not exist for many Indigenous cultures. Whereas settler knowledge views spring as preferable to winter, many Indigenous American epistemes impose no hierarchy among the seasons. Each one is equally important to the well-being of the planet. Such assumptions on my part are to be expected. I did not grow up with Indigenous pedagogical training. Even with extensive research, I am still an outsider and will get some things wrong. That is part of the process. Learning requires failure and humility to receive correction. This attitude is essential when working with marginalized communities with which you are not affiliated.

An Indigenous Approach: How Collaboration Shifted Our Learning and Tour
Jessica Mundy

As a white, cisgendered, middle-class woman who was raised in the southern Appalachian region of Virginia, my educational background is filled with people who look and think like me. This also means that I have found that there are large gaps in that education, formal and informal, as I begin to approach my own process of "re-learning." Being a part of the creation of TCU's Indigenous Campus Tour pushed me and my peers to think outside of dominant Anglo-American cultural "ways of knowing." Owen Lloyd Ol-

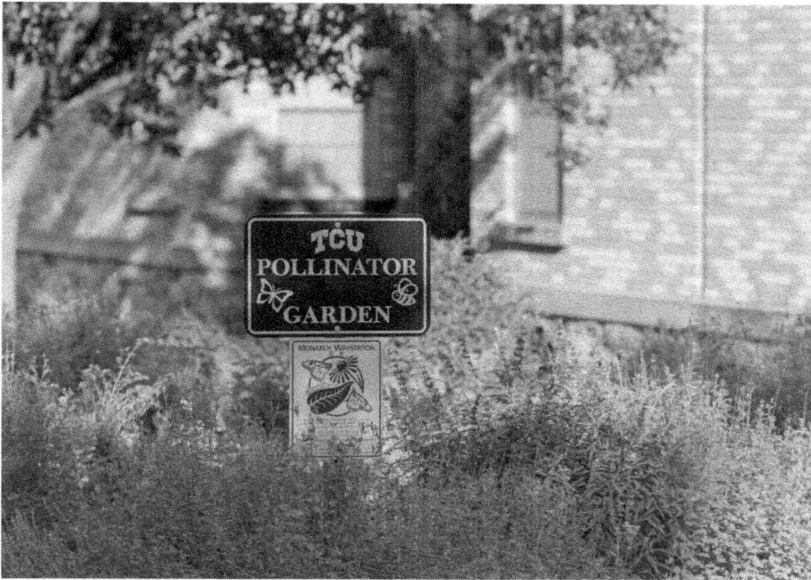

TCU's Pollinator Garden. *Photo courtesy of TCU Marketing and Communications.*

iver, creator of the University of Washington's Indigenous Campus Tour, states that "native knowledge systems are rooted in the natural landscape that ties language and sacred history into what is known as 'Place.' Place of the first peoples has been intentionally and continuously entangled with colonial assimilation and destruction."[4] Additionally influenced by the scholarship we read in class, my own need to break away from settler knowledge systems was evident.

As non-Indigenous students gathered in a classroom, we created an initial list on the whiteboard of landmarks and buildings that we thought would be good starting points for our tour. Soon after, we were fortunate to be able to meet with members of the Indigenous community to set our project on the right path. In these meetings, community mentors emphasized the importance of incorporating the land and nature into the tour, something that we students had neglected to include. So, with a new focus, a new direction based in collaboration, and bags of corn kernels graciously given to us by elder Annette Anderson to help ground us and clear our minds, the class turned to the land for memories, destabilizing western thinking that had caused us to over-emphasize human-made structures on campus.

I had the pleasure of researching TCU's Pollinator Garden, a stop that was not initially included until Indigenous community members told the class of the importance of the garden and plants and animals within. The pollinator garden represents a strange paradox on TCU's campus. In 2017, when faculty and students first proposed the Native American monument, which acknowledges the land the campus sits on as the ancestral homelands of the Wichita and Affiliated Tribes, a small garden to surround the monument incorporating "traditional Native American food (e.g., corn, beans, and squash) and medicinal (e.g., sage and sweetgrass) plants" was part of the proposal.[5] TCU did not approve the garden, and the monument, erected and dedicated in 2018, sits in a bed of non-native ground cover. The pollinator garden emerged as a later project by a non-Indigenous student and was supported by the TCU Sustainability Committee and the groundskeeping staff.[6] In honoring this request but not the others, it might seem as if TCU prioritizes pollinators over Native people. This rejection is uncomfortable to acknowledge. However, elder Annette Anderson helped us see how important *any* Native sacred plants growing on our campus are, and how we are in relation with pollinators and plants. For example, the garden includes sage, a plant that is extremely important in various Indigenous communities.

In the words of TCU's Land Acknowledgement, our campus is "a space we share with all living beings, human and non-human."[7] The pollinator garden is not only a symbol of that relationship, it is an active partner. This bright and colorful spot stands out from the highly cultivated norm of TCU's landscape and reminds us of a more Native way to approach the Land and the non-human beings with which we share it.

Through our communication with members of the Indigenous community, we were able to shift our own ideas towards ones that encapsulated the importance of land and nature, the value of route making, and the power of storytelling. A campus tour is not a clear-cut list, nor should it be. It should reflect a path forward. But that path cannot be and should not be created through one single voice.

The Arkikosa River's Significance to a
Campus Landmark and Indigenous Life
Lori Salazar

At first, I didn't think that the beloved campus landmark Frog Fountain had any possible linkage to Indigenous life or history, since it was built and placed on campus in 1969, well after the removal of Wichita peoples in this area. While listening to local Indigenous community members, however, I learned to look beyond the landmark itself and see the valuable resource that flows through the fountain, which for centuries has provided life-giving properties to Indigenous communities and our city. The water that flows through Frog Fountain and through our Fort Worth community has as one of its sources the Trinity River,[8] once called the Arkikosa River by the Caddo people. The river provided physical and spiritual sustenance to tribes that included the Wichita as well as the Caddo, Waco, Cherokee, Seminole, Muscogee Creek, Kickapoo, Taovayas, Tawakoni, Kichai, Ionies, and other Caddoan speaking tribes who lived along the river during varying periods of history. Some of the state's earliest documentation of Indigenous life dates to more than fifteen thousand years ago along this river. In 1690, Spanish colonizer Alonso de Leon renamed the river "La Santisima Trinidad" or "the most holy Trinity." The river later became known as the Trinity River.

My research led me to understand how the Republic of Texas began to establish what would become Dallas and Fort Worth in the wake of the genocide and forced expulsion of the Wichita and Affiliated Tribes and other Texan Indigenous communities in order to exploit the Arkikosa River and surrounding lands. On 14 May 1841, General Edward H. Tarrant, who became the namesake for Tarrant County (where TCU is located), led the Texas militia to Village Creek and used violence to force the removal of the Indigenous groups living in the North Texas area.[9] The Republic of Texas and the U.S. army established forts every one hundred miles throughout the state. These forts were implemented as a plan to "defend the western frontier" to accelerate European American settlement in the region. In 1849, the state established a fort at the confluence of the Clear and West Forks of the Trinity River, an area we know today as Fort Worth.[10] When TCU moved from Waco to Fort Worth in 1910, one of the reasons TCU's campus site was chosen was due to its proximity to the Trinity River. Although Joseph

TCU's Frog Fountain as it has appeared on Native American and Indigenous Peoples Day annually since 2016. Carl Kurtz (Citizen Band Potawatomi, TCU '14) sets up a lodge on the campus commons each year and shares knowledge with classes and passersby throughout the day. *Photo courtesy of TCU Marketing and Communications.*

Addison Clark, the father of the founders of TCU, didn't participate in the battle of Village Creek, he contributed as a land speculator to Euro-American colonization practices to re-distribute North Texan lands to non-Indigenous individuals.[11]

In researching how the water flowing in the Arkikosa River provided spiritual and physical sustenance to Indigenous peoples within the Fort Worth area, I was able to learn about the Indigenous history that is often forgotten in the origin stories of the DFW area and North Texas. I learned how the Republic of Texas and the U.S. government were motivated by greed and power to exploit the land and natural resources like water to forcibly remove Indigenous peoples from their ancestral homelands. As a Latinx student with ancestral roots in Texas, I value learning about Indigenous histories and disrupting colonial narratives. I have learned to analyze my own historical knowledge of Texas and question which voices throughout history have been forgotten or silenced due to colonialism. With this realization, I want to be an ally who is able to work with local Indigenous communities to keep their histories, autonomy, and sovereignty of their land and resources. The water flowing through Frog Fountain, like the ebb and flow of the Arkikosa River, reminds us that the Wichita and Affiliated Tribes, Tawakoni, Taovayas, Kichai, Ionies, Cherokee, Muskogee Creek, Kickapoo, Comanche, Caddo, and Seminole Nations continue to persevere against all odds.

Native American Artwork and TCU's Indigenous People's Walking Tour
Shafiq M. Said

Art and artistic expression are foundational elements in the aesthetics of most university campuses. However, the type of art that is deemed appropriate and valuable for public display has been, historically, deeply influenced by the pervading culture of whiteness in which PWIs such as TCU are steeped. The Portrait Project, a grassroots effort initiated at TCU in March of 2018, which surveyed all portraits across TCU campus, found that out of the twenty-two portraits on display in lobbies and boardrooms there were no portraits depicting persons of color or images of Native Americans or Indigenous people. When we began work on TCU's Indigenous Campus Tour, my peers and I were aware of this absence of representation as something that TCU faculty and administration are beginning to strive to correct. I chose to focus on the part of the walking tour focusing on art. As a Palestinian-American, I understand the importance of representation and that honoring those peoples on whose homeland our campus is built is a vital step in acknowledging the harm and violence associated with the taking of that land.

In the Fall of 2020, TCU opened the doors to The Harrison, a newly constructed, 86,000 square-foot administration building. TCU commissioned two portraits, displayed in a first-floor conference room, by contemporary Comanche/Kiowa artist J. NiCole Hatfield (Nahmi-A-Piah): "Based on Quanah Parker" and "Based on Mrs. Jack Treetop-Standing Rock 1908." The first of the paintings depicts Quanah Parker (ca. 1845–1911), the last chief of the Quahada Comanche Indians and a figure associated with Indigenous resistance to white settlement in Texas. Hatfield's second portrait is based on a photograph of a Lakota woman, Mrs. Jack Treetop, featured in Frank Bennett Fiske's (1883–1952) Standing Rock portraits. In painting these proud Indigenous figures, Hatfield states, she "acknowledges them as

Based on Quanah Parker by Comanche/Kiowa artist J. NiCole Hatfield (Nahmi-A-Piah). *Photo courtesy of TCU Marketing and Communications.*

Based on Mrs. Jack Treetop- Standing Rock by Comanche/Kiowa artist J. NiCole Hatfield (Nahmi-A-Piah). *Photo courtesy of TCU Marketing and Communications.*

well as honors them by giving them a voice in our contemporary world."[12] By choosing to paint portraits of Quanah Parker and Mrs. Jack Treetop based on historical photographs and adapting these paintings through her own critical lens as an Indigenous artist, Hatfield is reclaiming these images for the Native community.

Hatfield's portraits exist alongside several other pieces of art on campus as part of TCU's effort to begin to pay respect to the art and artwork of Native and Indigenous peoples through the inclusion of Native representation around campus. Recently there has been a resurgence of interest in Native American artwork, both within Indigenous communities and the broader art world. Artists like Hatfield are reclaiming traditional practices and adapting them to contemporary contexts, creating innovative works that challenge stereotypes and celebrate Indigenous identity. Moreover, Native American art has increasingly become a platform for social and political activism, addressing issues such as land rights, environmental conservation, and cultural sovereignty. By working to incorporate such artists and artwork within the aesthetic of its campus, TCU can create spaces for intercultural dialogue and systemic change.

Conclusion
Theresa Strouth Gaul

TCU's Indigenous Campus Tour's origins as a course project exemplifies the 3E's framework Frederick Gooding, Jr., describes in his essay in this volume. Education comprised the students' preparatory reading and the new information they absorbed as they conducted their research on Native history in North Texas and the Indigenous meanings associated with each stop on the campus tour. Exposure came through the transformative conversations they engaged in with Native community members, who acted as collaborators and mentors to them as they conceptualized the tour. And experience came with their production of the tour, their receiving of feedback from Indigenous and non-Indigenous participants, and their reflection on and processing of their learning through the writing of a conference paper, this essay, and conversations with tour groups. The incorporation of these three levels of learning took this project from a mere assignment to a learning experience that changed the way they looked at campus, made them aware of the biases and limitations of their own cultural perspectives, and helped them understand the benefits of collaboration. In turn, those who participate in the TCU Indigenous Campus Tour also encounter the 3E's, continuing a circle of learning: standing in and moving through the campus space, meditating on familiar campus landmarks from a new vantage point based in information that has been suppressed in their past education, and leaving them pondering questions about their relations with others that they may never have asked before. As Anderson explains in the next essay in this collection, projects like this have the potential to transform students' perspectives and future paths toward respectful, ethical, and empathetic engagement with people, communities, and the land we inhabit together.

Gaul et al notes

1.   See Scott Langston, "Diversity, Equity, and Inclusion and Understanding the 'TCU' in TCU," TCU Office of Diversity & Inclusion website, https://addran.tcu.edu/files/DEI-Understanding-the-TCU-in-TCU-April-2019.pdf.

2.   Examples of what students read are: Alyssa Mt. Pleasant, Caroline Wigginton, and Kelly Wisecup, "Forum on Materials and Methods in Native American and Indigenous Studies [Special Section]," *Early American Literature* 53, no. 2 (2018): 405–537; Sam McKegney, "Strategies for Ethical Engagement: An Open Letter Concerning Non-Native Scholars of Native Literatures," 79–87 and Niigaanwewidam James Sinclair, "Responsible and Ethical Criticisms of Indigenous Literatures," 301–8, both of which are in *Learn, Teach, Challenge: Approaching Indigenous Literatures*, ed. Deanna Reder and Linda M. Morra (Waterloo, ON: Wilfrid Laurier University Press, 2016). Examples of other campus tours we examined included the Indigenous Walking Tour at the University of Washington and the Racial Geography Tour at the University of Texas at Austin.

3.   Mt. Pleasant et al, 208.

4.   Owen L. Oliver, "Indigenous Walking Tour at the University of Washington," 2021, Owen Lloyd Oliver website, https://ais.washington.edu/sites/ais/files/documents/indigenous_walking_tour_at_the_uw.pdf.

5.   "Building TCU's Relationships with Native American Communities to Increase Diversity: A Proposal for an Annual Commemoration and Garden," private collection of Scott Langston, 1 March 2017.

6.   "TCU Pollinator Garden Earns Texas Certification," TCU News, 25 September 2023, https://www.tcu.edu/news/2023/tcu-pollinator-garden-earns-texas-certification.php.

7.   "Native American Land Acknowledgment," TCU Office of Diversity & Inclusion Website, April 2021, https://www.tcu.edu/native-american-indigenous-peoples/about/native-american-land-acknowledgment.php.

8.   "Fort Worth Drinking Water Quality Report," City of Fort Worth Water Department, 2016 https://www.fortworthtexas.gov/files/assets/public/v/1/water/documents/water-quality-reports/water-quality-report-2016.pdf], 1 and Arkikosa name

9.   Scott Langston, "TCU's Relationships with Native Americans and the Land, 1838–2014," in *Being in Relation: Indigenous Peoples, the Land, and Texas Christian University, 1873–2023*, eds. C. Annette Anderson, Theresa Strouth Gaul, and Langton (Fort Worth: TCU Press, forthcoming 2025.

10.   "Fort Worth History," City of Fort Worth website, accessed 18 April 2024 https://www.fortworthtexas.gov/about/history.

11.   Langston, "TCU's Relationships."

12.   "J. NiCole Hatfield," *Indigenous Goddess Gang*, 1 March 2018, https://www.indigenousgoddessgang.com/goddess/j-nicole-hatfield.

Judge Softly: TCU Students Walking Alongside Native Communities as Allies

C. Annette Anderson (Chickasaw and Cherokee)

Pray, do not find fault with the man that limps
Or stumbles along the road
Unless you have worn the moccasins he wears,
Or stumbled beneath the same load.

MARY T. LATHRAP, 1895

The Indigenous Campus Tour at TCU adapts a campus tour into a creative experiential lesson on Indigenous understanding and empathy. The tour helps visitors, students, staff, and faculty members shift the university community away from long-standing academic approaches that rely on detached observation and research on Native peoples. The tour is a move toward genuine respect, communication, and understanding with the original stewards of TCU land and the local Native peoples who can build healthy, solid futures for TCU graduates. Native Nations are some of the fastest-growing corporations. Students familiar with the histories of these Nations have an advantage in future opportunities. Activities such as the Indigenous Campus Tour can provide more accurate perspectives on the land where TCU resides and the Native cultures and peoples who love this land for all eternity.

Professor Theresa Gaul brought together individuals from the Native community with faculty members and eight graduate students, all of whom were enrolled in the course American Literature to 1900: Cultural Encounters in the Archive offered in the TCU English Department in fall 2023, to begin conversations and deeper understandings of TCU's history in relation to Native histories. The first conversations took place under the watchful eyes of Quanah Parker's portrait painted by Comanche/Kiowa artist J. Ni-Cole Hatfield (Nahmi-A-Piah) in a conference room in The Harrison building on TCU's campus.

The development process of the Indigenous Campus Tour reminded me of the lines of Mary Lathrap's poem, quoted above, which have often been attributed to Native people.[1] Lathrap's writing suggests that we must experience what others experience to understand them. Working on this project required that students engage with this thought process. This was a challenge to students to stand on the land and view it from a Native lens of the past, present, and future.

The Indigenous Campus Tour is this type of challenge. The tour is also an opportunity. Its development attempts to define Native understandings through experiential land-based learning. It is an act of empathy that forces one to discover the differences between the internal thought processes of a culture versus the external portrayal of that culture through film, TV, written works, and oral stories. Doing this work is incredibly challenging especially when that culture has been misinterpreted, sensationalized, and relegated to an outcome, much like the dinosaur bones at a natural history museum. For some participating students, the campus tour process might have been their first face-to-face discussion with a living person from one of the many Native Nations on this continent since none of the students were Native, nor did they have any prior connections with Indigenous communities.

At the first meeting, I could sense the burden these students felt as they were asked to think, experience, and feel the TCU campus, its history, the land, and the environment from a Native perspective. These students did not want to be a part of anything that might be construed incorrectly. It is hard to know if these students represent the broader student population at TCU, but they had fantastic talent, openness, and honesty, which touched a deep part of my heart and soul. Approaching the first dialogues between Native community members and the students creates many nervous thoughts for a community member. I soon realized that the students were also nervous about the entire process leading up to and including the experience. The students were verbally clear about their fears and caution. They did not want to do anything wrong or accidentally hurt someone or a group because of an unintentional mistake. We had not even started, and they already had set the parking brakes on their cars. They recognized the difficulty of empathizing from outside a culture.

They had well-formulated internalized standards regarding ethnicity and culture. As Native people, we rely so much on our intuition, "the knowing," and within minutes of the introductions, these students expressed an unmistakable sincerity. Was this through their educational training, personal and family experience, or the result of extraordinary intuition? I am still determining. I was in awe of these students and their forthright verbalization of the hesitancy and potential threat they felt stepping into this role.

The topic of developing a Native-driven perspective on the campus map had the potential for misunderstandings and awkwardness. They could not see any reason why they had the right or validation to do this project. They were not Native. What if they overstepped? What if they were using their privilege as graduate students to judge what others feel or experience in this world?

It is so hard to help people understand our culture from the outside looking in. We have had hundreds of years of training in trust given and trust broken, but our value systems and spiritual beliefs lead us to continue to extend our trust to new people. We may know only a few people will ultimately prove themselves trustworthy. But we value these few special people and want them to help us voice our needs and wants. We need these strong young people to help carry the truth of our stories, even if they are not in our culture. As Native people, we can empower others whom we trust and encourage them to share our experiences with others.

At the first meeting, Professor Gaul was one of the first to speak up, address the students' concerns, and reassure them that they were only obligated to participate in the project if they felt comfortable after our discussions. From my perspective, it was about "good intent," or what we refer to as the "good medicine" that should be in everything we do. Our actions should be approached without expectation of benefit or other return. Yes, this project may be for a grade or result in the students getting secondary recognition, but our hope and prayer is about the final result.

Ultimately, their reason for participating in this project came from good hearts and in the best way possible. For clarification, a Native view of the word *good* does not fit within the dichotomies of good vs. bad or right vs.

wrong. It is a broad view involving thoughts, feelings, behaviors, expectations, spiritual intents, and outcomes. Could these students step outside their upbringing and colonial societal values, which have shaped their worldview? How difficult would this be? How will they know if they have interpreted Native views and understandings accurately, and what were the reasons behind their thoughts?

It is not easy. Attempting this project took courage. Since there are no right or wrong answers, these students stepped into another's shoes, not knowing the outcome. They are allowing their names to be permanently etched into the World Wide Web for the next one hundred years and attached to this project. What they did this year might be questioned and have a different meaning twenty years from now. We see it happen every day in the political arena and on social media. Words said privately or in writings at one point in history were not considered offensive, insensitive, biased, or harmful and could take on different meanings twenty years later. No one would want their son or daughter to experience this stress, yet these students ultimately dared to proceed with this project. So, although I had faith and confidence in these students' "good intent," they were their own most prominent critics in approaching this project.

One unique perspective on this project is asking the students to understand that we are the only original stewards of this land among all marginalized groups in this society. The full impact of influence brought to this continent from other countries and the policies toward Native people by what is now known as Texas resulted in the small numbers we have today. The land where TCU now resides is very close to land where many, many people died at the hands of the military, Texas Rangers, and people who somehow felt entitled to our land. Despite this history, we repeatedly must trust and hope for the good intentions of others. We understand that treaties are broken, and we are used to lies and manipulation, but when we meet "good" people, we try to cherish and nurture those relationships.

When I relocated from Oklahoma to Houston, Texas, to attend the University of Houston School of Social Work, I found that nowhere in all of the classes, including multicultural sensitivity classes, did we focus on Native culture. It was as if Texas could only acknowledge people of color who were Black and Hispanic. It was very confusing to realize that it was not just at the college level where our culture was buried in unmarked graves; it was in the

TCU students reflect on the TCU Native American Monument while taking the Indigenous Campus Tour. *Photo courtesy of Annette Anderson.*

entire state public school setting. I raised two daughters in the Plano Independent School District. Their education taught them that our culture was non-existent. They would learn in school that Native people were extinct, and yet twenty-four hours earlier, they had spent the whole day dancing and playing at the powwows. It made no sense to my children, and it made no sense to me. Students coming to TCU may have had the same lack of experience with Native cultures. The impact of an Indigenous Campus Tour could change the view and understanding of the land where students spend their days in classes.

The design, thought process, and collaboration involved with the TCU students remind me of the 3Es to creating and engaging community described by Frederick Gooding, Jr., in an earlier essay in this volume. First is education. The process of identifying students' level of education regarding Native culture and its cultural relationship to the land where TCU stands was the first thing to consider. Finding a shared, basic knowledge base regarding Native people was important. Sovereignty, geography, commonality and diversity among Nations, spirituality, and history held the key message: we are still here, and we are still a vibrant community. Even when students are current on Native understandings, there is fear about meeting and interacting with people of our culture. Perceptions of the stoic, warring, fierce savage are frightening to people outside the culture.

The second concept is exposure. Learning about our culture in history books is like learning to ride a bicycle by only watching a YouTube video. We must meet face to face and share a meal or have human conversations about everyday life to dispel the fear and apprehension that takes place when you have no exposure to the culture.

Last is experience. This means going beyond a one-time meeting to dedicating significant time between and among people to bring a level of comfortable interactions based on what we have in common. We must share a genuine curiosity about what we don't know about each other. I remember a funny conversation between myself and a non-Native volunteer. I said that the NASA group (the Native American Student Association at University of Texas at Arlington) was coming to our event. She told me years later how disappointed she was that the astronauts did not show up. She explained that she honestly did not have a clue how the federal agency had any connection to our Native organization, but she was excited (and disappointed) anyway. NASA did attend the event; she just never made those connections. Our slang, our humor, and our language, even when speaking common English, can cause confusion. These students at TCU involved themselves in all three of these levels of connection.

These students have the potential to be excellent allies. You can see their insight reflected in their writings, which are shared in the preceding essay in this volume. Their awareness and cautious approach were reassuring for the first-round table discussions. We all experienced normal "unpleasant awkwardness," which happens when people from outside the culture do their best to test the waters without making a mistake. This awkwardness in today's world also saddens me because it inhibits some of our natural curiosity

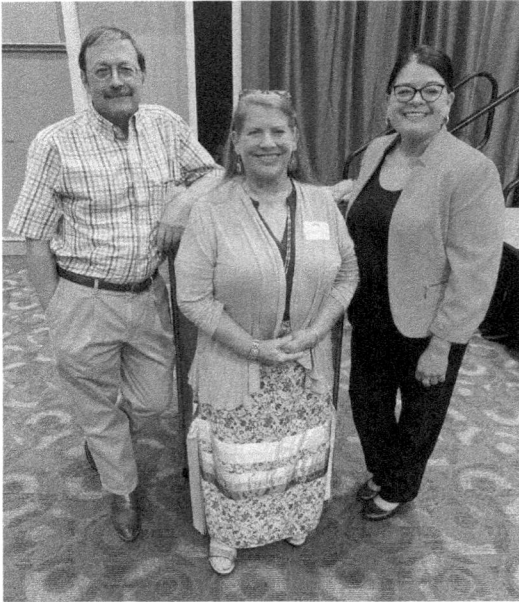

Anderson (center) with TCU's inaugural Native Nations and Communities liaison, Scott Langston (left) and Terri Parton, President of the Wichita and Affiliated Tribes. *Photo courtesy of TCU Marketing and Communications.*

Anderson (far right) discusses the importance of sacred plants with students in a TCU class at the Pollinator Garden. *Photo courtesy of Annette Anderson.*

about people very different from ourselves. I am very grateful these students ultimately accepted this challenge. I hope they gained some personal understanding that will help them when faced with other challenges outside their comfort levels.

In this class, these students showed a genuine concern about approaching a project on behalf or in reflection of a culture outside their own. We are one to three percent of the population. We need the support and voices of people who are willing to learn and then carry our voices through to others, to help us be heard without taking over our fight. These students represented what it means to be a true ally. An ally walks next to us, not in front or behind us. An ally reflects our long-standing history of adopting people into our culture with the same rights, respect, and responsibility of people who came into the circle by blood. An ally uses their ears in a higher proportion than their voice. They use their bodies for action more than their words. They keep us in the periphery of their vision so they don't accidentally misunderstand or misinterpret. An ally should be afforded the ability to ask direct and open questions without having their motivations and intentions questioned.

This exercise of the Indigenous Campus Tour stretches the comfort level of students. I hope that it becomes incorporated into every new student's experience on the campus so that they can hear Native voices before they are lost in the next generation. I want to thank Professor Gaul and the students who took this professional and academic leap of faith. I hope we continue to walk the road together and explore more ways we can share these experiences with others.

Anderson notes

1. "'Judge Softly' or 'Walk a Mile in His Moccasins' — by Mary T. Lathrap," *James Milson – Writing & Things*, accessed 18 April 2024, https://jamesmilson.com/about-the-blog/judge-softly-or-walk-a-mile-in-his-moccasins-by-mary-t-lathrap/

Asian Pacific Americans in Higher Education and the Politics of Identity at TCU

Carrie Liu Currier

IN THE HALLS of higher education, Asian Pacific Americans (APAs) represent a unique challenge as a group to study. Although APAs are minorities in the larger backdrop of American society, in higher education their situation is complicated by a variety of factors that cause them to be considered differently from other historically underrepresented racial and ethnic groups. At the heart of the problem is that when APAs are treated as a monolithic group, they appear to be overrepresented in higher education. As a result, universities often overlook APAs as a marginalized group deserving of special consideration when it comes to race-conscious initiatives designed to increase diversity on campus. In addition, it can be difficult to determine where exactly APAs fit in diversity debates, with the model minority stereotype creating the false sense that APAs have successfully overcome any adversity associated with racism and discrimination. There is, however, much to be learned by studying APAs. This chapter adopts the 3Es framework of education, exposure, and experience from the introductory chapter by Frederick Gooding, Jr., to shed light on a wide range of issues impacting Asian Pacific Americans at TCU.

This chapter begins by deconstructing demographics to educate on the diversity of the APA population, their place in our institution, and how they have been deminoritized in higher education. Deminoritization occurs when APAs are no longer seen or treated as a minority group due to shifting public perception, especially in reference to affirmative action.[1] Next, I expose racism and unconscious biases impacting APA faculty on campus, drawing on my personal experiences over the past twenty years at TCU as an APA faculty member and as a scholar of APAs in higher education. These examples can help build solidarity between APAs and other Black, Indigenous, and People of Color (BIPOC) faculty on campus and illuminate institutional areas in need of improvement. Finally, I offer suggestions on how we can focus on the experience of building community for APAs to make TCU a better place for all.

Overrepresented and Under Attack

A fundamental starting point for understanding the Asian Pacific American experience in higher education is to define who is captured under the umbrella of APA. The term Asian is frequently used to refer to a wide range of individuals representing sixty percent of the world's population.[2] In the American context APA includes first generation Asians in the United States from any of forty-eight different ethnicities, with origins in more than two dozen Asian countries. It also is used to refer to those who are of Asian heritage who were born and raised in the United States, and even those of Asian heritage who do not see themselves as American at all but are just temporarily located in the United States. This broad categorization is problematic because the experiences of those individual groups are quite distinct and should not be viewed as a monolith.

The East, Southeast, and South Asian experiences in the United States have been remarkably different. Discriminatory policies like the Chinese Exclusion Act (1882) and Executive Order 9066 (1942), which established Japanese internment camps, historically created barriers and a form of second-class citizenship for many East Asians. In the current political climate, Chinese Americans have again been singled out due to deteriorating Sino-U.S. relations. The trade wars initiated by the Trump administration in 2018 helped bring relations between China and the U.S. to an all-time low. This was followed up with the China Initiative (2018), which was designed to identify and investigate researchers with suspected ties to the Chinese government, leading to witch hunts of Chinese Americans under the guise of national security.[3] In 2020, anti-Chinese sentiment reached new highs with the onset of the global pandemic. When American politicians began refer-ring to COVID-19 as the "China virus," Chinese Americans became public enemy #1, and a surge of anti-Asian violence ensued.[4] This current wave of anti-Chinese racism has consequences for all APAs, who are experiencing indiscriminate physical harm in North Texas and nationwide.[5]

In contrast, the Southeast Asian experience is shaped by a different set of policies, where they have historically been viewed as war refugees in the aftermath of conflicts in Vietnam, Laos, and Cambodia. The Indochina Migration and Refugee Assistance Act (1975) provided financial assistance and resettlement for a limited group of Southeast Asians impacted by the Vietnam War. In addition, the 2024 Southeast Asian Deportation Relief Act under consideration by Congress further highlights the different plight of Southeast Asian immigrants and reinforces their perception and status as refugees. In comparison, South Asians, another geographically identified subgroup, are the fastest growing Asian population in the United States, yet they struggle to be seen by the general population as Asian at all.[6] Scholars studying this racial assignment incongruity for South Asians note the many challenges this creates because their experiences are unique but understud-ied.[7] Finally, in higher education there are a number of Asians on campus who are not Americans at all but are international students and faculty. For these individuals, their first experiences as a minority occur in the United States, since they are majorities in their home countries. Their encounters with racism may vary depending on national origin and the current political climate, but the discrimination they encounter on campus, especially at pre-dominantly white institutions like TCU, make them another distinct group to examine.

While each subgroup of the Asian population is different, universities ad-mittedly have aggregated these groups in their data, which is a disservice to the uniqueness of each subgroup and artificially inflates the size of the APA population.[8] It is for these reasons that APAs are mistakenly characterized as overrepresented in higher education and should be disaggregated to better reflect the diversity within the group. The unintended consequences asso-ciated with this misrepresentation are that APAs have been deminoritized and are overlooked when institutions consider how to enhance the diversity of their faculty, staff, or student body. Scholars have already noted the ways APAs have been omitted from consideration in race-conscious affirmative action programs, are scrutinized more heavily as an overrepresented group in STEM fields, and may actually be excluded from consideration in university funding opportunities and fellowships that target minorities.[9] However, it would be misleading to suggest that APAs have not benefitted from any of the aforementioned initiatives, since certain subgroups, such as Southeast Asians, historically have. The problem again lies in the fact that distinct sub-categories of Asians have been unfairly aggregated to disguise the complexity of the group, causing APAs to be deminoritized when it comes to institutional efforts to enhance diversity on campus.

An additional complication facing APAs with their BIPOC peers involves the perceived role Asian Americans have had in reversing race conscious admissions with the overturning of affirmative action in higher education. The Supreme Court cases *Students for Fair Admissions v. Harvard* (2023) and *Students for Fair Admissions v. University of North Carolina* (2023) have placed APAs in the spotlight as being anti-affirmative action, with the overturning of the use of race in college admissions. This mischaracterization effectively places APAs at odds with other racial and ethnic minorities. APAs should not be overgeneralized as against affirmative action, nor should they be portrayed as the enemy to their BIPOC peers. The underlying issue involves how APAs have been deminoritized as a result of aggregating the population in ways that unfairly identify them as overrepresented rather than as a collection of underrepresented groups.

The way APAs have recently been pitted against other BIPOC groups is not a new phenomenon. The model minority myth, a stereotype that suggests APAs have been more successful than other minorities, is a weak attempt to prove that racism and historical discrimination do not prohibit minorities from succeeding. While the stereotype appears to be a positive characterization of APAs, it should be deconstructed for its hidden and harmful effects. The origins of this myth date back to William Petersen's (1966) argument regarding the success of Japanese Americans who were able to improve their economic well-being after being interned during World War II.[10] However, scholars like Claire Kim (1999) have argued that the construction of Asian Americans as a model minority is an example of racial triangulation, where Asians are positioned as inferior to whites yet superior to Blacks.[11] This artificial hierarchy is essentially a tool of oppression, where APAs have been weaponized against Black Americans. Since 2020, with the resurgence of the Black Lives Matter movement, Kim (2023) has further argued that the model minority myth is even more harmful since it supports and reinforces anti-Blackness in America.[12]

As each of these examples show, APAs have struggled to be seen as a historically disadvantaged group in higher education because of improperly aggregated data. Moreover, even positive stereotypes, like the model minority myth, can take a toll on individuals when they create unrealistic expectations. The effects this has had on APA mental health have been well documented.[13] In addition, the model minority myth has placed APAs in an adversarial position relative to other BIPOC groups. Therefore, it is important to educate our community about the hidden forms of discrimination and racism that have contributed to these problems nationally, to better understand what we have seen locally at TCU. The next step is to expose some of the problems that have materialized on our campus over the last twenty years and examine what it means to do the work of race as it relates to APAs.

The APA Faculty Experience: Teaching, Research, and Service

The APA population has grown at TCU both in terms of faculty and students. According to the TCU Fact Book, APA faculty have increased from 4.4 percent in 2011 to 8.4 percent in 2023.[14] Despite these growing numbers, it is not uncommon for APA faculty at TCU or elsewhere to find themselves alone in their departments. In addition, the deminoritization of APAs described in the previous section has trickle-down effects where even our BIPOC colleagues are uncertain where we fit in the discussions about diversity. In 2020, while attending a luncheon for TCU faculty and staff of color, I was taken by surprise when one of my Black colleagues asked me in earnest, "Are Asians considered people of color?" This question is one that APAs have encountered on multiple occasions, prompting questions of belonging and what it takes to be seen as a minority on campus. In my twenty years as a faculty member at TCU, I have often struggled to be seen and for my work to be valued. Unfortunately, these experiences are not unique to APAs on our campus. The goal in this section is not to lay blame but to demonstrate how the politics of identity for APAs have evolved at TCU over the years so that we may help our institution and colleagues move forward in a more positive and progressive direction.

The APA faculty experience can be examined within the three pillars of our jobs: teaching, research, and service. In each of these areas, there are common themes that impact APAs in higher education, with additional examples from TCU offered to illustrate how they materialize on our campus. The first area to examine is teaching, where stereotypes about APAs shape expectations from our colleagues and students. APAs are expected to be concentrated in STEM fields, area studies, ethnic studies, and modern languages.[15] However, when these preconceived notions do not reflect reality, APA faculty find themselves having to justify or defend their chosen area of study.[16] In addition, APA faculty with non-Americanized or ethnic names may not even get hired or can end up with low student enrollment in their courses as a result of biases regarding English proficiency. Foreign and ethnic name discrimination is a problem for many APA faculty, with unfair assumptions made based on name alone.[17] For those APA faculty who do have accents, students can be quick to complain about the inability to understand their professor. Students avoid enrolling in classes led by those faculty or have asked to change sections because they question the faculty's English language skills. Since we know these unconscious biases materialize, faculty have been known to preemptively prescreen job applicants with foreign looking names to see if they represent a good "cultural fit," cloaking their own biases in a concern for the students.

For APA faculty, the challenge is not only getting hired but also surviving student perceptions on their teaching (SPOTs). APA faculty struggle with negative evaluations not only when it comes to accents, but also when students feel the faculty's identity does not match with their expectations regarding their behavior. Scholars have shown that the stereotype of APAs and especially APA women is that they are passive and docile, making them easy to challenge in the classroom.[18] If you break the stereotype and are seen as more assertive, you are evaluated harshly due to the cognitive dissonance it creates. Either case takes an emotional toll, creating racial battle fatigue, and it is not surprising APA faculty have difficulty with retention.[19] In my own classes at TCU, I have been openly called a bitch, a communist, and anti-American by my students. When I share this with my white male colleagues, they express shock, as they do not have similar experiences. When

I stand up to this abuse in class, I'm punished on my SPOT evaluations for not "treating students with civility and respect." In each of these situations, we can see how unconscious biases not only impact faculty hiring but can also lead to lower overall job satisfaction for APAs.[20]

When it comes to research, APA faculty who do work on race or ethnic studies can find it difficult to meet departmental standards, with consequences for tenure, promotion, and merit pay. Tier one journals dedicate less space to these topics, forcing faculty to publish in outlets of lesser value to their white colleagues. In addition, scholarship on the state of one's discipline and on Diversity, Equity, and Inclusion (DEI) are frequently minimized and devalued despite the fact it can help minorities feel seen and lead to institutional change. These examples of how BIPOC faculty in general experience epistemic exclusion, or the devaluation of their scholarship, communicate to such faculty that they are illegitimate members of the academy.[21] When the value of this research is rated as lesser than that of more "mainstream" scholarship in determining merit or promotion, it reminds us that the gatekeepers in the academy do not understand how racism and discrimination impact our employment. Even when this scholarship has been valued at institutions, the national attacks on Critical Race Theory are now threatening the academic existence of faculty working on race.[22] Research on these topics can be both healing and empowering. While some scholars may see it as a labor of love, it constitutes real research. The systematic study of questions that explain or predict phenomenon, creating knowledge to be shared with others, is the definition of research.

Finally, the last factor to consider is service. APAs, like other BIPOC faculty, have seen a significant increase in service commitments over the years, something scholars refer to as the minority tax.[23] With BIPOC faculty underrepresented relative to the size of our minority student population, the mentoring demands placed on each faculty member is significant, albeit emotionally fulfilling, and difficult to refuse. As the next chapter by Kelly Phommachanh will demonstrate, APAs struggle with a sense of belonging and seek out those who can relate to their situation. Mentoring our minority students includes everything from serving as advisors to their organizations to engaging in career and life counselling. One of the most valuable roles I have had is serving as an advisor to TCU's first and only Asian-interest sorority Kappa Lambda Delta (KLD), which was established in 2005 by TCU students Cleda Wang, Ambika Sharma, Jinpei Shan, Yusi Chen, Seo Hyun Jang, Diana Tran, and Lucy Xin. The creation of KLD was driven by the need for a space to grapple with APA issues and identity on campus; as an organization, KLD works to raise the visibility of APA students and APA issues on campus. In addition, my eleven years as director of Asian Studies helped me engage with more of our APA students, many of whom were not even declared minors. Among those seeking mentorship were APA community scholars and Asian international students, none of whom were interested in Asian studies but were simply looking for someone who might understand their perspective and experiences.

The minority tax has been especially steep with DEI, where new initiatives and efforts to diversify committees is placing high demands on minority faculty.[24] As an APA woman, I represent diversity in two categories, making me extra popular for those needing to balance out the distribution of white males on a committee. Some of these service requests, when they involve enhancing the university's DEI mission or efforts, are difficult to decline, especially when it gives APAs a voice. Yet the burden of speaking for one's group can also take an emotional toll, creating something known as racial battle fatigue, the cumulative toll of race-related stress emerging from constantly facing racially dismissive, demeaning, insensitive, and/or hostile racial environments and individuals.[25] For those who are untenured, it can be difficult to speak up on committees where racist or discriminatory remarks are made by one's colleagues. Moreover, as noted previously, APAs are sometimes selected for service because they are expected to be more deferential and submissive. Each of these situations takes an emotional and physical toll on APA faculty that does not stop when one leaves campus. While this section has exposed several negative trends regarding APAs in higher education that are unfortunately replicated here at TCU, it also demonstrates there are plenty of opportunities to create positive change.

Creating an Inclusive Community

While the first two sections of this chapter focus on education and exposure, this final section examines the experience of building community. While there is still a lot of work to be done to give APA faculty a sense of belonging at TCU, the Race & Reconciliation Initiative (RRI) is an important starting point where other BIPOC groups on campus have successfully brought is-sues of racism and discrimination as it relates to Blacks and Indigenous pop-ulations to the attention of the administration. The next step is to address other groups, where TCU now has an opportunity to be proactive rather than reactive when it comes to addressing the needs of its APA population. Up to this point, the RRI has not given sufficient attention to the experienc-es of APA faculty, staff, students, and alumni. While "Native American and Indigenous, Latinx, and African-American" populations are each highlighted as important groups in the RRI five-year plans, APAs are simply subsumed under the label of "other identities" and not explicitly identified, making them less visible as a marginalized group.[26] If the RRI has raised awareness about historical racism and inequality on our campus and is creating a space for APAs to reenter the discussion, it can do more to ensure APAs are ac-knowledged in the discussions about race and diversity on campus.

TCU has initiated several positive changes regarding some of the concerns in this chapter, including the dismissal of SPOTs in tenure and promotion evaluations, which can help mitigate the ways student biases harm minority faculty. In addition, as a private institution TCU is not restricted by state funding and has reaffirmed its commitment to DEI efforts, unlike other public institutions in our state. Both measures help in the recruitment and retention of minority faculty during what might be considered hostile times when it comes to doing the work of race on our campus and nationwide.

Regarding the APA population specifically, there are additional ways TCU can and should do better. One important change is to start disaggregating data on our APA population to capture the diversity within that population. Enhanced data collection based on geographical origin or ethnicity would allow us to see and study the APA population more closely to best determine strategies for increasing diversity and offering better institutional support. The myth of overrepresentation needs to be debunked. Recruitment, reten-tion, and inclusion of APAs can all be improved if we have a clearer sense of the many identities within our APA population. In addition, we need to create more community for APAs on campus. In the last two years, Asian Studies has morphed into Asian (area studies) *and* Asian American (ethnic) Studies, as well as a space for identity based APAs with no academic interest in these areas to come together. This agglomeration does a disservice to each entity. APA faculty and staff need to have an independent association with resources to support their identity group rather than just being assumed under the umbrella of faculty and staff of color, which does not provide the same sense of community. Whether it is an annual breakfast or luncheon, a workshop, or an APA advisory group, having a place for APA faculty and staff to meet and engage with one another to discuss issues relevant to us would make us more visible and give us a voice. It would also go a long way to help build a campus culture where everyone is respected and valued, an essential part of the RRI mandate.

This chapter has identified some of the important trends impacting APAs in higher education and identified some of the challenges that still lie ahead. It also serves as a call to action to make the APA population more visible. The hope is that by learning more about our APA faculty we can help bridge the gap between the APA community and the university's race and reconciliation initiatives to make TCU a more inclusive place.

Currier notes

1. Sharon S. Lee, "The De-Minoritization of Asian Americans: A Historical Examination of the Representations of Asian Americans in Affirmative Action Admissions Policies at the University of California," *Asian American Law Journal* 15, no. 1 (2008): 129–152.

2. Robert Gebeloff, Denise Lu and Miriam Jordan, "Inside the Diverse and Growing Asian Population in the U.S.," *New York Times*, August 21, 2021.

3. Colleen Flaherty, "After the China Initiative: Seeking Accountability," *Inside Higher Education*, September 20, 2022, accessed April 6, 2024, https://www.insidehighered.com/news/2022/09/21/scholars-targeted-china-initiative-seek-accountability.

4. See Luke Barr, "Hate crimes against Asians rose 76% in 2020 amid pandemic, FBI says," *ABC News*, October 25, 2021, accessed October 28, 2023, https://abcnews.go.com/US/hate-crimes-asians-rose-76-2020-amid-pandemic/story?id=80746198; Robert Hart, "Trump's Chinese Virus Tweet Helped Fuel Anti-Asian Hate on Twitter, Study Finds," *Forbes*, March 19, 2021, accessed May 2, 2024, https://www.forbes.com/sites/roberthart/2021/03/19/trumps-chinese-virus-tweet-helped-fuel-anti-asian-hate-on-twitter-study-finds/?sh=670e63b91a7c; Kimmy Yam, "Stop AAPI Hate group launches campaign to prevent candidates from using anti-Asian language," *NBC News*, September 21, 2023, accessed May 2, 2024, https://www.nbcnews.com/news/asian-america/stop-aapi-hate-group-launches-campaign-prevent-candidates-using-anti-a-rcna105886.

5. See Elizabeth Campbell, "Asians from diverse communities say they need to unite against hate crimes, racism," *Fort Worth Star Telegram*, March 27, 2021, accessed May 2, 2024, https://www.star-telegram.com/news/article250229185.html; Bud Kennedy, "Texas is third in hate incidents against Asian Americans amid coronavirus, group says," *Fort Worth Star Telegram*, April 16, 2020, accessed May 2, 2024, https://www.star-tele-

gram.com/opinion/bud-kennedy/article242027911.html; Terry Tang and Linley Sanders, "1 in 3 U.S. Asians and Pacific Islanders have faced racial abuse this year, poll shows," *LA Times*, November 14, 2023, accessed May 2, 2024, https://www.latimes.com/world-nation/story/2023-11-14/1-in-3-asians-pacific-islanders-faced-racial-abuse.

6.　Abby Budiman and Neil Ruiz, "Key Facts about Asian Origin Groups in the U.S.," *Pew Research*, April 29, 2021, accessed April 8 2024, https://www.pewresearch.org/short-reads/2021/04/29/key-facts-about-asian-origin-groups-in-the-u-s/.

7.　Jennifer Lee and Karthick Ramakrishnan, "Who Counts as Asian," *Ethnic and Racial Studies* 43, no. 10 (2020): 1733–56.

8.　Thomas Espenshade, Chang Chung, and Joan Walling, "Admission Preferences for Minority Students, Athletes, and Legacies at Elite Universities.," *Social Science Quarterly* 85, no. 5 (2004): 1422–4.

9.　See Deepa Shivram, "Southeast Asians Are Underrepresented in STEM. The Label 'Asian' Boxes Them out More," *NPR*, December 12, 2021, accessed 8 April 2024, https://www.npr.org/2021/12/12/1054933519/southeast-asian-representation-science; Carrie Liu Currier, "Breaking the Bamboo Ceiling: Challenges for APA Women in and Outside of the Classroom," *Journal of Political Science Education* 18, no. 2 (2022): 203–19; Yoon Pak, Dina Maramba, and Xavier Hernandez, "Asian Americans in Higher Education: Charting New Realities," *ASHE Higher Education Report* 40, no. 1 (2014): 1–135; Lowell Andrew R. Iporac, "Are Asians and Asian-Americans Excluded in Diversity, Equity, and Inclusion Initiatives?" *Bulletin Limnology and Oceanography* 29, no. 4 (2020): 132–33; Samuel Museus and Mitchell Chang, "Rising to the Challenge of Conducting Research on Asian Americans in Higher Education," *New Directions for Institutional Research* 142, Summer (2009): 95–105.

10.　William Petersen, "Success Story: Japanese-American Style," *New York Times Magazine*, January 9, 1966, accessed May 12, 2020, https://timesmachine.nytimes.com/timesmachine/1966/01/09/356013502.html?pageNumber=189

11.　Claire Kim, "The Racial Triangulation of Asian Americans," *Politics & Society* 27, no. 1 (1999): 105–38.

12.　Claire Kim, *Asian Americans in an Anti-Black World* (NY: Cambridge University Press, 2023).

13.　See Gayle Y. Iwamasa, "Recommendations for the Treatment of Asian American/Pacific Islander Populations," *Asian American Psychological Association*, 2012, accessed February 27, 2024, https://www.apa.org/pi/oema/resources/ethnicity-health/asian-american/psychological-treatment; Laura Uba, *Asian Americans: Personality Patterns, Identity, and Mental Health* (NY: Guilford Press, 2003); National Association of School Psychologists, "Supporting Asian, Asian American, and Pacific Islander Students and Families: Tips for Educators in K-12 Settings," 2023, accessed February 28, 2024, https://www.nasponline.org/resources-and-publications/resourcesand-podcasts/diversity-and-social-justice/social-justice/supporting-asian-asian-american-and-pacific-islander-studentsand-families-tips-for-educators-in-k%E2%80%9312-settings.

14.　Office of Institutional Research, "Texas Christian University Facts and Data," 2023, accessed 8 April 2024, https://ir.tcu.edu/facts-data/faculty-staff/.

15. Robert Teranishi, *Asians in the Ivory Tower: Dilemmas of Racial Inequality in American Higher Education* (NY: Teachers College Press, 2010).

16. Currier, "Breaking the Bamboo Ceiling," 206.

17. Yuhan Jiang. 2023. "How Name-Based Discrimination Affect Minority Groups," *Journal of Education, Humanities and Social Sciences* 9 (2023): 64–68.

18. Eunai Shrake, "Unmasking the Self: Struggling with the Model Minority Stereotype and the Lotus Blossom Image," in *"Strangers" of the Academy: Asian Women Scholars in Higher Education*, eds. Guofang Li and Gulbahar Beckett (Sterling, VA: Stylus, 2006), 178–94.

19. See William A. Smith, Tara J. Yosso, Daniel G. Solorzano, "Challenging Racial Battle Fatigue on Historically White Campuses: A critical race examination of race-related stress," in Christine A. Stanley, ed. *Faculty of Color: Teaching in predominantly white colleges and universities* (Bolton, MA: Anker Publishing, 2006), 211–237; Kieu Linh Caroline Valverde, Cara Maffini Pham, Melody Yee, and Jing Mai, "Killing Machine: Exposing the Health Threats to Asian American Women Scholars in Academia," in Kieu Linh Caroline Valverde and Wei Ming Dariotis, eds. *Fight the Tower: Asia America Women Scholars' Resistance and Renewal in the Academy* (Newark: Rutgers University Press, 2020), 110–163.

20. Luis Ponjuan, Valerie Conley, and Cathy Trower, "Career Stage Differences in Pre-Tenure Track Faculty Perceptions of Professional and Personal Relationships," *Journal of Higher Education* 82 (2011): 319–346.

21. Isis Settles, Martinque K. Jones, NiCole T. Buchanan, and Kristie Dotson, "Epistemic Exclusion: Scholar(ly) Devaluation that Marginalizes Faculty of Color," *Journal of Diversity in Higher Education* 14, no. 4 (2021): 493–507.

22. Sarah Schwartz, "Map: Where Critical Race Theory is Under Attack," *Education Week*, June 11, 2021, accessed on December 20, 2023, https://www.edweek.org/policy-politics/map-where-critical-race-theory-is-under-attack/2021/06.

23. See Wei Ming Dariotis, "Academic Symbiosis: A Manifest on Tenure and Promotion in Asian American Studies," in Kieu Linh Caroline Valverde and Wei Ming Dariotis, eds, *Fight the Tower: Asian American Women Scholars' Resistance and Renewal in the Academy* (Newark: Rutgers University Press, 2020), 382–418; Rene O. Guillaume and Elizabeth C. Apodaca, "Early Career Faculty of Color and Promotion and Tenure: the intersection of advancement in the academy and cultural taxation," *Race, Ethnicity, and Education* 25, no. 4 (2022): 546–63.

24. Carrie Liu Currier, "The Asian American Dilemma in DEI: Finding Space in the Diversity Debates," *Education Sciences* 14, no. 3 (2024): 305–22.

25. Wei Ming Dariotis, Nicholas D. Hartlep and Daisy Ball, "The Battle of Racial Battle Fatigue," in *Racial Battle Fatigue in Faculty: Perspectives and Lessons from Higher Education* (London: Routledge, 2020), 1–14.

26. TCU *Race & Reconciliation Initiative*, "Operation Triangulation: a Five-Year Plan," accessed May 2, 2024, https://www.tcu.edu/race-reconciliation-initiative/about/five-year-plan.php

Creating Community for Asians, Asian Americans, and Pacific Islanders at TCU

Kelly Palida Phommachanh

FOR STUDENTS who identify as Asian or Asian Pacific American (APA) at a private, predominantly white university like TCU, finding a sense of belonging is particularly complicated due to several factors, such as being treated as a monolithic group, being deminoritized in higher education, and being subjected to hidden forms of discrimination and racism.[1] By understanding the history of the Asian Studies program at TCU, as well as the importance of disaggregating data and experiences of Asian and APA students on our campus, this chapter explores how TCU can further develop and cultivate community and a sense of belonging for both Asian and Asian Pacific American students on campus.

Asian and Asian American Studies at TCU and Beyond

Asian American Studies programs in the United States emerged near the end of the civil rights movement of the late 1960s and early 1970s, thanks to the efforts of activists, scholars, and students, who challenged dominant narratives by striking to increase access and representation of Black, Indigenous, and People of Color (BIPOC) within higher education.[2] These strikes would also address the marginalization of Asian American communities not only in higher education but also in U.S. society. One of the monumental events was the 1968 Black Student Union / Third World Liberation Front Student Strike held at San Francisco State University (SFSU). This student-led strike helped to form the subsequent establishment of the College of Ethnic Studies, which included Asian American Studies as one of its foundational departments.[3] This strike, alongside similar movements at other universities, highlighted the demand for a curriculum that reflected the experiences and perspectives of marginalized communities, including Asian Americans. Following the establishment of the Asian American Studies program at San Francisco State University in 1969, other universities across the United States followed suit and began to establish similar programs in response to growing student activism and demands for ethnic studies.

At TCU, Asian Studies was introduced as the university's first area studies program in 1993, following the demands from students and the desire of faculty for a more inclusive academic exploration of Asia.[4] Initially led by Andrew Fort, professor of religion, the program subsequently flourished under the guidance of Carrie Liu Currier, associate professor and chair of political science, who served as its director from 2006 until 2018. Under Currier's leadership, the Asian Studies program at TCU expanded to be the largest ethnic or area studies program on campus. Currier oversaw the establishment of an official budget to support programming and events for students and faculty, the creation of a logo and slogan to better market the Asian Studies program, the development and promotion of Asian Studies courses across the curriculum, and the continuous recruitment of faculty to teach and students to minor in this area of study.[5]

Disaggregating the Data

As Carrie Liu Currier's chapter discusses in this collection, Asian and Asian Pacific American students and faculty are often excluded from discussions concerning their racialized experiences in higher education and the challenges they confront due to the detrimental model minority stereotype. This stereotype, with its problematic racial assumptions, characterizes APA students and faculty as diligent, highly educated, and exemplary among marginalized and minoritized groups in the United States.[6] The term "model minority" was first introduced to the public by sociologist William Petersen in 1966, where he highlighted the success stories of Japanese Americans.[7] Petersen attributed the success of Japanese Americans to their strong family bonds and exceptional work ethic, suggesting that other marginalized groups should follow this example to achieve the putative "American Dream." As Currier addresses in the previous chapter, although the model minority stereotype appears to be a positive characterization, the stereotype creates hidden and harmful effects.

The concept of the model minority stereotype has since become a divisive tool, further separating the Asian and APA communities from other minoritized and marginalized groups such as Black, Indigenous, Latinx, and other minoritized racial and ethnic identities. Given the context regarding the model minority stereotype, researchers must examine the various challenges faced by the broader Asian and APA communities. One way to do so is by disaggregating data to better understand and acknowledge the diverse ethnic groups that make up Asian, Asian American, and Pacific Islander categories.[8] While the TCU Fact Book provides a breakdown between "Asian" and "Hawaiian/Other Pacific Islander" identities as two of many possible student demographics and allows us to see the country of citizenship or permanent residence for all international students, this demographic break down is not possible to view for faculty or staff. The grouping of these diverse ethnicities often overshadows the distinctive struggles of various communities, and erases certain Asian, Asian American, and Pacific Islander ethnic groups.[9] As Currier shares in her own experiences at TCU, moreover, the model minority stereotype has led to experiences of exclusion from other non-Asian minoritized communities at the university. Data disaggregation for Asian, Asian American, and Pacific Islander communities assist those in the political arena, the education sector, and the general public to comprehend the true diversity of experiences and needs within APA ethnic groups.

Intergenerational Trauma

Trauma is prevalent among Asian ethnic minority families in the United States, like other communities that have been forcibly displaced as a result of conflict, slavery, genocide, religious or racial animus, and other forms of abuse.[10] Intergenerational trauma, especially stemming from war and displacement, can profoundly affect individuals and communities across multiple generations, depending on the gravity of the trauma endured.[11] Intergenerational trauma often involves the transmission of traumatic events from those who directly experienced them to subsequent generations.[12] Trauma manifests and affects people in a variety of ways, including psychologically and emotionally, such as through chronic stress and anxiety. Children and grandchildren of trauma survivors can also experience such lingering effects, even if they did not experience the trauma firsthand.[13] Researchers have also found high levels of depression, post-traumatic stress syndrome,[14] and attachment and trust issues linked to the children and grandchildren of trauma survivors.[15] Other studies show how the social and behavioral impact of trauma can manifest in parenting styles that can lead to overprotection or emotional distance. This in turn leads to low self-esteem and behavioral problems in the children of trauma survivors.[16] Some may even resort to substance abuse as a means of coping with their unresolved indirect trauma. Moreover, persons displaced from their original home experience a loss of cultural heritage and identity as well as a fragmentation of their community. This loss of social support structures can lead to weakened community bonds and a reduced sense of collective identity.[17]

Across U.S. universities and colleges, Asian and APA students may experience conflicts concerning their cultural heritage and overlapping identities.[18] The manifestation of intergenerational trauma often intersects with aspects of cultural identity, particularly as students endeavor to fulfill the demands inherent in pursuing their college degrees.[19] For Asian and Asian Pacific American students who cherish and identify strongly with their cultural backgrounds, the experience of attending a university that fails to recognize or celebrate their heritage can yield multifaceted harm. This discord may engender a sense of cultural alienation, wherein students perceive a lack of institutional acknowledgment or understanding of their cultural milieu.[20] Indeed, a student's cultural heritage, sexual orientation, socioeconomic status, and other facets contribute to their complex array of intersecting identities. Universities, understandably, must not only acknowledge this diversity but also proactively provide campus resources aimed at supporting students in making sense of their intersecting identities while pursuing their studies.[21]

Yet universities also confront the challenge of effectively reaching out to and supporting Asian and Asian Pacific American students grappling with intergenerational trauma, who may struggle to seek assistance and connect with peers.[22] The repercussions of intergenerational trauma can impede the development of interpersonal relationships for these students, complicating their ability to articulate personal challenges to peers, advisors, and faculty members.[23] Given the challenges faced by Asian and Asian Pacific American students grappling with intergenerational trauma, researchers at predominantly white higher education institutions like TCU must devise comprehensive action plans aimed at supporting these students throughout their academic journeys.

Understanding intergenerational trauma is essential for providing adequate support and resources to those affected. By acknowledging that Asian students should not be classified as monolithic, TCU can better address and respond to their needs, fostering a sense of healing and belonging. One of the ways that experts have suggested is through community support programs, such as the student organizations that can help build or rebuild social networks and provide collective healing spaces. Cultural revitalization projects can also help restore a sense of identity and community.

Sense of Belonging

As TCU strives to diversify its student body by recruiting students from diverse cultural, racial, and ethnic backgrounds that reflect a spectrum of lived experiences and intersecting identities, it is imperative for faculty, staff, and administrators to proactively engage in initiatives aimed at fostering a sense of belonging among these students within the campus environment. Sense of belonging refers to a psychological concept of how students perceive social support at their respective college or university, the feeling of interconnection, and the experience of being cared for and valued by their peers, staff, faculty, and the campus community as a whole.[24] Students can experience a sense of belonging in various ways, such as by getting involved in a student-led organization, seeing their intersecting identities represented both inside and outside the classroom, and noticing when their campus is being proactive in regards to institutional support that promotes diversity, equity, and inclusion.[25] It is crucial to recognize that contextual variables are likely to influence how students perceive their colleges or universities and can affect the relationship between campus environments and their sense of belonging.[26] For example, in the previous chapter, Currier was able to help APA students find their sense of belonging on campus by serving as the advisor to TCU's first and only Asian-interest sorority on campus, Kappa Lambda Delta, which was established in 2005.

Concurrently, there is a pressing need for these institutions to ensure the safety and security of students, particularly when incidents of racially charged attacks that target students' identities occur.[27] The dearth of safety measures and responsiveness becomes palpable when perpetrators of such attacks are found to be affiliated with the same academic community. This raises critical questions about the commitment of institutional leadership to principles of diversity, equity, and inclusion. Indeed, the urgency of the situation is underscored by the erosion of trust experienced by marginalized and minoritized student populations toward the faculty, staff, and administrators in times of crisis.[28] Potential ramifications for Asian Pacific American students who perceive their predominantly white institutions as unsafe encompass a spectrum of outcomes, including but not limited to psychological trauma, social disengagement, and withdrawal from academic pursuits.[29] During the COVID-19 pandemic, there was a national increase in violence against Asian Pacific Americans.[30] As Currier stated in the previous chapter, many American politicians referred to COVID-19 as the "China Virus," thus spreading xenophobic and harmful rhetoric. During this time, TCU's Office of Diversity, Equity, and Inclusion hosted an online panel discussion event titled "#StopAsianHate: Standing in Solidarity Against Anti-Asian Rhetoric" to address the concerns of TCU faculty, staff, and students regarding the multiple crimes and violence that targeted Asian Pacific American communities.[31]

The formation of student-led organizations is another way in which APA students at TCU can create their sense of belonging on campus. During the 1990s, students representing diverse Asian ethnicities undertook concerted efforts to assert their presence and articulate their concerns within the TCU community, prompting TCU faculty to adopt an Asian Studies minor.[32] Through initiatives spearheaded by organizations such as the United Asian Community, Students for Asian Indian Cultural Awareness, and the Asian Student Association, a plethora of social gatherings and educational sessions were organized, aimed at spotlighting the multifaceted cultures and narratives within the Asian student cohort at TCU. In 1999, TCU's Asian community united to orchestrate the inaugural "Asian Festival," an event intended to offer a nuanced exploration of various Asian cultures through food, traditional performances, and information sessions. [33] Student-led organizations Kappa Lambda Delta (KLD) and the South Asian Inter-cultural Association (SAICA), both of which focus on ethnic identity, emerged soon after, a pivotal moment on our campus, particularly for students hailing from marginalized and minoritized backgrounds. In the latter half of the 2010s, TCU witnessed a notable surge in its international student population, constituting five percent of the institution's overall student body. [34] A substantial proportion of these international students hailed from Vietnam. In response to this demographic shift, Vietnamese students on campus coalesced in 2013 to establish the Vietnamese Student Association (VSA), with a mission centered on fostering cultural awareness, amplifying the voices of Vietnamese students, and nurturing a sense of solidarity among TCU's diverse student body. [35] Such endeavors supported the increased awareness and presence of the various ethnically diverse Asian groups settling in the Dallas-Fort Worth metroplex.

Implications for the Future

The work of building community and a sense of belonging and its relation to students at private, predominantly white institutions like TCU should be continuously explored by researchers and administrators. In order to do so, understanding intergenerational trauma is essential for providing adequate support and resources to those affected. By acknowledging that all Asian students should not be classified as a monolith, TCU can better address and respond to their needs and foster a sense of healing and belonging. Cultural revitalization projects executed through student groups and supported by the university's office of student affairs can also help restore a sense of identity and community. The Race & Reconciliation Initiative (RRI) can also help us to understand the unique and diverse history of TCU's Asian Pacific American communities, through greater attention in its research of students, faculty, and staff from these vital and diverse communities. It is imperative to understand that a sense of belonging will look different for every student, faculty, and staff member. TCU can create a community that is inclusive of its Asian Pacific American faculty, staff, and students by understanding the history of Asian Studies and supporting its current efforts. Additionally, disaggregating the data and experiences of Asian, Asian American, and Pacific Islander students would better equip those working to create a sense of belonging and community within academia. As RRI's Oral History Project focuses its efforts in the future on the experiences of APA students, faculty, staff, and alumni, TCU can better educate itself about the lived experiences of APA communities through stories told through the voices of these individuals. By providing such forums, TCU can empower this community and create a sense of belonging in which all feel welcome and appreciated.

Phommachanh notes

1. Carrie Liu Currier, "The Asian American Dilemma in DEI: Finding Space in the Diversity Debates," *Education Sciences* 14, no. 3 (2024): 305–22, https://doi.org/10.3390/educsci14030305.

2. "Asian American Studies: Our History." San Francisco State University. n.d. https://aas.sfsu.edu/about%26from.

3. Karen Umemoto, "On Strike!" San Francisco State College Strike, 1968–69: The Role of Asian American students," *Amerasia Journal* 15, no. 1 (1989): 3–41.

4. Texas Christian University Institutional Research. "Fall 1993 Fact Book," (1993). https://ir.tcu.edu/wp-content/uploads/2021/05/TCUFactBook1993.pdf.

5. "Asian Studies." n.d. AddRan College of Liberal Arts. https://addran.tcu.edu/academics/majors-minors-programs/asian-studies.php.

6. Robert T. Palmer and Dina C. Maramba, "The Impact of Social Capital on the Access, Adjustment, and Success of Southeast Asian American College Students," *Journal of College Student Development* 56, no. 1 (2015): 45–60.

7. OiYan Poon, Dian Squire, Corinne Kodama, Ajani Byrd, Jason Chan, Lester Manzano, Sara Furr, and Devita Bishundat, "A Critical Review of the Model Minority Myth in Selected Literature on Asian Americans and Pacific Islanders in Higher Education," *Review of Educational Research* 86, no. 2 (2016): 469–502.

8. Dina Maramba, "The Importance of Critically Disaggregating Data: The Case of Southeast Asian American College Students," *AAPI Nexus: Policy, Practice and Community* 9, no. 1–2 (2011): 127–133.

9. Hiram E. Fitzgerald, Deborah J. Johnson, James Allen, Francisco A. Villarruel, and Desiree Baolian Qin, "Historical and Race-Based Trauma: Resilience Through Family and Community," *Adversity and Resilience Science* 2 (2021): 215–223.

10. Grant N. Marshall, Terry L. Schell, Marc N. Elliott, S. Megan Berthold, and Chi-Ah Chun. "Mental Health of Cambodian Refugees 2 Decades After Resettlement in the United States." *Jama* 294, no. 5 (2005): 571–579.

11. Cindy Sangalang and Cindy Vang. "Intergenerational Trauma in Refugee Families: A Systematic Review." *Journal of Immigrant & Minority Health* 19, (2017): 745–754 https://doi.org/10.1007/s10903-016-0499-7

12. Rachel Yehuda and Amy Lehrner, "Intergenerational Transmission of Trauma Effects: Putative Role of Epigenetic Mechanisms." *World Psychiatry* 17, no. 3 (October 2018): 243–257. Doi:10.1002/wps.20568. PMID: 30192087; PMCID: PMC6127768.

13. Rachel Lev-Wiesel, "Intergenerational Transmission of Trauma Across Three Generations: A Preliminary Study." *Qualitative Social Work* 6, no.1 (2007): 75–94. https://doi.org/10.1177/1473325007074167

14. Sammy Alhassen , Siwei Chen, Lamees Alhassen, Alvin Phan, Mohammad Khoudari, Angele De Silva, Huda Barhoosh, Zitong Wang, Chelsea Parrocha, Emily Shapiro, Charity Henrich, Zicheng Wang, Leon Mutesa, Pierre Baldi, Geoffrey W. Abbott , and Amal Alachkar, "Intergenerational Trauma Transmission is Associated with Brain Metabotranscriptome Remodeling and Mitochondrial Dysfunction." *Communications Biology* 4, no.1 (June 24, 2021): 783. doi: 10.1038/s42003-021-02255-2. PMID: 34168265; PMCID: PMC8225861.

15. Zlatomira Kostova and Vanya L. Matanova, "Transgenerational Trauma and Attachment." *Front Psychol.*15 (April 8, 2024):1362561. doi: 10.3389/fpsyg.2024.1362561. PMID: 38650899; PMCID: PMC11033415.

16. Nimrah Afzal, Siyan Ye, Amy C. Page, David Trickey, Mark D. Lyttle, Rachel M. Hiller, Sarah L. Halligan, "A Systematic Literature Review of the Relationship Between Parenting Responses and Child Post-Traumatic Stress Symptoms." *Eur J Psychotraumatol.* 14, no. 1 (2023): 2156053. doi:10.1080/20008066.2022.21560 53. PMID: 37052099; PMCID: PMC9788707.

17. Ciano Aydin, "How to Forget the Unforgettable? On Collective Trauma, Cultural Identity, and Mnemotechnologies." *Identity*, 17, no. 3 (2017): 125–137. https://doi.org/10.1080/15283488.2017.1340160

18. Alina Siu Wong, "In Flux: Racial Identity Construction among Chinese American and Filipina/o American Undergraduates" (PhD diss., University of Michigan, 2011).

19. An Huynh, Christine J. Yeh, and Phuong Tang, "Intergenerational Trauma and Resilience among Second-Generation Southeast Asian Americans." *Asian American Journal of Psychology,* (2024). Advance online publication. https://doi.org/10.1037/aap0000343

20. Sharon Rae Jenkins, Aimee Belanger, Melissa Londoño Connally, Adriel Boals, and Kelly M. Durón, "First-Generation Undergraduate Students' Social Support, Depression, and Life Satisfaction," *Journal of College Counseling* 16, no. 2 (2013): 129–142.

21. Samuel D. Museus, Varaxy Yi, and Natasha Saelua, "The Impact of Culturally Engaging Campus Environments on Sense of Belonging," *The Review of Higher Education* 40, no. 2 (2017): 187–215.

22. Amanda Alexandra Tom, "Examining the Barriers to Seeking Counseling and Mental Health Services on College Campuses in The Asian American Student Population" (PhD diss., Azusa Pacific University, 2021).

23. Jeannie Sheng Lee, J. S., "The Impacts of Intergenerational Trauma on First Generation Hmong American College Students" (Master's thesis, California State University, Fresno, 2021).

24. Terrell L. Strayhorn, "Exploring Ethnic Minority First-Year College Students' Well-Being and Sense of Belonging: A Qualitative Investigation of a Brief Intervention." *American Journal of Qualitative Research* 6, no. 1 (2021): 42–58.

25. Emily Laff, "Vietnamese Student Association Seeks to Bring Cultural Diversity to Campus," *TCU 360,* Nov. 9, 2015, https://tcu360.com/2015/11/09/vietnamese-student-association-seeks-to-bring-cultural-diversity-to-campus/.

26. Samuel D. Museus and Ting-Han Chang. "The Impact of Campus Environments on Sense of Belonging for First-Generation College Students." *Journal of College Student Development* 62, no. 3 (2021): 367–372. https://doi.org/10.1353/csd.2021.0039.

27. Angela R. Gover, Shannon B. Harper, and Lynn Langton, "Anti-Asian Hate Crime During the COVID-19 Pandemic: Exploring the Reproduction of Inequality," *American Journal of Criminal Justice* 45, no. 4 (2020): 647–667.

28. "#STOPASIANHATE: Standing in Solidarity Against Anti-Asian Rhetoric" 2021, https://what2do.tcu.edu/event/stopasianhate-standing-in-solidarity-against-anti-asian-rhetoric/

29. "Addressing Asian American/Pacific Islander College Students' Mental Health Needs. Expert Recommendations," *National Center for Institutional Diversity* (January 27, 2022). https://medium.com/national-center-for-institutional-diversity/addressing-asian-american-pacific-islander-college-students-mental-health-needs-4413a55f49b7

30. Angela R. Gover, Shannon B. Harper, and Lynn Langton, "Anti-Asian Hate Crime During the COVID-19 Pandemic: Exploring the Reproduction of Inequality." *Am J Crim Justice* 45, no. 4 (2020): 647-667. doi: 10.1007/s12103-020-09545-1

31. "#STOPASIANHATE: Standing in Solidarity Against Anti-Asian Rhetoric," A panel discussion about the Recent Events and Rhetoric Misrepresenting and Endangering Global Asian Communities and Asian Americans. *TCU's Office of Diversity, Equity, and Inclusion* (April 6, 2021). https://what2do.tcu.edu/event/stopasian-hate-standing-in-solidarity-against-anti-asian-rhetoric/

32. Michael Bou-Nacklie. "AddRan Looks to Hire Faculty Member to Teach Chinese," *Daily Skiff.* (Feb. 22, 2007), p.1

33. Mel Korte, "Asian Festival," *Daily Skiff* (April 21, 1999), p.1.

34. "TCU International: Foreign Students and Study Abroad Programs on the Rise." *TCU 360* (Nov 26, 2013). https://tcu360.com/2013/11/26/19070tcu-international-foreign-students-and-study-abroad-programs-risei/

35. "TCU's Vietnamese Student Association Celebrates Community Through Sharing," *TCU News* (May 14, 2021). https://www.tcu.edu/news/2021/Vietnamese-student-association-celebrates-community.php

TCU and Fort Worth Mexicanos During the Progressive Era (1900–1924)

Cecilia N. Sánchez Hill

IN THE FIRST FEW DECADES of the twentieth century, local and state leaders in Texas and the Southwest did not believe it was their responsibility to care for or educate Mexican-origin children.[1] State and local leaders did not recognize Mexicanos as permanent members of society but rather as "a species of farm implement that comes mysteriously and spontaneously into being coincident with the maturing of the cotton . . . He has no past, no future, only a brief and anonymous present."[2] Even though Progressive Era (1900–1924) education reforms created state mandatory school attendance laws beginning in 1915, there were no accountability measures to these laws until 1948 when the Texas Education Agency (TEA) tied attendance to state funding. Prior to the changes to the law in 1948, districts received state funding based on the number of school-aged children who lived in their city or county, whether or not those children attended school. After 1948, TEA required districts to maintain and report their daily attendance to receive state funding. In addition to mandatory attendance laws, education reformers in the early twentieth century professionalized teaching by establishing certifications, reorganizing schools into districts with county superintendents who reported to a centralized state apparatus, and restructuring curriculum to emphasize English-only teaching and assimilationist pedagogical strategies, such as teaching only a patriotic version of U.S. history that prioritized American norms.

Because city and school officials did not demonstrate a commitment to addressing the needs of Mexican and Mexican American children at this time, local churches, funded largely by the elite white society of Fort Worth, provided these young Mexicanos with clothing, food, and schooling services. Public school administrators in the city did not seek out Mexicans in their communities, nor did they welcome them onto their campuses. The large attendance in these church and community missions highlights Mexicanos' beliefs in the value of education. It was in this context that, in 1915, TCU professors and students established a Mexican mission for children. Although TCU faculty and students contributed to the nation's assimilationist goals for immigrants, they were guided by a desire to provide needed services to the poor; such missionary goals are in stark contrast to those funding the missions, who hoped to gain acceptance into high society as patrons of those less fortunate.[3]

The 1880 census is the first time ethnic Mexicans appear in Fort Worth. The census listed nine unmarried men as common laborers. By 1910, there were 548 Mexican-born and 149 U.S.-born ethnic Mexicans living in 121 households in Fort Worth. Of these 121 households, 74 percent were family units consisting of a male head, wife, and children.[4] These Mexican households lived in scattered barrios across the city known as "Little Mexicos." Like many other Mexican migrants in Fort Worth, for example, Santiago Diaz's family left their homeland during the violent Mexican Revolution in the 1910s. Diaz's father, Abran, found work in Fort Worth with the railroad. The family, which included two younger siblings and his mother Telesfora, settled in one of the downtown Mexican barrios.[5]

While Jim Crow laws did not fully segregate Mexicans or legally exclude them from public spaces, Juan Crow norms ensured city leaders and white residents racialized Mexicans in Fort Worth, relegating them to their own small communities. Churches often had separate services or seating sections for Mexicans. Orphanages in the city did not welcome Mexican children. The public schools in the city did not offer any language services, diminishing the possibility that non-English speaking students would be successful in school. It is unclear whether any of the children from the 121 households attended public school in Fort Worth in 1910: the Black and white binary that categorized Mexicans as white in official government documents obscured such documentation, and Mexican children are not mentioned in the Fort Worth Independent School District (FWISD) board meeting minutes until 1923. At the October 6, 1923, board meeting, Mrs. Robinson, a representative of the Broadway Presbyterian Church in El Papalote, a Mexican barrio just south of downtown, requested permission from the FWISD school board to sell paper bonnets to girls at various schools to raise money for a charitable endeavor. The church hoped to raise enough funds to build a room "to teach the Mexican girls."[6] In the first couple of decades of the twentieth century, it was Catholic, Presbyterian, and Methodists churches that took on the role as educator for Mexican children in Fort Worth.

In September 1912, the Daughters of Isabella, a Catholic women's organization, established the first Mexican mission in Fort Worth at the intersection of Bridge and Franklin Streets, just behind the Tarrant County Courthouse in one of the first Mexican barrios, La Corte. The mission, which focused on education, began with just five children; by mid-October, it had increased to twenty-seven pupils. After this quick growth, the Daughters of Isabella relocated to Our Lady of Guadalupe Mexican Mission at Peach and Hampton Streets, less than a mile away. According to a *Fort Worth Star-Telegram* article titled "Mexicans Are Taught American Ways in Newly Established Missions Here," a second mission school opened in 1913 in the North Side for the increasing number of Mexicans living in that community. The leader of the new San Jose mission, Father Pohlen, who was of German ancestry, had graduated from a college in Mexico City and "spent much time among the Mexicans, learning their customs, language, and characteristics." Mexicans "have a great desire to learn things," he told the *Star-Telegram*; "they seem almost wild to learn English." In addition to learning English, these mission schools taught their students "the right way to live" and cleanliness habits. This education went beyond the daily instruction in the classroom. Father Pohlen and the Daughters regularly visited their students' homes "to see if they are profiting by their lessons."[7] Even though these religious institutions utilized subtractive methods of Americanization efforts that stripped the child of their native language and culture with the goal of replacing them with American ideals, they recognized a need to care for the Mexican community.[8] Neither the city nor the school district attended to any of the needs of Mexican children in Fort Worth during these years.

Throughout the first few decades of the twentieth century, the *Star-Telegram* reported on the dire conditions of Mexicans in Fort Worth and the efforts of elite white women in addressing these problems. Reporters and their interviewees condescendingly informed readers that "little" or "tiny Mexican children" with "little brown faces" and "brown hands" were in "a sadly neglected state."[9] To help these ostensibly tiny, brown, and barefoot children, white women raised money at prestigious gatherings in high profile locations where they played card games to win donated prizes and applauded each other for their charitable endeavors. On March 1, 1914, the *Star-Telegram* reported that "in the ball room of the Westbrook [Hotel] fifty tables were arranged for the benefit card party . . . for the purpose of aiding the work of the two mission schools for the Mexican children." The party was "a great success financially and socially."[10]

From time to time, these philanthropic white women also put Mexican children on display to demonstrate the success of their efforts. In May 1914, eighty-three Mexican children who attended the two mission schools performed short plays in both Spanish and English at the Mount Carmel Academy, "as examples of their progress in learning the English language."[11] The *Star-Telegram* announced the event and invited the public to attend. Although these women were providing the means for religious institutions to address the needs of Mexican children that the city and the public schools ignored, all parties involved had individual motivations for their benevolence. Their charitable undertakings led to mention of their names in the society pages of the newspaper; their efforts aided upper levels of society in preparing "the little Mexican children to be useful citizens."[12] Also, their continued support of these mission schools quietly enforced racial segregation, ensuring that Mexican children would not attend public schools with their white children. In an article reporting on the attendance of Mexican children at the mission schools, the author stated that the high interest of Mexican parents in these schools proves that "a separate school for the Mexican children is more satisfactory than a mixed one." The author speculated on why Mexicans supposedly preferred to attend their own separate schools: "Mexicans are unable to dress in a way which will compare with the American children and even the poorest of them are extremely sensitive about this fact."[13] Fort Worth's elite white society used these reasonings to attempt to maintain white-only schools.

In 1915, a third mission school opened in Fort Worth in the growing Mexican community of North Side, under the leadership of Mateo Molina, a former TCU professor who was then a student at Brite College (now, Brite Divinity School). Molina was joined by Clara Case, a professor of Spanish at TCU, in teaching these one hundred enrolled students; seven additional female public school teachers joined Molina and Case as instructors. Molina, described as a Spaniard in the *Skiff* (TCU's student newspaper) and in the *Star-Telegram*, may have been Mexican. The 1915 *Horned Frog* yearbook stated that Molina "came from Mexico to be a missionary."[14] For the people of Fort Worth, identifying as Spaniard rather than Mexican elevated a person's status in society. Molina's time at TCU began a few years earlier in 1909, when he was hired as a professor of Spanish and French. He held a graduate degree from the Valencia Institute in Spain and had extensive experience teaching English in schools in California and at the West Texas Military Academy in San Antonio.[15] Molina taught both introductory and advanced courses in Spanish and French. After teaching for a few years, Molina enrolled in the Seminary Baptist Mission as a divinity student, then transferred to Brite in 1915. Prior to the opening of the mission in the North Side, Molina provided both language classes and spiritual guidance to Mexicans in Fort Worth. According to the society pages of the *Star-Telegram*, Mrs. W.J. Storms reported to the Central Methodist Study Circle that Professor Molina taught Spanish at a "nonsectarian Mexican mission" to "barefoot and illy clad" Mexican children so that they "may enter the public schools." Molina also provided church services on Sundays to the children and led many to be baptized at the Broadway Baptist Church.[16] In 1916, a year after graduating from Brite, he left Fort Worth to serve as a pastor at a church in Oklahoma.

Clara Case, like her fellow TCU educator Mateo Molina, recognized the needs of Mexicans on both sides of the border and used her skills and talents to provide services that they had not received from either local government. In 1899, she opened a Christian mission in Mexico under the direction of the Christian Women's Board of Missions. Within a few years, the mission grew from just a handful to almost five hundred students.[17] Case returned to TCU in 1912, but as the *Skiff* explained, after "three years of efficient and faithful work building up the Spanish Department," she felt a call to continue the work she established at the mission in Mexico.[18] When she was at TCU, Case participated in the TCU Volunteer Band, an international association that trained students and faculty to work in missions outside of the country, even though she already served in a foreign mission. TCU's program had missionaries in India, Jamaica, and Canada with the Salteaux

"Indians."[19] The global chaos of the Great War, however, cut her missionary work much shorter than she planned, and she quickly returned to TCU, where she and Molina began their mission work.[20]

In January 1915, Molina's mission school opened its doors to both children and adults ranging in ages from seven to sixty. The school operated with the assistance of the Ministerial Association of TCU and was one of several charitable activities conducted by the university. Prior to beginning work in any mission, TCU volunteers first "devote[d] a month to each field, studying first the geography, race, and customs of the people, their literature and culture" and the specific needs of the mission. The *Skiff* reported that "Don Mateo Molina" was "conducting a mission and night school . . . among the Spanish speaking people of North Fort Worth."[21] Molina stated that most of the students of the new mission were employees of the packing house and their children. He believed his mission met needs of the Mexican community that the school district or the city could not. Operating from 7 p.m. to 10 p.m. on Mondays and Fridays, his mission school reached adults and children who worked during the day. Molina claimed that "in many cases both the father and mother work in the packing houses all day, and the older children are required to stay at home and look after their younger brothers and sisters." He also stated that some families "are too poor to send their children to school." Ultimately, Molina hoped that the efforts by him and his eight teachers would "develop their pupils into sturdy and intelligent American citizens," similar to the goals of public education at the time.[22] The school began by providing English classes but had plans to implement math classes for both basic and professional skills. On Sundays, Molina preached and taught the Bible to Mexican adults while Case provided services to the Mexican children. Molina's preaching and teaching of the Bible drew on the immigrant experiences of his audience, who were establishing new homes in Fort Worth, and he made his lessons applicable to "fit the lives of these people."[23]

Although TCU students continued to support Mexican missions in Fort Worth after Molina left, their involvement never reached the levels provided by Don Mateo. Brite students volunteered their time in Mexican missions too. The campus chapter of the Young Women's Christian Association taught Mexicanos English, sewing, and cooking and raised money to fill children's stockings. In addition to spiritual services, Molina had a desire to provide schooling to Mexican children and adults who needed to learn English and other basic skills to increase their opportunities in Fort Worth. As both a language professor and a divinity student, Molina reached beyond the ivy-covered borders of the university to address the needs of the Spanish-speaking people of Fort Worth. As Sean Atkinson's essay explores in narrating the history of establishing Mariachi Sangre Royal de TCU in the chapter to follow, there are many other ways for TCU faculty, staff, and students to engage with the Mexicano community here in Fort Worth today. While the current Spanish-speaking community's needs are not the same as they were more than a century ago, the TCU community would do well to look to the example of Molina and consider how to use their means and myriad areas of expertise to help Mexicanos and other Latinx people feel welcome in Fort Worth and at TCU.

Hill notes

1. This chapter is adapted from Chapter 1, "'Mexicans Are Taught American Ways': Fort Worth's Mexican Schools" of my dissertation, "Brown Erasure: Mexican Americans and the Teaching of History in Cold War Texas", completed at TCU in April 2024.

2. Pauline Kibbe, Latin Americans in Texas (Albuquerque: University of New Mexico Press), 1946, 176. Kibbe was a field associate to the Executive Committee on Inter-American Relations in Texas during World War II. She summarized her findings in Latin Americans in Texas. Cynthia E. Orozco, "Kibbe, Pauline Rochester," Texas State Historical Association website, Last modified February 21, 2017, Accessed December 12, 2019, https://tshaonline.org/handbook/online/articles/fkign.

3. The term Mexican American describes American citizens of Mexican ancestry or origin. The term Mexican refers to people of Mexican origin living and attending school in the United States that are not U.S. citizens. I will sometimes use Mexicanos to include both groups. The term white is used to identify the dominant group in American society who have historically benefited from racial and social privileges.

4. Kenneth Hopkins, "The Early Development of the Hispanic Community in Fort Worth and Tarrant County, Texas, 1849–1949," *East Texas Historical Journal* 38, no. 2 (October 1, 2000), https://scholarworks.sfasu.edu/ethj/vol38/iss2/9.

5. Santiago Diaz, Interviewed by Moisés Acuña-Gurrola, Fort Worth, Texas. October 17, 2015, Latino Americans: 500 Years of History, Fort Worth Public Library Digital Archives.

6. Fort Worth Independent School District Board Meeting Minutes, September 25, 1923.

7. "Mexicans Are Taught American Ways in Newly Established Missions Here," *Fort Worth Star-Telegram,* December 21, 1913.

8. An additive method would allow the student to maintain and celebrate their culture while learning a new one. For more on the subtractive schooling method, see Carlos Kevin Blanton, *The Strange Career of Bilingual Education in Texas, 1836–1981* (College Station: Texas A&M University Press, 2007) and Angela Valenzuela, *Subtractive Schooling: U.S.-Mexican Youth and the Politics of Caring* (Albany: State Univers of New York Press, 2017).

9. "XMAS Program for San Jose Mission," *Fort Worth Star-Telegram,"* December 6, 1914; "Mission to be Aided by Carnival," *Fort Worth Star-Telegram,* September 5, 1915; "Install New Officers on Next Sunday," *Fort Worth Star-Telegram,* January 2, 1916; "Monster Cake Brings Joy to Poor Children," *Fort Worth Star-Telegram,* May 6, 1921.

10. "Society: Benefit Card Party," *Fort Worth Star-Telegram,* March 1, 1914.

11. "Two Mexican Schools to Hold Exercises," *Fort Worth Star-Telegram,* May 29, 1914.

12. "Mission Children Thanksgiving Guests," *Fort Worth Star-Telegram* November 29, 1914.

13. "School for Mexicans Now Well Attended," *Fort Worth Star-Telegram,* September 15, 1915.

14. *Horned Frog,* 1915.

15. "The New Faculty," *Skiff,* September 17, 1909.

16. "Society," *Fort Worth Star-Telegram*, February 16, 1913.

17. "State Convention of Christian Church is Now in Session in This City," *Skiff,* May 20, 1905.

18. "L.D. Anderson, T.C.U. Alumnus, is Elected President of School," *Skiff,* March 10, 1916.

19. "Members of Volunteer Band Elect Officers For the Year," *Skiff,"* October 2, 1914.

20. "Enmity in Mexico Too Keen, Teacher Returns to Texas," *Fort Worth Star-Telegram,* June 27, 1916.

21. "Missionary Work in T.C.U.," *Skiff,* February 19, 1915.

22. "North Side Mission School Educates by 'Short Orders,'" *Fort Worth Star-Telegram,* January 3, 1915.

23. "Missionary Work in T.C.U.," *Skiff,* February 19, 1915.

Embracing the Culture of Our Community: The Story of Mariachi Sangre Royal de TCU

Sean Atkinson

IT WAS A BEAUTIFUL October evening in Fort Worth, and the lights in the Van Cliburn Concert Hall at TCU dimmed. The sold-out audience—the first sell-out crowd in the new concert hall that opened 18 months earlier—was settling in for the second half of the last concert of the 12th Biennial Latin American Music Festival, featuring not only the TCU School of Music's newest ensemble, Mariachi Sangre Royal, but several high school mariachi groups from Fort Worth and the award-winning professional group Mariachi Sol de México. The final selection for the evening included all of the mariachi groups in a rousing arrangement of "El Son de la Negra," concluding a true celebration of mariachi music, culture, and community.

Community, culture, and music are inextricably linked. Mariachi music, born in Mexico in the late eighteenth century, has come to define not only a musical style that is uniquely Mexican, but also a strong cultural bond for communities of Mexican and Latinx people living in the United States. With over 30 percent of Fort Worth's population identifying as Hispanic, a population with which TCU has traditionally struggled to connect, it was surprising that TCU had not until recently embraced mariachi with an ensemble of its own.[1] What follows is the story of how TCU's first mariachi ensemble, Mariachi Sangre Royal, was started. What began as a student-led organization has now become a vital piece of the fabric that adds to the identity of the School of Music, opening new connections to the Fort Worth community and providing a space in which mariachi music can be celebrated.

Mariachi is a difficult word to define. It can simultaneously refer to a genre of music, the group or ensemble, or the individuals in the ensemble. But no matter how it is defined, one thing above all else stands out, and that is its deep connection to Mexico and Mexican culture. In the mid nineteenth century, the precursor to the modern mariachi ensemble came into existence in central Mexico. These groups formed in mainly rural areas of the country and provided music for community events and celebrations. It was not until after the Mexican revolution, in the early twentieth century, that mariachi music would become a national symbol for the country. For those unfamiliar with mariachi music, modern mariachi ensembles typically consist of trumpets, violins, guitars, and two specific string instruments that help to distinguish mariachi ensembles. The *guitarrón* is a six-string bass guitar and the *vihuela* is a smaller five-string guitar. Many mariachi groups also feature a harp, but one element that is always present is singing. Every member of a mariachi ensemble is expected to sing, either as part of the group or as a featured soloist. Singing is one the great equalizers in mariachi music, allowing it to be a welcoming and inclusive ensemble. In most other instrumental ensembles, the barrier to entry is the ability to play an instrument, but everyone can sing on day one in mariachi, regardless of previous instrumental experience.

The music of mariachi ensembles is quite diverse. Polkas, marches, folk tunes, and arrangements of almost anything else (including the TCU Fight Song) are fair game;[2] the distinctive instrumentation of the ensemble helps to create its unique sound. The strummed string instruments provide a harmonic and rhythmic foundation, while the trumpets and violins carry the melodic lines. Costuming is another vital component in mariachi culture and a symbol of pride for the mariachis in the group. The garb of the typical mariachi is that of a *charro*, or cowboy. This typically consists of ornate pants, a short jacket, a *moño* (large neck bow), boots, and a *sombrero*. The complete set of clothes, or *traje*, are quintessential to the overall aesthetic of mariachi, often customized for each specific group. Mariachi Sangre Royal, for example, features *traje* with the TCU logo, custom embroidered *moños*, and a Horned Frog on the back of the jackets. But before the customized *traje* and before there was mariachi at TCU, there was a student on a mission to see Sangre Royal become a reality.

Juan Pablo de Leon and Gabriela Cruz, violin, during the world premiere of Sangre Royal, a piece commissioned by TCU for Wind Band and Mariachi. September 28, 2023, in the Van Cliburn Concert Hall at TCU. *Photo courtesy of TCU Marketing and Communications.*

Emanual (Manny) Arellano (BM in Music Education, '23) came to TCU with a passion for music. Transferring into the School of Music from Tarrant County College (TCC), Manny hit the ground running in the fall of 2019. With the help of Laura Singletary, an associate professor of music education in the School of Music, he ticked off an item on his to-do list: find other students on campus passionate about mariachi music and get an ensemble started. According to Arellano, "mariachi was the missing link for me and a way to connect deeper to my roots. The Mexican population in Fort Worth and at TCU is pretty large, and I felt like mariachi needed to be part of campus life."[3] The group needed a name, so Manny settled on Mariachi Sangre Royal de TCU. *Sangre royal* translates as "royal blood" and is a nod to the royal purple color of TCU and its venerable Horned Frog mascot that can shoot blood from its eye when threatened. By the end of that first semester, Manny had found a core group that held regular rehearsals. If Singletary acted as the group's faculty sponsor, then she was there to learn from them, and Manny's passion for mariachi was infectious in a way that led to her next research project in music education.

Inspired by what she was seeing with the student group, Singletary reached out to the mariachi instructors at North Side High School, just minutes away from TCU. Ramon Niño and Wendy (Imelda) Martinez lead Mariachi Espuelas de Plata ("Silver Spurs") at the high school. The ensemble has earned recognitions at local, regional, state, and national competitions over the years, making Niño and Martinez some of the leading experts in mariachi education in the state. Both have also served as the president of the Texas Association of Mariachi Educators. It was from these instructors that Singletary wanted to learn more about how mariachi was being taught in schools and how it compared with instructional methods she was more familiar with in band, orchestra, and choir. Her observations have led to some interesting findings that could have significant ramifications for music instruction across all genres and age levels. Singletary noted that "there is [a] tremendous list of musical things like phrasing and breathing and tone quality and articulation and all the things you would talk about in a traditional band or orchestra class, but the mariachi directors are right there showing the students what to do. Modeling is more of a teaching tool here than anywhere I have seen."[4] Teaching in this way, through active modeling of desired outcomes, is not only a tradition of mariachi music, but also something from which music rooted in Western historical traditions could benefit.

Unfortunately, only months after starting her observations at North Side, Singletary's time learning from Niño and Martinez was cut short, as the COVID-19 pandemic ended her ability to observe mariachi rehearsals. Yet the relationships she formed with the instructors in that program would prove invaluable for the future of Mariachi Sangre Royal.

In the fall of 2020, with the COVID pandemic still in full swing, operations in the School of Music were stretched to a breaking point. Regular ensembles struggled to make in-person class restrictions work effectively, and members of all the instrumental ensembles were forced to be physically distanced from one another, resulting in, among other things, the need to split the larger ensembles into smaller groups. Student organizations across campus, including Mariachi Sangre Royal, were all but impossible to keep going, especially those that relied on in-person meetings to function. Despite these setbacks, Manny and the ensemble members kept working towards building the group as much as they could.

By the following summer of 2021, I was appointed director of the School of Music and began looking for ways we could broaden our outreach to the Fort Worth community, especially to peoples with whom we had struggled to connect. That is when I learned about Manny's student mariachi group and Singletary's research into mariachi music education. The path forward seemed simple enough: incorporate the student group into the School of Music and create an ensemble that not only exposes the TCU community to this music and helps to create a bridge to the Hispanic community in Fort Worth, but also provides the opportunity for music education majors to learn how mariachi is taught and pick up those valuable lessons that Singletary had observed at North Side. However, three major obstacles stood in the way: instructors, instruments, and *traje*.

Finding instructors for the ensemble turned out to be the easiest piece of the puzzle. I was fortunate to have Singletary connect me with Niño and Martinez, who enthusiastically agreed to be the instructors of the new ensemble. They would continue at North Side High School, but the TCU ensemble would be scheduled to rehearse in the evenings, which allowed them to come to campus twice a week and lead the rehearsals. Additionally, Niño and Martinez were also able to help with the instruments and *traje*, leveraging connections they've made over the last twenty years with instrument

Members of Mariachi Sangre Royal de TCU performing during the 2024 Reconciliation Day. *Photo courtesy of TCU Marketing and Communications.*

manufacturers/distributors and *traje* makers. An anonymous donation to the School of Music facilitated the purchase of everything so we could get the ensemble moving as quickly as possible.

The fall of 2022 was the official start of Mariachi Sangre Royal in the School of Music. Even though the instruments and *traje* had not yet arrived, our intrepid mariachi instructors did not hesitate to let us borrow some of North Side's instruments so rehearsals could begin. Things were going so well that first semester that we decided to include the ensemble as part of the College of Fine Arts Gala that December. In front of a large audience of arts supporters from the community, Sangre Royal made their debut in their full *traje*, which, as luck would have it, arrived on campus the morning of the Gala.

From there, Sangre Royal has quickly developed into a major ensemble for the School of Music. As of the writing of this essay, there are now two distinct mariachi ensembles, one for beginners and another for students with more experience in mariachi music. Tarrant County College students can also join the ensemble, furthering TCU's positive reach into the community. TCU students enrolled in the ensemble do not simply learn how to play a different kind of music. They are immersed into a new cultural experience, requiring them to reconcile their own lived experiences with the music they play, the language they sing, and the other students in the ensemble. For Latinx students, the ensemble offers a sense of belonging, knowing that the university supports a musical and cultural art form from Latin America.[5] One of the desires of the Race & Reconciliation Initiative is to integrate race into the TCU student experience, and a thriving mariachi ensemble embedded on campus has become an important piece of this integration.

The group frequently performs for campus events, including an alumni tailgate for a football game, the annual Scholarship Dinner, during the campus celebration of TCU's sesquicentennial anniversary in October 2023, and as part of the annual Reconciliation Day in 2024. They recently competed in November 2023 at the 29th Annual Mariachi Extravaganza in San Antonio and won 3rd place in the Collegiate Division.

This brings us back to the Latin American Music Festival, held in October 2023. The crowd for that final concert was standing room only, and most of the audience was attending their first concert on campus since the pandemic. The event, the first of its kind to feature such extensive mariachi music at TCU, was also widely reported.[6] It was awe inspiring to see such wide-ranging community support for music that is a part of the cultural fabric for so many residents of Fort Worth. Such an event could not have happened without the dedicated hard work of a handful of people who believed that mariachi had a place at TCU. I hope that Mariachi Sangre Royal de TCU continues to grow, thrive, and foster stronger connections between TCU and Fort Worth's Hispanic community for many years to come.

Atkinson notes

1. The latest data from the U.S. Census Bureau show that 35.1 percent of Fort Worth residents identify as Hispanic or Latino, and 29 percent specifically identify as Mexican. U.S. Census Bureau, American Community Survey, 2022 American Community Survey 1-Year Estimates, Table DP05, generated by Sean Atkinson, using data.census.gov, https://data.census.gov/, April 12, 2024.

2. Mariachi Sangre Royal participated in the final celebration event for the TCU Sesquicentennial Anniversary, and as part of the event several School of Music groups joined together in a musical mash-up. The conclusion was, of course, the TCU Fight Song played by all of the groups together, so an arrangement of the song had

to be made for Sangre Royal. The group has gone on to perform the fight song arrangement on their own at concerts, festivals, and competitions. Nothing, I think, better symbolizes the ambitions to connect mariachi culture with the TCU community than a mariachi version of the Fight Song.

3. Jeff Wilson, "The Music of Mexico," *TCU Magazine*, February 6, 2024, https://magazine.tcu.edu/endeavors-2024/mexico-music-mariachi-fort-worth/.

4. Ibid.

5. See Kelly Phommachanh's chapter, which focuses on student sense of belonging within the APA community on campus.

6. Cristian ArguetaSoto, "Area High School Mariachi Bands Sound Off at TCU Latin American Music Festival," *Fort Worth Report*, October 5, 2023, https://fortworthreport.org/2023/10/05/area-high-school-mariachi-bands-sound-off-at-tcu-latin-american-music-festival/.

Index

Page locators in *italics* refer to images.

Add-Ran Christian University, 10–13
Add-Ran Male and Female College, 7–10; racial segregation at, 8
African American and Africana Studies (AAAS), 61
Ailen, Riley, 24
alcohol: at Add-Ran Male and Female College, 9
All-America City Award: won by Fort Worth, Texas, 27
Allen, Joe, 15
Altamirano, Elba, 33
Alvarado, Texas: Joseph Addison Clark's sawmill in, 6
American Education Research Association (AERA): *Reconcile This!* podcast and, 103
Anderson, C. Annette, 129, 133–34, *148*; on Indigenous Campus Tour, 142–49
Anderson, Sue, 109
Apaches: enslavement and, 3
Arellano, Emanual ("Manny"): Mariachi Sangre Royal and, 183, 184
Arkikosa River, 135–37
Arlington State College: racial integration of, 37. *See also* University of Texas at Arlington
Asian American Studies program, 162–63
Asian Festival, 58, 168
Asian Pacific Americans (APAs), 150–59; as TCU faculty members, 154–57; TCU student organizations for, 58, 156–57, 166–68; as TCU students, 32–33, 162–68
Asian Student Association, 58, 167–68
Asian Studies: at TCU, 41, 60, 157, 158, 163
athletics: Mexicano stereotyping and, 20; racial integration of, 41, 43–45, 49; student advocacy and, 61–63
Augustine, Jay: as *Reconcile This!* podcast guest, 101

Bailey, Roosevelt, 15
Bates, Bertice, 35
Baylor University: racial integration at, 30–31, 37, 43
Bell, Reva, 35, 41
belonging: Asian Pacific American (APA) students and, 166–68
Ben Kori, Abdullah, *31*, 32
Black Alumni Alliance, 57
Black people: as freshman class "presidents" at TCU, 15–16; in Fort Worth, Texas, 13; higher education for, 21, 114–15; portraits of, 67; racialized stereotypes of,

at TCU, 11–12; as TCU employees, 8–10, 11, 14–15; as TCU faculty members, 41, 67; TCU student organizations for, 57; as TCU students, 33, 35–39

Black Student Caucus (BSC), 57

Black Studies: at TCU, 41, 45

Bland, Sandra: death of, 86

Bonham, Kenneth, 25

Boschini, Victor J., Jr., 50–51, 108; on Deferred Action for Childhood Arrivals (DACA), 53–54

Boyd, Whitnee, 102

Briscoe, Roland, 15

Brite Divinity School: Jewish Studies program at, 61; Mateo Alvarez de Molina at, 24, 175, 176; racial integration of, 35–37; student volunteers to Mexican missions from, 177

Brown, Patsy: portrait of, 67

Brown Lupton Student Union: Intercultural Center at, *65*, 66–67

Brown v. Board of Education (1954), 29, 30

Bryant, Marian Brooks, 38

Bunche, Ralph, 45

Cantrell, Vida, 32

Carroll, Michael, 63

Carter, Amon G., 13

Carter, Jordan: as *Reconcile This!* podcast guest, 99

Case, Clara, 175–77

Cash, James, *42*, 43, *44*, *82*

Cash, Juanita, 35, 43

Charlie, Mike, 58

Chen, Yusi, 157

Chiariello,, Haylee, 128–29

Chicano studies: at TCU, 40

Chicanos: as TCU students, 33, 40. *See also* Latinx; Mexicanos

Chiles, Dorothy, 111

China Initiative (2018), 151

Chinese Americans, 151–52

Chinese Exclusion Act (1882), 151

Civil War: Clark family in, 4–6; enslaved people in Tarrant County, Texas, during, 13; TCU's founding and, 1–2

Claiborne, James Lee, 35

Clark, Addison, 1, *14*; Add-Ran Male and Female College and, 8; in the Civil War, 4–5; Disciples of Christ and, 7, 48

Clark, Ella Lee (wife of Randolph), 9–10, 108–9, 114

Clark, Joseph Addison (father of Addison and Randolph): Add-Ran Male and

Female College and, 8; Black rule feared by, 5; in the Civil War, 5–6; Disciples of Christ and, 7; enslavement by, 2, 5–6; land speculation by, 135–36

Clark, Joseph Lynn (son of Randolph), 106–7: on Black education near Thorp Springs, Texas, 10; on Charley Thorp, 8, 9; on the Civil War, 4; on Kate Thorp, 10; on Robert E. Lee, 6

Clark, Randolph, 1, *14*, 109; on Addison Clark's Civil War service, 5; Add-Ran Male and Female College and, 8; on Charley Thorp, 9, 109, 114–15; in the Civil War, 5; Disciples of Christ and, 7, 48; on Jarvis Christian Institute, 21; racism of, 25; on TCU's mission, 1

Clark Hall, 14

Cleburne, Texas: Joseph Addison Clark in, 6

Clemson University: enslavement and, 101

Clinton, Hillary, 53

Coalition for University Justice and Equity (CUJE), 51, 56

Cockrell, E. R., 22

Cockrell, Lousie Dura, 22

Cold War: TCU's racial integration and, 29–30, 37, 41

Cole, Hattie, 15

Cole, Linzy, 43

Colonial Country Club (Fort Worth, Texas): racial segregation at, 27–28

Colony, the (Hood County, Texas, Black settlement), 109, 114

Comanches: enslavement and, 3

Community Scholars Program, 49, 59, 60

Comparative Race and Ethnic Studies (CRES), 61

Confederacy, the: TCU's founding and, 2. *See also* Civil War

Conference on Inclusiveness, 49

Conzonire, Katie, 108

COVID-19 pandemic, 86, 98; Asian Pacific Americans (APAs) and, 152, 167; Mariachi Sangre Royal and, 184

Cruz, Gabriela, *182*

curriculum: racial diversity in, 39–41, 45, 60–61

Currier, Carrie Liu, 60, *83*, 163–64, 167; on Asian Pacific Americans (APAs) experience at TCU, 150–59

Curry, Aaron, 63

Dallas, Texas: Anthony C. Thorp in, 114; Charley Thorp in, 110; William J. "Jack" Hammond's sermon in, 20

Dallas Truth, Racial Healing and Transformation, 103

Daughters of Isabella, 174

decolonization: racial integration and, 30

Deferred Action for Childhood Arrivals (DACA), 53–54

DEI Committee, 56

de Leon, Alonso, 135

de Leon, Juan Pablo, *182*

DeLeón, Arnoldo, 40

desegregation (racial): alumni letter protesting, *34*; defined, 26; of Fort Worth independent school district (ISD), 29; J. M. Moudy's statement on, *36*, 37–38; TCU's challenges with, 38–39; of Texas universities, 30–31, 38. *See also* integration (racial); segregation (racial)

Diaz, Abran, 173

Diaz, Santiago, 173

Diaz, Telesfora, 173

Dibbles, Larry, 44

Disciples of Christ: Add-Ran Christian University at, 10; Clark family and, 7, 48; on enslavement, 7; Jarvis Christian College and, 21, 38, 46; Ku Klux Klan opposed by, 20

Diversity and Inclusion, Office of, 56

diversity, equity, and inclusion (DEI), 51, 56, 158, 166–67; Asian Pacific American (APA) faculty members and, 155, 157

Diversity Council, 49

Divine Nine Pillars, 64, *65*, 66

Dixon, Brandon: as *Reconcile This!* podcast guest, 99

Dixon, Jamie, 62

Donati, Jeremiah, 63

DuBois, W. E. B., 21

Duncan, David, 115

Duncan, Dock, 111

Easley, Aaron C., 12

education: community creation and, 89–91, 147

Education, TCU School of: racial integration of, 35, 41, 43

Ellington, Duke, 45

Elliott, Vida, 25

Ellmann, Holly, 112

enslavement: Disciples of Christ on, 7; of Indigenous people, 3; Joseph Addison Clark and, 2; in Fort Worth, Texas, 13; Moody Lee and, 10; Pleasant Thorp and, 8; resistance to, 4; in Tarrant County, Texas, 13; TCU's founding and, 2; in Texas, 3

ethnocentrism, 20

Executive Order 9066 (1942), 151

experience: community creation and, 91–93, 147

exposure: community creation and, 91, 147

Felder, Vada Phillips, 35, 36

Feldman, Ariel, *83*
Ferrari, Michael ("Mick"), 48–49
Ford, Darius, *82*
Forrester, W. H., 9
Fort, Andrew, 60, 163
Fort Worth, Texas: Add-Ran Male and Female College in, 7; Black community in, 13–14; enslavement in, 13; Ku Klux Klan in, 19; Mexicanos in, 20–21, 28–29; racial integration in, 29; racial segregation in, 13–14, 27–29; TCU's move to and early history in, 13–25
Fort Worth Independent School District (FWISD): desegregation of, 29, 173–74
Fort Worth Star-Telegram: on Mateo Molina, 176; on Mexicanos, 174–75
Floyd, George: murder of, xv, 51, 82, 83
Franchione, Dennis, 62
Frog Fountain, 93, *94*, 135, *136*

Garnett, Ervin, 44
Gaul, Theresa, 61, 142–43, 144
Gay Street Elementary School (Fort Worth, Texas), 35
George (enslaved person), 5
George, Amiso, *83*, *84*
Giddings, Jennifer, 43–44, 45
Godspeed, Daniel, 35
Gooding, Frederick, Jr.: 3E framework of, 85–89, 139, 146–47, 150; on Race & Reconciliation Initiative (RRI), xv, 86–94; as *Reconcile This!* podcast producer, 98–104; RRI Oral History Project (OHP) and, 107, 120
Grady, Kai: as *Reconcile This!* podcast producer and editor, 99
Granbury Depot, 109, *110*, 115
Greek life: Asian Pacific Americans (APAs) and, 156–57, 167; cultural sensitivity training for, 54; racial integration of, 46
Green, Abe, 15
Greensword, Sylviane: on Charley Thorp, 106–17; as *Reconcile This!* podcast guest, 100–101, 102; RRI Oral History Project (OHP) and, 90, 120
Gregory, Dick, 45
Griffin, Thomas, 45
Guardiola, Mayra, 53–54
Gurrola, Moises, 90

Hall, Johnnie, 32
Hall, Van ("Hoss"), 32
Hamilton, Lottie Mae, 35
Hammad, Hanan, 61, *83*
Hammett, Joyce, 34

Hammond, William J. ("Jack"), 20, 28

Harris College of Nursing: racial integration of, 37, 41

Harrison, The: portraits in, *66*, 67, 115, 137, 139, 143

Hatfield, J. NiCole: portraits by, 67, 137–39, 143

"Hell's Half Acre" (Fort Worth, Texas): Add-Ran Male and Female College at, 7

Hightower, Hattie, 114

Hightower, Hettie, 114

Hightower, Leona, 109, 111

Hightower, Simon, 109, 114

Hill, Cecilia N. Sánchez: on Mexicanos at TCU and in Fort Worth, Texas, 172–76; as *Reconcile This!* podcast guest, 101

Hispanic Alumni Association, 57

Historians of Latino Americans (HOLA) of Tarrant County, 29

"Hit the Negro Baby" game, 18

Hoang, Tiffany, *84*

Holmes, Debra Duncan, 111

Huckaby, Letitia, 115

Hunter, Arthur, 15

Hurdle, Ronald, 43, *84*; as *Reconcile This!* podcast guest, 102

Indigenous Campus Tour, 127–49; at University of Washington (Seattle), 133

Indigenous people: Cato Sells on, 22; enslavement of, 3; portraits of, 67; as TCU faculty members, 40, 128; TCU student organizations for, 58; as TCU students, 32, 34, 128. *See also specific confederations and tribes*

Indigenous Studies: at TCU, 40, 61

Indochina Migration and Refugee Assistance Act (1975), 152

infrastructure (TCU): racial diversity and, 63–68. *See also specific buildings*

integration (racial): defined, 26; in Fort Worth, Texas, 29; of TCU, 26–46. *See also* desegregation (racial); segregation (racial)

Intercultural Center, *65*, 66–67

intergenerational trauma: Asian Pacific American (APA) students and, 164–66

international students: first experiences as a minority by, 152; Intercultural Center and, 66; James Moudy on, 37; TCU student organizations for, 58, 168

Jackson, Ketanji Brown: on remembrance, xv

Jang, Seo Hyun, 157

Japanese Americans, 153, 164

Jarvis, Ida Van Zandt, 8, 21

Jarvis, James Jones, 8, 21

Jarvis Christian Institute (later College), 41, 115; founding of, 21; TCU's affiliation with, 38; TCU's exchange program with, 46

Jarvis Hall, 14

Jean, Botham: death of, 86
Jefferson, Atatiana: death of, 86
Jewish Studies, 61
Jews: as TCU students, 24–25
Jim Crow, 26; Jarvis Christian Institute and, 21; Mexicanos and, 173. *See also* segregation (racial)
Jones, Allene Parks, 37, 41; portrait of, *66*, 67
Jones, Benjamin, 11
Jones, Zorana: as *Reconcile This!* podcast guest, 102
Jordan, Jack, 32

Kaepernick, Colin, 54
Kappa Lambda Delta (KLD), 156–57, 167, 168
Kernell, Chebon, 61
King, A. L., 41
King, Martin Luther, Jr., 36
Knox, Donna Gay, 34
Korean War: racial integration and, 30
Krochmal, Max, 90
Ku Klux Klan, xv, 18–21, 24–25
Kurtz, Carl, 136

Lambiase, Jacquiline, 67
Land Acknowledgement, 127, 134
Langston, Scott, 61, *148*
Laphen, Lauren, 108
Lathrap, Mary T, 143
Latin American Music Festival, 180, 186
Latinx people: Mariachi Sangre Royal and, 186; *Skiff* on, 12; TCU student organizations for, 57–58. *See also* Chicanos; Mexicanos
Latinx Studies: at TCU, 60–61
Leach, Jimmy, 45
League of United Latin American Citizens, 57
Leatham, Miguel, 61, *83*
Lee, Louis, 108
Lee, Moody: enslavement by, 10
Lee, Opal, 114
Lee, Robert E.: Joseph Lynn Clark on, 6; *Skiff* on, 12
Lee, Roswell, 107, 108
Lentz, Blake: as *Reconcile This!* podcast guest, 103
Lester, Lea: as *Reconcile This!* podcast guest, 103
LeVias, Jerry, 43

Lindsay, Jeremiah, 15
Linn, Maxine, 34
Little Mexico (Fort Worth, Texas, neighborhood), 28–29
"Lost Cause" rhetoric: at TCU, 11
Lunger, Harold, 36
Ly, Michael, 58

Madigan, Tim, 112
Magee, Rhonda V.: as *Reconcile This!* podcast guest, *100*, 101
Majestic Theater (Fort Worth, Texas), 36
Mammoth Pageants, 22; program for, *23*
Mariachi Sangre Royal, 180–86
Martin, Trayvon: killing of, 53
Martinez, Peter, 29
Martinez, Wendy: Mariachi Sangre Royal and, 183–84
Matthews, Aundrea: as *Reconcile This!* podcast guest, 102; RRI Oral History Project
    (OHP) and, 121–25
Mayfield, Earle, 19
McBride, Ann: portrait of, 67
McNair Programs, 59
Melton, Amos: TCU's racial integration and, 39, 41
Mexicanos, 172–76; English-language instruction for, 177–78; in Fort Worth,
    Texas, 20–21, 28–29, 173; stereotyping of, at TCU, 20–21; racial segregation
    of, 173; at TCU, 22, 24, 175–77, 180–86. *See also* Chicanos; Latinx
Middle East Studies, 61
Ministerial Association of TCU, 20, 177
minstrel shows, 18
Mitchell, Hodges, 44
Mitchell, Robyn, 58
mock slave auctions, 46
model minority: Asian Pacific Americans (APAs) as, 150, 153–54, 160–64
Molina, Marcela, *84*
Molina, Mateo Alvarez de, 22, 24, 175–78
Montes, Pablo, 102–3, 128
Moore, Caylin, 63
Moudy, James M., 44; TCU's racial integration and, 26–27, 30, *36*, 37–33
Mount Carmel Academy (Fort Worth, Texas), 175
Moy, Tommy, 32–33

Nace, Karen, 109
National Association for the Advancement of Colored People (NAACP), 53, 67
National Panhellenic Council (NPHC), 66
Native American Advisory Circle, 128, 130; members, *148*

Native American and Indigenous Peoples Day, *136*
Native American and Indigenous Peoples Initiative (NAIPI), 58, 61, *83*, 127–28
Native American Monument, 64, 128, 134, *146*
Native American Student Association (NASA; University of Texas at Arlington),
147
Native and Indigenous Peoples Day Symposium, 127–28
Native and Indigenous Students Association (NISA), 58
Negro War Industries Training School, 29
Niño, Ramon: Mariachi Sangre Royal and, 183–84
Nungaray, Albert, 128
Nursing, Harris College of: racial integration of, 37, 41

Oliver, Owen Lloyd, 132–33
O'Neal, J. C., 32
oral history: RRI Oral History Project (OHP), 119–26, 169
Organization of Latin American Students, 57
Our Lady of Guadalupe Mexican Mission (Fort Worth, Texas), 174

Parker, Quannah: portrait based of, 67, 137–39, 143
Parker, Wheeler, Jr.: as *Reconcile This!* podcast guest, 101
Parton, Terri, 61, *148*
Patterson, Gary, 62
Penn, Otis Albert, 34
Perkins, Marcellis, 67, 109; Portrait Project and, 115; as *Reconcile This!* podcast
producer and editor, 90, 98–104
Pete, Gail, 40
Peterson, William: model minority concept and, 162–63
Phommachanh, Kelly Palida, *84*; on Asian Pacific American (APA) community,
162–69; as *Reconcile This!* podcast guest, 103
Pittman, Jim, 44
Plume Award: winners, *83*, *84*, *112*
Pollinator Garden, *133*, 134, *148*
Porterfield, Austin, 28
Portrait Project, 67–68, 115, 128; Indigenous people and, 137–139

Rabb, Shaun, 104
Race & Reconciliation Initiative (RRI): effects of, 94; Frederick Gooding Jr. on, xv,
86–94; oral history project of, 119–26, 169; origins and mission of, xv, 86–87;
sign of, *87*; sticker of, *81*; Victor J. Boschini and, 51
Race & Reconciliation Initiative Heritage Trail, 81
racial epithets: in *Skiff*, 16, 18, 20
Reconciliation Day: first (2021), *92*, 93; second (2022), *82*, 106, 112–13; third

(2023), *83*; fourth (2024), *83, 84, 185*, 186

Reconcile This! podcast, 90, 96–104, 115

Red Scare (First), 18–19

Reed, Leon, Jr.: as *Reconcile This!* podcast guest, 102; RRI Oral History Project (OHP) and, 124–25

Reed Hall, 15, *16*

Rhodes, Ray, 44

Rice University: racial integration at, 30, 38

Ridglea Country Club (Fort Worth, Texas): racial segregation at, 27–28

Ridglea Wall, 27, *28*

Righton, Kelcia: as *Reconcile This!* podcast guest, 103

Ripley Arnold Housing Project (Fort Worth, Texas), 28–29

Rivera, Jesus, 24

Rodriguez, Claudia Tiffany, *84*

Ross Avenue Christian Church (Dallas, Texas): William J. "Jack" Hammond's sermon at, 20

Rouse, Federick, III: as *Reconcile This!* podcast guest, 101–2

Ruffins, Mollie, 109

Sadler, M. E.: alumni letter protesting desegregation to, *34*; TCU's racial integration and, 31, 35, 38–39, 41

Sadler Hall, 14

Saffell, Mary, 108

Salas, Briana, 108

San Francisco State University (SFSU), 163

Sanders, Claire, *83*

Schells, Regina, 115

Schells, Royce, 111

Scholarship Dinner, 186

Sears, Witt, 110

secession: of Texas, 4

segregation (racial): at Add-Ran Male and Female College, 8; in Fort Worth, Texas, 13–14, 27–29, 173; of Mexicanos, 173. *See also* desegregation (racial); integration (racial)

Sells, Cato, 22

servant house, 15, *16*

Sesquicentennial Plaza, *67*, 68

Shan, Jinpei, 157

Sharma, Ambika, 157

Sierra, Wendi, 128

Singletary, Laura: Mariachi Sangre Royal and, 183, 184

Skiff (TCU student newspaper): on Booker T. Washington, 21; on Jerry LeVias,

43; on Jews, 24–25; on Ku Klux Klan, 19–20; on Lost Cause, 11; on Mexicanos, 24; on minstrel shows, 18; mock slave auctions promoted in, 46; on Rabindranath Tagore, 22; racial epithets printed in, 16, 18, 20; racialized reporting in, 11–12; on Willis Duke Weatherford, 22; on Yu Yui Tsu, 22

slavery. *See* enslavement

social media: as academic resource, 102; political polarization and, 53; TCU student activism and, 56, 58–59

South Asian Inter-cultural Association (SAICA), 168

South Asians, 152

Southeast Asians, 152

Southern Methodist University (SMU): racial integration at, 30, 36, 37, 43

Spurgeon, John, 18

Star-Telegram (Fort Worth, Texas): on Mateo Molina, 176; on Mexicanos, 174–75

Steele, Karen, *83, 84*, 90–91, 101

STEM Scholars program, 59, 60

Strong Players Are Reaching Kids (SPARK), 63

student activism and advocacy, 47, 52–63

student life: racial integration and, 45–46

student-led organizations: advocacy by, 56–59

Students for Asian Indian Cultural Awareness, 58, 167–68

Students for Fair Admissions v. Harvard (2023), 153

Students for Fair Admissions v. University of North Carolina (2023), 153

Sweatt v. Painter (1950), 35

Tagore, Rabindranath, 22

Talbert, Florence Cole, 22, *23*

Tan, Tabitha, 58

Tarrant, Edward H., 135

Tarrant County, Texas: Black population of, 13; Mexicano population of, 20

Tarrant County College: Mariachi Sangre Royal and students from, 185

Tawil, Randa: as *Reconcile This!* podcast guest, 99

Taylor, Claire, 34

Taylor-Randle, Loriessa, 111–12

TCU Volunteer Band, 176

Testa, Nino, 67

Texas Education Agency (TEA), 172

Texas Wesleyan University: racial integration at, 29

Thomas, Cornell, 49

Thomas, Rhondda: as *Reconcile This!* podcast guest, *100*, 101

Thompson, S. H., 15

Thorp, Anthony C., 114

Thorp, Charley, 8–10, 21, 106–17

Thorp, Charlie, 114
Thorp, Colonel, Jr., 110–11, 115
Thorp, Colonel, Sr., 109, 114
Thorp, Daisy, 111
Thorp, Henry Pleasant, 109
Thorp, Jude, 8, 108
Thorp, Julia, 110–11, 109
Thorp, Kate Lee, 8, 107, 108, 109
Thorp, Kitty, 109, 111, 114
Thorp, Mary, 115
Thorp, Pleasant, 7, 106, 114
Thorp Springs, Texas: Add-Ran Male and Female College at, 7–10, 106–7; Charley
    Thorp in, 110; field trip to, 109
Tomlinson, LaDainian, 63; as *Reconcile This!* podcast guest, 101, 102
Tomlinson Student-Athlete Development Endowment Fund, 63
Torrey's Trading Post No. 2 (outside Waco, Texas), 3
Tran, Diana, 157
Treetop, Jack, Mrs.: portrait based on, 67, 137–39
Trinity River. *See* Arkikosa River
TRIO programs, 59–60
Trosino, Cassie: as *Reconcile This!* podcast guest, 99
Trump, Donald, 53–54; trade wars of, 151
Turner, Darron, 57
Tsu, Yu Yui, 22

Ubuntu (concept), 88–89, 93–94, 108, 115; Reconciliation Day and, 106
United Asian Community, 58, 167–68
United Daughters of the Confederacy (UDC), 11; program, *12*
United Latino Association, 57
United Latinx Association, 57
Universities Studying Slavery (USS) consortium, 91, 97–98
University of North Texas (UNT): racial integration at, 30
University of Texas at Arlington: Native American Student Association (NASA) at,
    147; racial integration at, 37
University of Texas at Austin: racial integration at, 30
Upward Bound, 59

Vasquez, Victor, 33
Vietnam War, 52, 152; racial integration and, 30
Vietnamese Student Association (VSA), 58, 168
Village Creek, Battle of (1841), 135–36
von Daacke, Kirt: as *Reconcile This!* podcast guest, 101

Waco, Texas: Add-Ran Christian University at, 10–13, 110
Waits, Edward M., 25
"Walking Colors" silent march, 53
Wang, Cleda, 157
Washington, Booker T.: *Skiff* on, 21
Wassenich, Mark, 105; TCU's racial integration and, 38
Weatherford, Willis Duke, 22
Weatherly Hall: racial segregated food service in, 35–36
Weinberg, Nicole, 103
White, Haywood, 15
Whitekiller, Kathleen, 58
Wichita and Affiliated Tribes, 13, 64, 132, 137; white expulsion of, 135–36.
    See also Native American Monument
Williams, Lee, 109
Williams, Mary Michael, 108
Willis, Jenay, *84*; on oral history, 119–26
Wood, J. Lindley, 24
Wooster, Donald E., 40
World War Two: racial integration and, 29; Charley Thorp's descendants in, 114

Xin, Lucy, 157

Young Women's Christian Association (YWCA), 177

www.ingramcontent.com/pod-product-compliance
Lightning Source LLC
Chambersburg PA
CBHW030819270326
41928CB00007B/799